SUN AND DAUGHTER SIGNS

SUN AND

BY NAOMI WAGMAN

EDITED AND INTRODUCED BY SYLVIA SHERMAN,
DIRECTOR, AMERICAN SCHOOL OF ASTROLOGY.

DAUGHTER SIGNS

SIGNS

AN ASTROLOGICAL GUIDE TO CHILD CARE

Max Padell inc.

SUN AND DAUGHTER SIGNS

First Edition

Copyright © 1974 by Max Padell Inc.

All rights reserved. This book may not be
reproduced in whole or in part, for any
purpose whatever, without permission from
the publisher. For information, address
Max Padell Inc., 830 Broadway, New York,
N.Y. 10003.

Printed in U.S.A.

Library of Congress Catalog Card No. 73-87928
ISBN 0-87538-000-X

DEDICATION

To the Sagittarians without whom this book would not have been conceived and the Moon-child whose inspiration and love of life led to its completion. May it give them a morsel of pleasure, delight and insight.

CONTENTS

CAPRICORN December 22nd - January 19th

AQUARIUS January 20th - February 19th

PISCES February 20th - March 20th

APPENDICES

INTRODUCTION

WHEN you think about it, does it not seem to be a deliberate "Supreme" plan that there is a prolonged gestation period before the birth of an offspring? With humans the nine months of pregnancy certainly serves to prepare the mother-to-be psychologically, mentally and emotionally for acceptance of the duties ahead of her. The gradually heightened anticipation built up during those prenatal months can lead her to want to care for, to love, and to prepare her child for the trials and tribulations he may have to meet during his future life.

Therefore, it is the responsibility—in fact, the outright duty—of parents to use every facility, every source of knowledge, and every available tool to help them in the serious upbringing of their children.

Astrology is certainly one very powerful and vital area to utilize in the understanding of different personality traits, which can act as aids in the blending of mother and child characteristics.

What is astrology? How can you use it to help you?

Astrology is a para-science which delves deeply into the psychological make-up of an individual based on the exact position of the planets in the heavens at the moment of birth, which, to an astrologer, is the first independent breath of a new born baby. From the precise positions of the planets, a competent, knowledgable astrologer can mathematically predict future events as well as trace back past incidents of one's life. The expert sets up a horoscope, which is a chart of the planets' positions as if one took a picture of the sky at the moment of birth, providing one's "fingerprint" in the heavens.

Throughout the Ages it has been found that the non-believers of astrology were those who did not exert themselves and take time to investigate the exactness of how it works. Anyone who seriously entered the study of astrology in order to refute it eventually ended up as an avid practitioner.

Astrology is as real as the stars and the planets we see embedded in the Milky Way. These are the same twinkling stars Babylonian shepherds idly watched on the long nights as they tended their sheep. I believe that astrology was discovered through these shepherds who first tracked the path of the ever-changing sky pattern. In any event, it was the Babylonians who were the first people to record their findings of the heaven's movements and their effects. These findings involved the best time for mating their sheep for healthy offspring, as well as the proper time for shearing the animals for good wool and better future growth.

Much of this is evident through myths and legends found on ancient tablets and on the pictorial walls of century-old ruins.

The earliest treatise on astrology called "Tetrabiblos", written around 150 AD by Claudius Ptolemy, is still being reprinted, studied, and respected by modern-day astrologers.

So many famous people throughout history were devotees of astrology. Among the physicians of history who regularly practiced astrology were Pythagoras, Hippocrates, Campanus, Paracelsus, Broughton, Nostradamus and Culpepper. Some famous mathematicians and astronomers who were astrologers were Galileo, Copernicus, Lilly, Napier, Kepler, Brahe, Flamsteed, Newton, Jung, Ben Franklin and Thomas Jefferson.

Comparable authors involved in astrology are Goethe, Dryden, Shelley, Sir Walter Scott, Byron, Dante, Shakespeare, Spencer and Aquinas.

So you can see that today's astrologers keep pretty famous company among their predecessors.

Dr. Len Broughton, a New York physician and astrologer in the 1800's wrote in his book "Elements of Astrology", a narrative concerning John Dryden, poet and astrologer, as follows:

"When Mrs. Dryden commenced in labor of her son, Charles, Dryden left his watch in charge of one of her ladies in attendance, with a strict injunction to notice the exact moment of the child's birth. In about a week after her confinement, Mr. Dryden took the occasion to tell his wife that he had calculated the child's horoscope. . . . He went on to tell her that if he lives to his eighth birthday, he will come near a violent death. . . .When young Dryden arrived near his eighth year, it was arranged that Mrs. Dryden should spend the summer vacation with her Uncle Mourdant, and Mr. Dryden was invited to the county seat of the Earl of Berkshire, his brother-in-law. . . . Dryden insisted on taking Charles and they parted in anger.

On the child's eighth birthday it was arranged by the Earl of Berkshire that his guests should go hunting, and Dryden, to keep the child out of mischief, set him to a double lesson in Latin, with a strict injunction that he should not go out of the house. Charles was performing his duty in obedience to his father, but as ill fate would have it, the stag made towards the house, and the noise alarming the servants, they hastened out to see the sport. One of the servants took young Dryden by the hand, and led him to see it also; just when they came to the gate, the stag being at bay with the dogs, made a bold push and leaped over the court wall which was low and old, the dogs following threw down a part of the wall ten yards in length, under which Charles lay buried. He was immediately dug out, and after six weeks languishing in a dangerous way, he recovered. . . ."

The father's calculations proved but too prophetic. The above is an example of the exactitude with which astrology can be calculated and interpreted by reliable astrologers.

At last, astrology has begun to receive the dignity and stature that it so rightfully deserves. This is due to the innate curiosity and unquenchable thirst for knowledge that cropped up among us as a people. I have always stated that, if astrologers had been given grants for the purpose of extensive research comparable to those that astronomers and scientists have received in the past, we astrologers would have been far more advanced than we are today. Whatever accomplishments that we did achieve to date have been through frustratingly laborious efforts.

I have been delving into the study of astrology since the age of seven, becoming more serious about the subject during my college days. At that time there were few books to be found and hardly any teachers were available. I bought every book I could find with the word "astrology" on it, regardless of its academic quality. Because I could not find any instructors, I went from one astrologer to another to have my horoscope interpreted. With each seer I would ask, "How did you arrive at such a conclusion?" or, "On what basis did you make that prediction?" Piece by piece, with the help of rare books and the words of wisdom from seasoned astrologers, I struggled to teach myself the fascinating study of the past, present, and future. I also became involved with astrological societies and attended whatever sparse lectures I would hear about. I ferretted out and mingled among other astrology "bugs" with whom I could share knowledge and compare notes.

It was for these very reasons that I founded the American School of Astrology in West Orange, New Jersey, with its own extensive book shop. Here others who have the interest and desire to pursue the occult can have a place to study, easily finding the necessary books on the subject.

Now, through this book you have the opportunity to delve deeply into the inter-relations of mother and child in order to gain a better understanding of how to deal with situations which might be anticipated for each sun sign. Remember that this book is limited to sun signs only and cannot take the place of the intrinsic value of individually cast horoscopes measured by the exact time, place and date of a person's birth. An exact individual horoscope takes into consideration not only the sun's position but that of all the known planets . . . Mercury, Venus, Mars, Jupiter, Saturn, Uranus, Neptune, Pluto, as well as the luminary, the Moon, and a number of sensitive points, such as the Midheaven and the Ascendant of the horoscope.

You may be interested in knowing how astrology can help mothers with their children. One mother recently engaged me to help her daughter astrologically. She and her daughter could not decide which of two schools the child should attend. I calculated the young girl's horoscope and then proceeded to analyze it in relation to the two schools, judging their spheres of influence by using their dates of incorporation. Taking into consideration their locations as well, I did select that seat of learning which would provide the better influence on this girl. She is now doing excellently at that chosen school. Another mother desperately called upon me to help her son who was blatantly indulging in the abuse of drugs. She was able to convince her skeptical son to consult with me. I determined through this boy's chart that he was trying to escape from his complex home problems. Through my careful and diplomatic guidance, I caused him to recognize his great potentials. He has since not only stopped partaking of hallucinatory escapes, but today he is ambitiously studying toward his Ph.D. degree. He has also established his own successful rehabilitation center under the auspices of a national charitable organization and is now helping other youngsters in need of understanding guidance in order to make their retreat from drugs.

In your great responsibility as a parent, try to understand your child's problems through his eyes, remembering that you were once a youngster yourself. Perhaps through the guidance and knowledge of astrology you can hold your patience, keep your sense of humor, express your love and understanding, have faith in his motives, and radiate confidence in his abilities.

When you can fathom the other fellow's way of thinking and his attitude toward himself or toward others . . . and this book can help you do just that . . . you will succeed in taking your child by the hand to give him a good start through life's path.

Help him to win and achieve what he wants. Yet, if or when he loses to someone else, you must be there to help him face the painful fact that circumstances are not always to his liking. Thus, he must learn to live by the rules of life in cooperation with society.

Through astrology you can discern that each child is an individual who is entitled to have different and distinct likes and dislikes, his own exclusive personality and many varied desires. Help him to be a well-developed person so that he will grow strong in character as well as strong in body. His ego must be nurtured. As wholesome food is needed for a healthy body, so is wise counselling necessary for the development of a well-rounded personality.

Through astrology you can anticipate the sensitive areas of your child's physical health needs. You can also note certain intensity periods of his life when his vigor and well-being must be observed more closely.

Through astrology you can note the extent to which your child would want or need religious and philosophical guidance in his formative years, in order to extend to him a solid ideological outlook among his peers.

Through astrology you can evaluate whether your child would

be naturally slow or quick in his development; such as, when he should take his first steps or speak his first words. Will he instead have a physical or mental impediment to hinder his abilities? Advanced awareness of any deterrents could possibly aid in correcting them early in his life.

Through astrology you can see to it that your child will develop a proper attitude toward his own and others' worth. You must help him respect the use of money and resources as a tool for evaluating what is a necessity, what is a convenience and what is a luxury.

Through astrology you can foresee what circumstances would influence his attitude toward other people, such as his parents, his sibling, if any, his friends and his educators.

Through astrology you are better equipped to guide your child into the proper type of professional usefulness according to his best abilities. You can help nurture his talents into a satisfying vocation.

Through astrology you can learn about your child's latent talents. Certain astrological configurations can indicate his interest in the fine arts, in science, in literature, or any other endeavor.

Through astrology you will recognize that your child, who is a natural imitator, will place his own connotations on your behavior according to his own astrological personality. Therefore, you must always be conscious of your child's potential conduct.

Through astrology you can become aware of the styles, the colors, the clothes, the environment with which your youngster will be happiest. He has distinct preferences which would keep him happier and more comfortable while he learns, eats, romps and sleeps.

During previous times each child was brainwashed to believe that parents, right or wrong, were always to be considered perfect. Today parents have stepped off their pedestal out of the awesome role of rulership into a new pattern of sharing with their children. Parents, as long as they recognize that they have faults, will keep an open mind to educating and improving themselves. This must in turn benefit all those who come into contact with them, particularly their own children. Only through astrology can one measure a child's potential difficulties many years before he becomes an

WHo KNO
So THE IDEAL PARENTS WHO KNOWS
ASTROLOGY.
OF COURSE,

adult. Only through astrology can we prepare that child with better guidance long before these problems are irrevocable.

So read the contents of this book meditatively and reflectively. You may not agree with all of its suggestions and you will have your own strong opinion about your child.

The aim of this book is to present the author's interpretation and evaluation of the astrological sun signs of the mother, the child, and their probable relations to each other.

Though this book is written basically for the layman, the interpretations of each sun sign are quite apt. They can be applied to almost any combination of sun signs in their dealings with each other. Many relationships that might otherwise be strained or confused may well be helped and nurtured by the revelations that astrology can offer. This book is a good tool to use. In this way one can reach a new plateau in reference to astrological know-how, perhaps to pursue the subject even more deeply and thoroughly.

Between these covers this book will enable you to find a start in your pursuit of harmonious living as a mother . . . or even as a child. The author has created a subtle and useful blending of astrological characteristics for you to adapt to your needs.

Nature's clock cannot be denied but can be used to great advantage when there is awareness and an understanding of it.

SYLVIA SHERMAN
West Orange, N. J.
May, 1973

The Ram, the Bull, the Heavenly Twins,
And next the Crab, the Lion shines,
The Virgin and the Scales;
The Scorpion, Archer, and Sea-Goat,
The Man that bears the Water-Pot;
And Fish with glittering tails.

—Isaac Watts

SUN AND DAUGHTER SIGNS

THE
ARIES
MOTHER

March 21st — April 19th

AS an Aries mother, it is most probable that you are overly concerned with your liberty and freedom of movement. Becoming a mother, therefore, can be regarded as an impediment or handicap to your independent spirit. You have the versatility and gray matter necessary, however, to make an extremely smooth adjustment to this new obligation.

This role will provide you with an opportunity to display your supremacy as ruler of the roost, but you must avoid going overboard and becoming a dictator of the empire.

You must force yourself to impose restraint and discipline and to gain fulfillment from learning to be the best there is as a mother who is well-adjusted, giving and sensitive.

For you this can be translated to mean self control and denial in many instances. The anticipation and prospects must be put in proper perspective, those you maintain for yourself and those you have a right to impose on your children. Interspersed with generous portions of your mental perspicacity, you should be able to handle the challenge competently.

The primary function with which you must concern yourself is that of developing and maintaining an acceptable level of fortitude and moderation when necessary. Exercise half the patience your own mother had to possess and be magnificiently municifent in allowing for the contingencies of childhood.

You are quite adept at building buffers and barricades to safeguard yourself from the slings and arrows of outrageous fortune.

These intrenchments make you appear cold and calculating, devoid of warmth and compassion. Now, to a child, these defenses can appear to be the walls of Jericho. Until he is old enough and aware he will not know that those walls can tumble down.

Since you do have the inherent warmth, generosity, and mental capacity, you and no other can be the best guiding light for your child. Your storehouse of knowledge should be thrown open to him, and he should delight in sharing and learning with you.

The standards which you set for yourself cannot interfere with your discernment of others' needs or criticism of their behavior. It is quite feasible to discipline and motivate a child without foregoing or suppressing the natural curiosity that opens up new pathways to exploration that will bring you both fulfillment.

Your aesthetic nature and creative talents are there for your child to emulate. Use them to expand his interests and develop his independence but avoid being hyper-critical. If he does not meet your standards for performance in any area, do not declare war and ready the battlefield. Try gentle persuasion. Should you fail, be patient and compensate yourself with his other achievements. His aspirations will revolve around the praise and affection he receives from you—subliminal motivation.

As you value your own individuality so highly, do not hesitate (lest you be lost) to acknowledge that which belongs to your child. Do not attempt to make him a rubber stamp, no matter how ego-gratifying. Grant him the freedom you yourself need. He is a part of you and that should suffice. From you he has inherited a blend of qualities. Now allow him to cultivate his own traits and develop his personal character. The rapport between the two of you will come sooner and endure all the perils of life if you force yourself to be a wise woman early in the career of child rearing.

As you have come to realize during your own lifetime, life does not consist of black and white areas alone. The major portion of our time (and even yours) is plodding along through the gray areas, and so extremes too are relegated in proper perspective to the right and wrong times. You are such a wonder-woman that it should require little of you to avoid suffocating your child, depleting your reserves of love, understanding, and praise. Place yourself in the precarious position of giving your all and you make it impossible for him to give enough in return. Your feelings bruised, you can lick your wounded pride in a grudging way that will consequently be deleterious to him.

From the positive angle, giving just enough will provide him with the self confidence needed to give you pride in his endeavors as he strives to follow your example in a continuing quest for the vital and stimulating things in life. How you dole out your affection is the key.

One pitfall to avoid is playing "Can you top this?" with your child's future. Your leadership qualities are strong and admirable. He can't escape your competency. Children are intuitive and he senses your need for followers. Inundate him with too much of this good thing and his own personality will drown the very first time and not have the strength to try for a third time. Teach him to mimic you in your drive for independence and he can also learn to swim the first time out without benefit of a life preserver or water wings.

Setting him foot-loose is not the equivalent of an Emancipation Proclamation. You need him just as he needs you and perhaps a little bit more. The familial ties are close as are all your warm-hearted relationships. So they will remain even if he is liberated. Give him his privacy so that you will both appreciate your independence and togetherness. You are much more apt to be left alone if you deny him his freedom.

The planet Mars blesses you in its own way with a pugnacious streak that you seem to enjoy. Heated discussions and frequent arguments are routine for you and satisfy your need for finding the best route through an obstacle course. Regard the role of mother as one that must not only be mastered but sometimes requires a stunt-man to keep you from being disqualified. Only with this approach will you come to realize the value of the small tasks and routine chores that come with the job. You are not above it all until your child has a fully developed character, pertinent interests, and a sense of well-ordered balance about him.

Yes, you are older and wiser but that does not give you license to make all the decisions or impose your superior opinions and tested solutions. How will he ever know how right you are unless he learns for himself. Draw him out, listen to him, and let him try his way. You may even learn a new trick or two yourself as an added extra. More important, he will value you and your persuasive ways to a greater degree.

The first time you sit and sigh to yourself over all you have relinquished for this child, grab hold and stop. With your mental capabilities, your physical drive, and stubborn nature, there is no earthly reason for you to be a martyr and give up career interests or hobbies. Few women have the capacity for both and, of those few, you can best cope. This is not just to save your soul and flatter your ego but will complement the child as well.

Once upon a time, not too long ago, an Arian made a mistake and the world did *not* stand still or even slow down. Since then, many more Arians have admitted to failures and errors of human judgment, and the world still turns. Everyone of us has doubts and uncertainties, and even rams have them too. Should you ever achieve the improbable state of perfection you couldn't live with your smug self and could not ask mere mortals to do so. As soon as you can openly admit to a small mistake, your social face will soften and gain warmth. It's a part of delayed adolescence. Now, on a greater scale, make the same allowances for your truly immature child and he will evolve into a wiser and softer grown-up. Thee is no need for either of you to be punished just because there is a resemblance to *homo sapiens*.

This brings you down from the tower onto the gray terra firma again. This land is fraught with roads of compromise which are international two-way highways; those paved with gold are narrow one-way streets, usually dead-end. No major mishaps can occur to either of you when there's room to turn around.

Please don't ask him to be a chapter ahead in Dr. Spock's book or even right on. There will be as many rules of thumb and schedules for his behavior as there are books in print. If he is a month behind in being weaned or learning to write, or if he is just on schedule, leave him be. If he is physically fit and not a child genius this does not make him a second class citizen. Spend more time imbuing him with the human qualities of understanding, generosity, sensitivity, and sociability and tune yourself in to these qualities too. From this, too, all good shall come to pass and no one knows how this could snowball.

Being something of a peacock, you will be just a bit tempted to parade your child around or hold a showing for your ingenious creation. Yes, he is yours and mighty nice at that, but not to be displayed or worshipped as a perfect achievement or extension of yourself. All who know you certainly are aware of your prowess, intellect, and super-human drive. If your children follow suit, let them be discovered on their own; if not, then leave well enough alone lest you harbor ill feelings for his lack of achievement, and exact a toll of one sort or another because of your injured pride.

As an Aries mother you embody all the qualities, good and bad, of the Aries female. You are reckless and intelligent, enthusiastic and headstrong, efficient and full of drive. Many of these qualities can keep you bouncing from one debilitating denouement to another if you do not learn to temper your energies with a dash of endurance and conciliation.

With all your positive qualities as a teacher and leader, your warmth and sense of right and wrong are the makings of a marvelous mother. Watch the negative aspects of possessiveness, domination, and pride and your love for your child will be amply rewarded.

Each child, of course, has his individual sun sign, too, and it will be of enormous help for you to gain knowledge of what you must face in developing a relationship with children born under different signs of the Zodiac.

THE
ARIES
CHILD

THE children of Aries are the first of the zodiacal calendar and the harbingers of spring. The key for this sign is "I am" and don't ever forget it or take it too lightly. Aries is symbolized by the horns of a ram which resemble the small shoots of a plant breaking through the ground. As the plant bursts forth, it is impatient to find the warmth of the sun and proceed with the business of living. Therein lies your guide. In his or her own fashion you will be cued in on who is now top banana in the household. Your baby is glad to be alive and joyous much of the time as he or she delights you with coos and gurgles from the crib. At the same time the infant is restless to get on with life and will show the basic characteristics of his nature—activity, energy, creativity, and, yes, impatience, frustration and irritability. The Arian baby has all of these traits and displays them very quickly. He is happy to be here and wants you to know it.

You can expect that the coos and gurgles will commence upon awakening, unless, of course, your baby is hungry or needs a changing. Under these circumstances the coos will be cries, and the gurgles, bellows that scream with a sense of urgency to bring you running. It would be wise to learn from the outset, no later than the day of arrival back home, that you should anticipate baby's every need. The cries that can emanate from the wee one emerge with such gusto and are filled with such frustration that you will be sure he has a pin sticking into him. You'll learn to adapt and distinguish quickly, and then you will have many delightful hours ahead. Your baby will be lovable, cuddly, and lusting for all the attention you and others can give him, thus, in turn, pleasing you. If the attention is lacking, you run the risk of finding your-self with a little ram on your hands.

As soon as he is a bit older, but just a little bit, you start to impress upon this little being that the world does not and can-not revolve entirely around him. Many kind words and caresses will be necessary to placate him as you gradually start to keep him waiting for you. This is not just a suggestion but a necessity. It must be built into the baby's character as early as possible. A calm atmosphere is of the utmost importance in the early years. Remember that this does not hold true as far as he himself is concerned. He may make the walls tremble his own special brand of wails and vibrations, but woe to anyone that disturbs his tran-quility. He will be alarmingly alert and active at times. A waving about and flailing of arms and little legs is par for the course as is the red face that appears during those long minutes of waiting for mother.

Aries is ruled by the planet Mars which symbolizes activity. As your baby starts to crawl and move around, he will be a little ball of energy and more than slightly active. A wise move would be to remove all sharp and hard objects from his area of play. This Fearless Fosdick will set out to perform daring feats, striking fast with a fistful of courage. Almost every Aries infant is acci-dent-prone and will have an above average number of cuts, bruises, and bumps. So he really does need your protection. Use your finesse when he gets old enough to understand. A no-no will bring about a defiant outburst of some kind. Anything within his grasp that is a source of potential danger is something you can be sure he will have an encounter with, often more than one. Do your best to develop those eyes in the back of your head.

Prime importance must be placed on instilling cooperation into his character at an early stage. Arians are concerned mainly with themselves and are most aggressive in their own self-interest. Start by teaching him, or her, to share material possessions, toys, etc., with other children. At times he will do so with marvelous and surprising liberalism. However, those who bruise his ego or abuse him would best profit by leaving town rather than face the wrath that will be incurred.

Sylvia is a perfect example of the bright-but-bossy Aries baby. She is ahead of her playmates in learning new tricks and discovering the world. In the process of passing on this information to the other kiddies she will share her knowledge and her possessions as long as she reigns supreme as the undisputed know-it-all. As soon as someone else within her play group discovers and introduces a "first", she has lost the game of "one-up-manship" and will toddle away dragging all her toys behind her. More often, pushing them out of reach or into the "new discoverer" is up her alley. She has even been known to toss those toys right out of sight or at the traitors that have turned away from her. After such a scene she comes flying into Mama's waiting arms for comfort. Beware.

The Fire brings warmth, and you may be suffocated and smothered at times with affectionate kisses and hugs. Very few are inhibited in this area, and if they are, it is due to some emotional experience and not basic nature. Be sure to caution all babysitters that your child should be treated with kid gloves. A sharp reprimand that would work with other children may throw him into a temper tantrum and, let's face it, babysitters are hard to come by these days.

The usual disciplinary measure will be completely unavailing with your ram. He has a facility for self-administering blackouts and, therefore, does not learn from experience when the customary punishments are meted out. You will notice this after several rounds of having your efforts bring about only wrath and indignation. Remember, his spirit is a combination of Captain Courageous and the defiant devil. Deprivation and denial of expected delights will more readily motivate him to concur.

Exercising your lungs will be as ineffectual as spanking his bottom, so spare yourself the agitation. He has built-in earplugs on such occasions. The body stands before you, but his mind is most probably into the middle of next week. Rewarding him in a prudent manner for excellent (not just good) behavior will make the worm turn. Rest secure (if at all possible) in the knowledge that after the worm starts to turn, your child will come around surely and speedily, eventually reaching a loving and lovable stage. A true angel, though, he will never be.

The care and feeding of these children will be a little disconcerting at first but you'll learn how to handle this as well. Your child's tastes in food will be very definite as a baby and even more so as the years progress. There will be no compromises made without much subtle training. When he is fed something that he finds displeasing, watch out. The walls may need a new paint job. At an age when he can first handle silverware or a cup, you should keep a large supply on hand. Impatience that stems from a wait for food or displeasure with its taste will lead to much banging, breaking and denting of dinnerware.

Before you begin to think that you have a real problem child on your hands, let me try to dispel some of your qualms. Your child is one of extreme sensitivity whose emotions are easily bruised. This may seem to be a contradiction or conflict in personality but give it a little thought. Anyone that is concerned with, and aware of, self to such a degree must likewise be concerned with the opinions of others towards him. You must be very patient and precise in explaining on a level that will make sense to the child. When explaining, please be sure that in your own inimitable way you are absolutely truthful at all times. This again relates back to an understanding that the world does not function for his pleasure. Neither you nor others exist to please him. When handled correctly he will respond beautifully and probably overwhelm you.

Your child is also gifted with a vivid and fascinating imagination that will be of great use to him in later life. Don't break his bubble about fairies, Santa Claus, and the good ship Lollipop too early. Magic holds a fascination for him and fairly tales must have been written by a fellow Arian for Aries children to dream on. All children have imaginary friends and with your child's imagination even you can almost see and hear these friends.

When it comes to playtime, and toys in particular, expect a preference for anything red. The color signifies the vibrancy of the personality (small as it still is) and the element of fire which injects white heat into an already active and energetic youngster. The girls will have a passion for red dresses and flamboyant colors. By the way, the Arian girls are no different in their actions or determination. Never subtle (Aries children cannot be), the girls will appear somewhat more mellow, but underneath it all still burns the same fire.

Little Sylvia is precocious, as you would expect. She is, however, still the female of the species. Before she could stand, she had uncovered the wiles of femininity and Daddy is still all tied up in ribbons. A certain smile, a direct gaze, or a toss of her little head at just the right moment gets her man every time. Even though she is old enough to communicate more directly now, she has learned the value of coquetry; how it spares her punishment, the way a female's helplessness becomes her strength, and, most important, how to avert the severe decrees handed down by mother. The soul seems soft but the spirit is steely.

Arians are trail-blazers by nature but very prone to letting someone else finish up. The inception is theirs and once underway, their mind is already caught up in the details of another and more exciting challenge. When the time comes for you to discover and exploit the talents that your little wonder possesses, it should also be handled with kid gloves.

He is an investigator and a forerunner of all things new. Glee will spread over his face at the sight of a new toy or the thought of a fresh project—very often this will be mischievous glee. Here again is where you are a vital force. Too often the toy or project will be quickly abandoned, boredom will set in, and another "untried" grabs his attention with a fierce passion. You should, from the very beginning, make it mandatory that one thing be finished and done with before allowing the child to undertake something new. Even with playthings, see to it that the old is put away before the new is given its turn. Put those blocks back in the box before the game is dragged out. This will take some time and training on your part, as well as persistence. You must stick to your guns and help the child complete the project or he will be off and into something else before you know where he is at.

He will undoubtedly want to take lessons on every instrument known to the Boston Symphony. All forms of art and every Olympic sport will be on his list. Your child is more talented than most, so play fair for his sake. Let him sign up for lessons in music, or what have you, but on a short term basis. This will allow you both to feel the situation out and investigate the amount of prowess in any given area. Should he want to take additional lessons in a favored area of accomplishment, by all means encourage it and spur him on. Energy and perseverance will go into the learning of anything in which he has a real interest. Let the

Aries child pace himself in these lessons and that is the golden rule as far as school is concerned as well. Don't ride herd on your child. Nagging or criticism will be misinterpreted and the child can become easily discouraged.

Sylvia is proficient on the piano and clarinet, in horseback riding and softball, and in ballet and cookie-baking. All things she has learned well and abandoned just as readily. Once the undisputed champion of the student group, her interest vanished. After all is said and done, however, she still remains a respectable match in any of these areas even without practice. Now, tell me, is that all bad?

Now that you can rest assured that your child will never be on the analyst's couch, his physical health should be given some consideration. Oftentimes the Aries baby will run a high fever during the teething period and with all childhood diseases. So don't get overly alarmed. This is par for the course. Do have a good pediatrician on hand. Do not allow every injury to his being to strike terror in your heart. Much rest is needed for your little cherub to make up for all that activity during the waking hours. Add a lot of fresh air and you have the secret for refueling that bundle of energy. Like anyone else his battery will need recharging, but more than the ordinary amount. Aries, as you know, rules the head, and in later years he will be a sufferer of frequent headaches. See to it that regular eye examinations are part of his physical check-ups. Incidentally, energetic Arians are often subject to migraine headaches about which little can be done.

School can be a most exciting and yet frustrating experience for your Arian. Exploring will be an adventure, but he will tend to become lax again when it comes to studying. Forewarn his teacher about the consequences of nagging. When something is presented as a challenge to this child, he will respond with such fervor and energy that you should get out of the line of fire. He will go to any lengths to prove that he cannot be topped by another mortal who is just ordinary. Any application whatsoever on his part will result in the immediate and total comprehension and knowledge of the subject at hand. Should he be surpassed once or twice by his peers he will see to it that he will never be shamed again. You're going to have a whiz kid on your hands sooner or later.

When at play with his peers the Aries youngster will always be the one giving orders and trying to dominate. The quality of leadership is a plus factor but only when it is properly developed. Very gentle guidance is called for so that his enthusiasm will not be squelched. Too firm a hand will result in a rebellious, domineering adolescent who is poison ivy to his contemporaries. He will seek out those with weak and submissive characters over whom he can easily exert influence.

Rote learning is not his cup of tea. He is much too creative for such mundane things. Sluffing off homework could appear to you and his teacher as being pure laziness. You, at least, should know better. He simply feels that tending to homework is a loss of valuable time and he would rather be active in something else that will burn off some of his energy. Don't be distressed by the possibility that his marks in school will often not measure up to expectations. You and his teacher both know it is not due to a lack of intelligence, but rather that he lacks a consistency of purpose.

Sylvia has the highest I.Q. in her class since kindergarten. Once, when in the third grade, she was threatened with not passing on to the fourth. Her teacher realized that Sylvia was bright enough to make it but was upset constantly by her lack of attention and apparent rudeness. Once briefed by her parents, the teacher found devious means to keep her attention long enough to achieve the desired results— something to spark her interest long enough to have the right answer on the tip of her tongue. Luckily, he was able to accomplish this without creating a contest to "get to the head of the class". Just so long as the seat of thought is exercised, the report card grades are secondary. Nothing and no one will keep this boarding house reacher from arriving at her station in life.

His career possibilities will be limitless. Anything from soup to nuts is open to him. Any field can be mastered. Be assured that he will be an innovator in whatever he does. He will rarely be unreasonable about salary or income and will seek only what he feels he is really worth. Creativity abounds in his nature and it is very likely that the communications fields would be a natural for your child. Advertising, sales, or any form of public relations that requires personality plus are good possibilities. The arts are very probably another possibility. Any field that will sop up that drive, energy, and resourcefulness is where he will be found.

You must accept the birth of your child with open arms and an open mind. If well warned about what to expect, you will have few disappointments and much pride and pleasure from your little Arian. Above all, use discretion and diplomacy in handling your ball of fire. Even though you are in the driver's seat don't be tempted to become a driving force. The spirit of leadership is a blessing, but you as a parent have the initial responsibility for balancing the scales so that this characteristic does not turn your child into a domineering adult.

For babies born between March 21st and March 31st your child's personal planet is the same as his ruling planet—Mars. This influence will emphasize the stubborn and impatient streaks in your baby's temperament. Temper tantrums are more prominent with children born within this period, as well as more intense degrees of drive and impetuosity. Much success is to be gained by these particular children above and beyond the accomplishments of other Arian children and you have learned that those are usually above and beyond the ordinary child.

Babies that come into the world between April 1st and April 10th have the Sun as their very personal planet. This injects an overwhelming amount of warmth into the personality, tempering some of the adverse aspects of the Mars character. Pride and ambition are intensified under the sign of the Sun and give vent to the insatiable appetite for the new and undiscovered. First, there was the Sun . . . . Inspiration and originality will be dominant.

Those babies born between April 10th and April 19th have the added advantage of Jupiter as their personal planet. Jupiter is Lady Luck itself. The sensitive side of your child is more visible if he is born during this period. The traits that have dubbed the symbol for this sign to be the ram are also more noticable with these kidlets. Dignified, impetuous, and, oh, so lovable—you really have a bundle of contradictions here.

THE ARIES
MOTHER
AND HER CHILD

The Aries Mother And The Aries Child

Sometimes opposites attract, and sometimes not. With an Aries child possessed of your same strengths there will be head-on clashes that Mars never imagined. Impatience, impulsiveness, and iron wills come face to face—a stubborn child and an authoritative parent.

With a midget mirror reflection of yourself, you must use *self* discipline and not react instinctively. Think before you act or react. Do not feel for a moment that size and strength will solve the problem at hand. Be explanatory, logical, and persuasive. Do not push, menace, or carry a big stick. What a child cannot understand he cannot do.

Under the proper circumstances and with the rules of the game down pat, you can enjoy much from and with this child. Mutual awareness of each other's love and giving nature can cement otherwise loose ties. This child will be one of your greatest challenges but one from whom you can derive the utmost pleasure.

The Aries Mother And The Taurus Child

The Taurus child is one that will tax what little patience and forebearance exists within you. An indispensable cry for moderation is to be heard, since he operates at a deliberate and slow pace completely contrary to your nature. You can also be as deliberate in your haste to retard the habit of procrastination from becoming a full time hobby before he is operating at top speed. This must be done with understanding and without throwing you into a frenzy.

The Taurus child will often draw you to him magically and

14

send you into a rage just as miraculously. The more you exercise your authority and try to impose your will, the more apt he is to persist and behave like the bull he was born.

Be effervescent, exuding charm and persuasiveness and a prayer or two. Do not harp or nag. It's a waste of time and effort. This situation is one of those cases where a cheerful mother can lead to the brass ring whereas an authoritarian approach will bring instantaneous strife.

The Aries Mother And The Gemini Child

You'll mutter under your breath and be cranky with the Gemini twins who irritate you and keep you scurrying hither and yon. He is much like you. His restless soul and inexhaustible energy pleases you and keeps you from getting bored with either one of them.

The two of you will have much in common. A neverending exchange of ideas and vitality keep you both sparkling and invested with the job of being alive.

Whatever conflicts arise will undoubtedly end up bringing you more animation than agitation. You'll never be bored with each other and will go through life delighting in your relationship that always retains its stimulation and variation.

The Aries Mother And The Cancer Child

In order to obtain and retain a harmonious level of rapport with your moon child, you must expend a substantial amount of effort, all of which will be amply rewarded if you succeed. Through all stages of his growing years and on a frequent basis, this child will want things to remain "status quo" and not budge while you require excitement, thrills, and action.

No one-way streets can be followed here. It's the middle road —a two way street that is a necessity. Keep cool and keep the golden way. It's the only way.

If you play your cards right, your lunar love will exert a calming influence on you. At the same time, you can bring excitement and adventure into his placid and serene life style. Sharing and being together will bring understanding. You'll both be the wiser.

The Aries Mother And The Leo Child

Your extroverted little lion cub will bring you a tremendous amount of pleasure. A mutual admiration society will be established and the appeal each of you holds for the other should bring happiness to you both.

This child is at his best when he is somewhat *insecure*. A need for the exciting and adventurous is one that you should admire along with a zest for new places and new faces, a characteristic you have in common.

His natural curiosity and intellectual pursuits amaze you and bring moments of pleasure. Your lack of patience, however, will grow as you find his incessant queries, as he gets older, to be quite irritating and annoying at times.

With both of you as active participants, the mother-child relationship of give-and-take can start at a young age and last for a number of years to come.

The Aries Mother And The Virgo Child

This is one child who makes you feel uncomfortable and uneasy with his cool and logical attitude. He will prove to be invaluable to you simply by cajoling you to test your many, and sometimes unreal, dreams in practice.

He will eat away at your sense of duty and force you to face discomforting but crucial thoughts. There will be no getting out, no excuses, and no procrastination in doing what must be done as long as your Virgo child is within the view-finder or hearing range.

There will be times when you'll be peeved, feeling that this is more than you bargained for, but in more appreciative, somber moments you'll be as grateful for his concern with detail as you will be by his concern about your health and attitude.

You may feel your ego bruised a bit with his criticisms but if you listen, you may find your disposition improving. Keep an open mind and respond in kind. With a Virgo child you have a wise, young, old man or woman overnight. Hark his words.

The Aries Mother And The Libra Child

A Libra child is your opposite in the Zodiac and here again the old adage about opposites attracting holds water.

Your child's generous and warm nature will make you happy. You must keep on guard to avoid playing on his giving trait and taking unfair advantage. Do not take everything he is capable of giving, for he will let go of more than he can afford, emotionally and otherwise.

With Libra, you cannot be overly domineering and must curb this proclivity. Easy, but slow, and you are sure to make it. Let him know that you really have heart and that it is all for him. Reassure him often and sincerely. Be flexible and tune in to your child's compassion and generosity and there will be no conflicts. Do not come on too harshly. You can inflict unnecessary hurts and bruises on this tender child with just a few words.

The Aries Mother And The Scorpio Child

Your Scorpion can frighten the daylights out of you or make you tenser than you ever imagined. As an Aries mother the very time you spend together can set sparks aflame and emotions aboil.

The interplay of two such volatile personalities will bring you both (without your awareness) to do and say things completely out of character. Circumstances will not ever be casual or boring. A smooth-as-glass relationship is an impossibility, but then again there would be no challenge if that were to be the case. You will probably find such a situation pleasant and exciting.

The relationship will be predictably unpredictable, full of ups and downs, mysteries, and intrigues. It is possible to head off in any direction at any time. Do make sure that you as a parent step in to curb the free flying emotions, acting as a stabilizer so that the relationship remains one of stimulation and not intimidation. Sheer ecstasy can be yours almost forever if you remember to temper some of those delirious moments.

The Aries Mother And The Sagittarius Child

This will be a rewarding and gratifying relationship for the two of you, with many fringe benefits. You and your little archer will work and play well together, soul-searching amplifying your intellectual faculties. There is very little that will not bring joy, respect, and love into your time together at home or away.

The learning process will not be relegated to the little one either. He will be a force to reckon with and one that will buoy you up, in one way or another, to broaden your horizons, devote more time to your interests and, if you have the desire, to forge ahead with your creative talent to achieve some recognition for yourself.

Exploring new territories or returning to favorite places will be completely relaxing and most pleasant with your little Sagittarius. Each of you will spur the other on to spend more time on the road tripping on any sojourn that will give you new insights.

The only danger this relationship can encounter is one developing from your mutual tendency to seek too much too soon and reach for impossible heights. Very little else will interfere with a delightful and pleasurable mother-child alliance for years to come.

The Aries Mother And The Capricorn Child

This is another combination that will test your endurance and patience. The mountain-goat will intrigue you and keep you in a quandary much of the time. Put a harness on all impulsive words and deeds with the Capricorn child—proceed slowly and with caution. This child is equipped with such a strong protective instinct that he could easily rival a Cancer mother. Don't be misled by what you think to be a slow and easy-going pace and apparently passive mind. Look a little deeper and you will behold great treasures. That protective streak can sneak up on you if you should become too lax or complacent. You will find yourself with the roles reversed with the most capable Capricorn holding your hand while babysitting with you.

Understanding is a reciprocal trade agreement and one necessary for this familial bond to flourish. He will be willing to understand your wants if you acknowledge and bear with his beliefs, different as they may be·from yours.

The Aries Mother And The Aquarius Child

The Aquarian child has a great need for love, friendship, and affection, all of which he is willing to give in generous portions. He must also have your time and attention to test the affection that you often try to mask.

The relationship can be a happy one and fulfilling in an un-usual, mysterious way. Each of you will make elaborate promises which are well-intentioned at the time, but which cannot usually be kept.

It is essential, therefore that you become the stabilizing force that keeps your relationship on a well-grounded and tangible pla-teau. It is far too easy to slip into a pattern of building dreams that consistently remove you from the truth of your daily existence. Level off your dreams. Do not aspire to anything higher than a child can hope to attain, else the disappointments and setbacks leave scar tissue.

You Aquarian wonder will operate at a speed pleasing to you and his reflexes are equally in keeping with your standards. He may ride a mite slipshod, though whizzing along at this pace, and you should attempt to hold him back a little to make him cogitate and reflect before moving. This you can do together so you and your child can have a longer lasting relationship.

The Aries Mother And The Pisces Child

This is one child that must be handled with great tenderness and compassion. Doing so will be a difficult task for you since he will unearth and bring to the surface some of your innermost fears and desires. For some unknown reason, he makes you feel that you could be taken advantage of to an irrational degree. You will be concerned about giving more than you receive. You are an in-dividual who wants an even return for your investment, whether it be time, money, or emotion.

In a mystical way, the Pisces child can burrow beneath your defenses and see the fears beneath your exterior. He will be blunt even when it makes you smart with pain because it will be true. At the same time that you wince with the hurt and become irritated with him, you are aware of the merit of such a trait.

Truth will be the basis for your relationship, and it will be a happy one. Learn to handle the unforeseen, especially the unfore-seen actions that will bear your soul to him. Once you have learned to accept these truths calmly and with grace, they will be invaluable to you in future days.

While learning to live with the truth, you must also watch your Pisces child for a possible lack of ambition and persistence. Since you know this characteristic all too well, you can work toward the common goal of cultivating better habits.

This combination is not the easiest to digest, but the potpourri can intermingle to provide you with a palatable and delicious result. Pull all the components together in a cohesive bond and you will eventually find an admirable alloy of love and cooperation.

STAR GUIDE
FOR
ARIES

Symbol	●	The Ram
Ruling Planet	●	Mars
Element	●	Fire
Gender	●	Masculine
Key Words	●	I Am
Birthstones	●	Diamond, Bloodstone
Favorite Flowers	●	Red Rose, Sweet Pea
Best Colors	●	All Reds
Mineral	●	Iron
Favorite Music	●	Marches
Favorite Pastime	●	Travel
Lucky Number	●	3
Best Days	●	Tuesday, Thursday
Compatible Signs	●	Aquarius, Gemini, Sagittarius
Incompatible Signs	●	Cancer, Capricorn

FAMOUS PEOPLE
BORN UNDER
THE SIGN OF THE RAM

DEAN ACHESON
EDWARD ALBEE
HANS CHRISTIAN
  ANDERSON
PEARL BAILEY
WARREN BEATTY
LEONARD
  BERNSTEIN
BISMARCK
MARLON
  BRANDO
CHARLIE
  CHAPLIN
ILKA CHASE
JULIE CHRISTIE
WILLIAM P.
  CHRYSLER
HENRY CLAY
JOAN CRAWFORD
PERRY COMO
BETTE DAVIS   '
THOMAS E.
  DEWEY
ANATOLE
  FRANCE
ROBERT FROST
JAMES GARNER
ALEC GUINNESS

HOUDINI
WASHINGTON
  IRVING
THOMAS
  JEFFERSON
GEORGE JESSEL
NIKITA
  KHRUSCHEV
JOSEPH LISTER
CLAIRE BOOTH
  LUCE
HENRY LUCE
GUY DE
  MAUPASSANT
SHIRLEY
  MACLAINE
EUGENE
  MACARTHY
J. PIERPONT
  MORGAN
GREGORY PECK
MARY PICKFORD
LILY PONS
JOSEPH PULITZER
SERGEI
  RACHMANINOV
DEAN RUSK
OMAR SHARIF

SIMONE
  SIGNORET
HAROLD
  STASSEN
LEOPOLD
  STOKOWSKI
RICHARD
  STRAUSS
GLORIA
  SWANSON
LOWELL THOMAS
ARTURO
  TOSCANINI
ARNOLD
  TOYNBEE
SPENCER TRACY
MARK TWAIN
PETER USTINOV
VINCENT VAN
  GOGH
WERNER VON
  BRAUN
WILLIAM
  WORDSWORTH
TENNESSEE
  WILLIAMS
F.W.WOOLWORTH
WILBUR WRIGHT

22

THE TAURUS MOTHER

April 20th — May 20th

YOU Taurus women have the capacity to make superb mothers if you caution yourselves to remain ever mindful of those innate Taurus qualities that would work both for and against you. The fact that you have so much power to put a "stamp" on your children should be an incentive to you to make certain that only your most desirable qualities are constantly on display. Children, despite their individual signs, will tend to take on some of the characteristics of the mother, either consciously or unconsciously, taking into consideration the theory of environmental influences. Naturally, the influences of their own particular signs will have a mitigating effect here. The emulation will result just the same, usually to a noticeable degree. This plea for caution to Taurus mothers, or future mothers, is based on the very real danger that Taurus's natural tendency toward a domineering personality may have a harmful effect on children whose personalities are just in the making.

A Taurus mother may actually inhibit her child's mental or emotional development, even though she may feel that she is following the correct formula for the perfect, no-fail child. On the brighter side though, Taurus may be domineering and overprotective. You do treat your children in a consistent and rarely frazzled manner, and give them the feelings of constancy and stability that are so important to a child's mental and emotional development. You are almost like the Rock of Gibraltor, radiating stability and security, even if your own world is crumbling into ruin. Practically no adverse act of man or God can unhinge you to the point that your children lose even the illusion of security. Some may accuse you of lack of sensitivity, not realizing your ability to deal with trouble by bottling up your emotions. Everyone concedes that in times of adversity you can't be beat.

Taurus approaches motherhood in much the same manner as you approach every other aspect of life—with the forcefulness, perseverance and take-charge attitude that are your sign's most distinctive characteristics. Let's take one of your Taurus mothers in her first pregnancy. Now, she's just enough of a diplomat to smile sweetly, nodding her head to all those clamoring around her with their own brand of advice. But Spock or no Spock—she's going to do everything her way in the end. All we can do is hope and pray that her instincts are correct. And, as nature would have it, they usually are. One theory of child-rearing is that the mother should raise her children in the manner that comes naturally to her. This is the theory to which most of you adhere. The danger lurking here, however, is that your intuitive feelings about child-rearing are a little off mark. If they are, it's going to be an uphill battle for anyone or anything to set you straight.

The Taurus bull, more than individuals born under the other eleven signs, seems to be able to take just about anything in stride. You mothers, or future Taurus mothers, are least likely of all women to hold any resentment toward your pregnancies or children, whether they are the result of a divine plan or a not-so-divine accident. Your kids will never suffer in any way from your feelings, whether conscious or subconscious, that your life would have been a lot more glamorous without them. Since nobody, however artful, can ever hope to conceal an undercurrent of resentments forever, the Taurus mother gets a big gold star in this category. Resentment just does not compute in the Taurus's mind for very long, anyway. She hasn't time to think about past injustices or misfortunes in her haste to get on with life. You might say that the Taurus could bull his way through anything by sheer force of will.

The foregoing does not wrap up the motherhood championship for Taurus, however. Quite a few Taurus women view motherhood as a necessary evil. Although outwardly you do all the things a mother should do, you may be sorely lacking in the area of emotional involvement. Sure, you provide for your child's every physical need; you're a good (if a bit stodgy) cook, immaculate housekeeper, and confident inspiring nurse, but your attitude toward motherhood is frequently uninspired, and this lack of spirit may be transmitted to your children. I know of one Taurus mother, in particular, who prides herself on the high quality of her child care (it's her main vanity), but in whom the spirit of motherhood seems to be missing.

Taurus women tend to be strict mothers, a fact which can be attributed largely to your faith in your own judgment as to how things should be done. You're generally sticklers for order and neatness, even perfectionists. You prefer to get pesky little things like toilet training or comprehension of and respect for the word "no" over at a very early age. You frequently find yourselves boasting to other mothers (especially those with unruly children) how well behaved your little darlings are. Frequently they tend to view their children not so much as individuals, but as extensions of themselves. You may get unduly upset if your child falls behind in school or gets into a scrape of some kind because you feel that you have failed in some way in the eyes of others. This reluctance to accept your children as individuals with lives of their own is the main reason that Taurus mothers tend to have more trouble than mothers born under other signs with teenage children. No matter how children are brought up, they will all rebel to a certain extent when they reach adolescence. This rebellion is a bitter pill for Taurus mothers to take. To see your well-behaved darling suddenly do an about face, and become a threat to your orderly existence is, in some cases, more than you can bear. You may even feel like shutting these monsters out of your life entirely. The Taurus personality isn't noted for its tolerance of departures from what is considered to be normal behavior. For the Taurus mother to get through this harrowing period of her children's development takes a lot of love and understanding. Just remember that this is just a phase and that your children will be better people for having gone through it. You are bound to learn a valuable lesson in human nature and be a better person, as well. Love can get you through almost anything and pay dividends in return. Eventually you'll come to accept your children for what they are and do, even if you may not approve of what they are and do. This forced lesson in tolerance will carry over into other interpersonal affairs as well.

Here is a general guideline for the Taurus mother to follow.

These are just broad suggestions to cover a variety of situations from the moment of your baby's birth. You should start to think of him as a person with an identity all his own rather than just another responsibility to shine at. You have a tendency to say, "I have to", instead of "I want to". Nip that attitude in the bud and you'll always be thankful you did. Another pitfall to watch out for is calling your child "baby" long after he is climbing trees and hitting pop-ups. Get in the habit early of using his name instead, and you'll force yourself to think of the complete identity that fits the name. Don't be too harsh on your child when he begins what seems to be a systematic destruction of his environment. A little destructiveness is normal, and you can decide when to draw the line. Remind yourself that destructiveness and creativity often go hand in hand, and the suppression of the former may insure the suppression of the latter as well. This danger may not even occur to Taurus mothers who have allowed themselves to lapse into pure conventionality. But you have the concern of your children at heart and will not spurn advice if you realize the benefits that result.

Taurus mothers as a whole take their responsibilities seriously and are noted for being a solid success. Make sure you use these tips from astrology to help you through your new motherhood.

THE
TAURUS
CHILD

TAURUS is symbolized by the horns of a bull. If you were to see this sign, however, by itself, you might be inclined to say that it resembles the chin and Adam's apple of a human being. Your baby's key word is "I have" and you will become aware of this without delay. Further speculation on the symbol for your child could lead an observer to note the similarity to a crescent lying on its back, that might simulate a cup holding something. This will indicate to you the generally placid nature of your offspring as an infant. Just so long as he is being held and has a hold on that bottle, he will give you little trouble, far different in temperament from the Aries child. There will be much less fuss and ado about nothing, with your Taurus baby. A far greater degree of contentment comes in this little package, no flailing and thrashing about of arms and legs with this child. Love is ruled by Venus as is your baby's sign. It is love that will make your child respond. Just keep this in the front of your mind at all times. Comfort and love will keep him happy early in his life. Make big strides to create a warm and loving atmosphere and you will have a minimum of difficulty and frustration. Setting up and maintaining a schedule is of great importance for the Taurus child's well-being. It is practical, and he can sense the logic. He is an Earth sign, and the practicality of a routine and schedule fits the mold. Baby will look forward with great expectation to feedings, baths, and any event that becomes an established part of a daily routine in his life. You will be greeted with coos and gurgles every time, if you respond to this baby's needs. Once a routine is formed, it would be advisable for you to adhere to the schedule if you value the atmosphere you have created. Try to vary the hour of established routine and you can witness your little bull see red. Should you not be there when you should, the horns will be lowered, and a matador could not get a bigger rise out of your baby.

Above all, he will not be able to understand how you, the love of his life, could commit such an insulting deed. Look at it from his point of view. Here are the two of you, good friends. He would never run the risk of hurting you, would he? And you already know what the best method of handling such a situation is going to be. That's right, affection—cradling your baby, rocking him, and cooing a little yourself. Make sure that he understands you are sorry and it was not intentional. When he is completely calm, you know you have made your point. Taurean babies love to be sung to and, if mother has a good voice, try a lullaby or two. If your voice is not good, still sing, but only so long as your baby is young enough to not know the difference. Venus also governs music, and your child is like the savage beast that is soothed by music. He will have an excellent ear for music and very likely will become fairly accomplished in the field (particularly in singing). Don't run the risk of overdoing things if your talents are limited. Make sure he has a radio or record player of his own in later years.

While Taurus is ruled by Venus, it is an Earth sign which bespeaks solidarity and practicality. Your baby will not be quite the daredevil that the Arian child can be. As he starts to crawl around and later toddle, he will be apt to use caution and take things slow and easy. He will prefer to be sure of the ground under his feet. He will teeter and totter, moving along, grabbing onto each piece of furniture for support, as he wends his way along. There is no charging straight ahead for this level-headed youngster. He wants to be certain of just what he can do before he goes it alone.

One of the problems you can expect from your child, as an infant, will come when you try to break the bottle habit. A creature of routine, he will not take this intrusion very lightly. Weaning can be a traumatic experience and the earlier the better with this child. Naturally, your physician should be the determining factor here, but remember that if you wait too long he may start the first grade with bottle in hand. The bottle has become a routine and therefore, a part of him and his life. Watch out. It is a possession and your little angel's key word is "I have". Infringing on his basic nature can turn weaning him from the bottle into an act of sacrilege in his mind. Walk slowly and carry a small club. Your little tot is a wee bit stubborn when being prodded or pushed. Never, and I do mean never, push that immovable object around. Gentleness and patience will get you far, as will logical acts and explanations.

Ronnie is a typical little bull and holds on to *his* private possessions. When his mother first tried to separate him from his teething ring (long after he had a full set of choppers), she not only forgot the golden rule, "don't push", but was unprepared for the gritting of those same teeth, just as a bull hoofs the ground and lowers his head before charging ahead. It is no small wonder that those baby teeth were not ground down into powder before Mama did recall that it was basically a matter of mental combat. The Taurus child would just as soon avoid a confrontation with "el matador", so Mom changed her tactic to one that was firm but loving, suggesting extra playtime together if he would surrender. Suddenly the bull was a little lamb.

Later on you will find that some difficulty is to be encountered in the area of sharing toys and what have you with others. Far different from the Arian child, who is uncooperative because of his own interest in a toy, or a person, or the will to dominate, your child is a collector. Whether or not a particular toy is in use (it could have been buried and untouched in the back of his toy chest for two months), it is still his exclusive property. You have a job on your hands here. A sense of responsibility is wonderful, but the obsession with ownership of material items must be played down and tempered by you very early in the game. You won't run into the typical "instant mess" when playtime comes around. Your proud possessor will care for and handle his belongings with pride. Most likely, each toy will be whisked away before you have a chance to give the order (in a subtle way, of course). Do your job well. The loss of a material object will be catastrophic to your collector. If you install a sense of value early enough, it will mean a few less rough spots for you and far less scars for him.

Favorite playthings will fall into definite categories. As you may suspect, any toy with a musical twist is on the top of the list. Music boxes, little pianos, animals that speak in soft melodious tones will be preferred both in infancy and in later years, in more mature forms. Colors hold a special fascination for the bull; pastels, soft and delicate colors. Crayons will be purchased by the boxload, as he will adore the do-it-yourself aspect of coloring, books and paints. His reactions to this form of self-expression will be almost visible to you. His senses are tuned to the melodious (he hates loud noises), soft, and vibrant tones, and his disposition will be affected by these factors. The dark and startling colors will fall by the wayside, as will the harsher sounds in music.

Your youngster is a good child and will do as he is told most of the time. He may be somewhat slower than some of his peers, but then he will retain what he absorbs far longer. You are more fortunate than most parents and will reap great joys from your warm and affectionate child. Many bruises will adorn your body from tight embraces and fervent kisses. There will be no question about where you stand in his affections. The boys will be boys all the way down the line—basically athletic, mischievous, and impish. The little girls will be femme fatales as soon as they are old enough to wink and flash a seductive smile at Daddy to get their way.

With typical bullish perserverence, Taurus will try, try, and try again to succeed when he has decided that something is worth his efforts. The determination contained within that little being would very likely stagger a real-life, full-grown bull. Allow twice as much time as necessary for him to even lift a finger. His need for achievement is so great, he won't take the chance of acting too hastily. Be firm when *you* take the first steps toward speeding him up. No one but you will have the motherly patience it takes to wait for him to move, and even you have difficulty. Do not hesitate or leave room for argument. Treat any rebellion with swift dismissal, showing little or no emotion. If this treatment starts too late you may never live to see him break the four-hour mile. His speed, or lack of it, will mushroom as he ages.

You are blessed, believe it or not, in having a child who adapts to schedules easily. As a result, your offspring will be a patient learner, accepting the discipline and rigidity of school schedules without a ripple or wave after the first day or week. Never forget that "I have" attitude. At the very beginning, school will symbolize the taking away of mother, his most prized posses-

sion. The bull will charge that first day, so beware! Any child
has difficulty in adjusting to the new and insecure atmosphere of
his first days at kindergarten or nursery school, and understandably so. No child wants to be left in strange surroundings without
"mom", and your child will hold your hand until it is wrenched
away. Then his teacher can expect him to raise cain. Please clue
her in on what it's all about so that she may prepare your child for
what is to come. Tell him why it has to be this way. Pull no punches
and tell it like it is. If at all possible, try to have your child meet
the teacher in advance of that frightening day so that some of the
strain will be removed. This may be your first opportunity to take
a look-see at your child in a social situation of this magnitude. You
will find that he is somewhat shy, and consequently needs a gentle
shove with some encouragement behind it. This timidity is part of
a positive nature. Your little Taurean is basically a receptive child.

Ronnie is not only receptive, but obedient to an inordinate,
degree. He is the type of child who rarely needs to be reprimanded
in school. If he were subject to punishment, he would delight in
writing, "I will not stick chewing gum in Sandy's hair again", one
hundred times, doing it so neatly that he would deserve an A+
for penmanship. Once, his teacher asked the class to draw pictures
for the bulletin board. Ronnie went home and created a new little
something every night to bring to school the following day. Teacher
tried to stop him. She tried, and tried, and tried, finally placing
Ronnie in charge of room decorations as a solution to a very common problem.

You can expect relatively little trouble at school, despite the
bullish tendencies of the adorable one. If he is teased or taunted
in any way, or misinterprets any action or word of a peer or
teacher, that streak may come shining through in the classroom.
Hope that his first teacher is an affectionate one, because she is
your stand-in at the outset. He will want to follow instructions and
will be able to, because he listens well and means well.

Do not ever push your youngster into the limelight in front
of guests. He is shy and the underlying aversion to a shove will
only create a negative situation in such circumstances. The scene
can be counted upon to remain tranquil almost all the time; that
is, as tranquil as it can be with a child. You will run into far fewer
problems with your Taurus child than most mothers. Always get

your point across in times of trouble or doubt by emphasizing and playing up the sweet and loving, not the rigid and disciplinary.

Taurus rules the area of the throat, and health problems will most likely be centered in this area. In infancy, it is important to constantly check this area since the tot can hardly be expected to tell you if he has a sore throat. At the first sign of fever, call a doctor. Be sure that you and he check the throat area for infection. More often than not, you will have found the trouble spot. You can relax when it comes to eating habits. Good, plain food is your best bet now. Later on, he will have a proclivity to a sweet tooth. Hold back on the rich foods, also. Being moderate and keeping it simple will establish balanced appetites that will hopefully become an unbroken routine. Sensible habits can be established now. Taureans can become gourmets with insatiable appetites for the sweet and the rich, which must be under constant control.

A Taurus child may well inspire the next book in a series called The Sensuous Child. His pleasures are thoroughly received and his instinctive appreciation for the finer things does not hinder his beautification program. Few people are so gifted with an ability to sing with delight when something truly pleases them. Fortunately, he also is endowed with good taste. He is a sensualist with superior style.

Your practical child possesses quite a bit of stamina. This will stand him in good stead as he grows older; to carry him through the college years with ease if he decides to go on. Money is ruled by Taurus and it will not be wasted on his education. If a means to the end is a college education, he will do well what is necessary and expected of him. He will study, get the marks required, and then go on to a money-making position. Many Taurean children will work their way through school, even when it is not mandatory from a financial standpoint. Your child is cooperative and understanding and, above all, practical.

That collector tendency is influenced by the money aspect of the sign. Ronnie, now a teenager, still has his teething ring tucked away in a box along with his first crayon, a-b-c's with a gold star, some baby teeth, string, twenty-five cents from his first allowance, etc., ad infinitum. By the time he marries, he will need three spare rooms to store his memorabilia. More than anything, he likes to collect money in any form; penny by penny, new bills, or scrunched up raggedy ones. But this has its merits too. As time goes on, your adolescent will develop good tastes that are expensive. He will work for what he wants and cherish his purchases. He likes beautiful things and appreciates the beautiful items that money can buy. You will find his choice in clothing, fabrics, etc., will reflect his sense of color, extending later on to the furnishings in his own house. He will expect that you provide a home that is tastefully furnished for him.

Taureans are builders by nature. Should a musical talent exist, expect that the first choice for a career will lie in the entertainment field. If not, a myriad of possibilities exist in the professional field. Large corporations are built on and by Taureans, and your offspring prodigy may well become an organization man. The Aries child may create the ideas but the Taureans will develop and build the foundations; some as carpenters, architects, and contractors.

Once you have overcome the road to frustration, motivating this child will not be such a chore. You must recognize his constancy and consistency, and then presto, the bull will meekly nuzzle up to you. The Pavlovian system is most successful even if it goes against your grain. Tempt him with a reward (materialistic, most likely) for cooperation and good behavior. Set realistic and attainable plateaus for improvement within a structured program.

Smother your Taurean child in a blanket of love and affection and reason with him as you would with an adult. This magic formula produces well-rounded stable adults who are givers from the heart. Keep the sensual in the foreground and you will have little frustration and much pleasure from your bull. A sensitive and sentimental soul always, he will always do what is right. He will delight in surprising you with a thoughful gift or gesture. You can be sure that in his adult life he will be a most considerate spouse.

Children born between April 20th and April 30th have the double aspect of the planet Venus in their chart. Sociability and benevolence are brought to the fore under these circumstances. The artistic in the basic nature will be more highly developed than those born later on under the sign. So inclined will this child be to sympathize and rush to the aid of others that he should take care that he is not used by those not so dear. Tenacity will be sustained as will the habits and routines into which all activity will fall.

For birthdays between May 1st and May 10th, the personal planet is Mercury, which is the rational force that makes an organizer of men. The strength and optimism of this child will inspire the respect of others, making him a soothsayer of sorts. Mercury rules the memory and powers of expression, injecting the studious and confident facets into the personality. Sometimes overly conservative, this child may deliberate longer and delve deeper before making a decision, which will usually almost always be the right one.

The planet Saturn is the personal one, of those born between May 11th and May 20th. Saturn governs time and makes people born under its influence patient, thoughtful, and very cautious. Endurance tests will always be won by these subjects, who possess limitless reserves of stamina (evenly paced) and persistence. These children will make few compromises, but will seek help and assistance when it means advancement on a personal or professional level. They are incredibly able to see things as they really are and face the real facts.

THE TAURUS
MOTHER
AND HER CHILD

The Taurus Mother And The Aries Child

As a Taurus mother with an Aries child, you will often be gratified by your child's desire to be a leader in all things and by his frequent success. Although your child quite often seems too engrossed in his own goals and achievements, do not delude yourself into believing that he does not appreciate how hard you have worked and how much you have sacrificed, personally, in order to give him every possible advantage. Your Aries child may adopt certain attitudes or participate in certain affairs that you cannot condone, but you will never be far apart during your lifetime.

Aries have the most disturbing perceptiveness sometimes, and this perception is just about intense enough to see through that unflinching rock-steady exterior of yours. If you've got something gnawing at your weary brain, you can count on your Aries child to come through in a pinch to cheer you up.

The Taurus Mother And The Taurus Child

In a relationship of this kind, there is bound to be a serious lack of communication. Both of you are the close-lipped type who would almost rather face a firing squad than get involved in a heart-to-heart talk, especially with someone you love. Not only will you have difficulty in unburdening your soul to others, but your Taurus child will have difficulty in unburdening his soul to you, which could relieve his own ennui, anxieties and tensions.

You'll have to overcome this longstanding habit in order to help your child attain his full potential. In the process, you'll help yourself achieve yours. You'll find, that much like yourself, your Taurus child seems to be shouldering most of the work in group activities and getting little of the credit. Don't let this happen to your child.

Give him all those things you, yourself, thrive on; affection, honesty, peace and harmony.

The Taurus Mother And The Gemini Child

As a Taurus mother, you are very likely to find yourself irritated, perplexed, and outsmarted by your changeable and enigmatic Gemini child. You might as well just learn to live with that mercurial little creature, because he is a master of debate and complicated arguments and can't be beat especially by one so logical as a Taurus (even a Taurus mother).

They are loving children but sometimes become undemonstrative, toward you, especially when they reach adolescence. This is usually okay with you, Taurus, because you are not an openly demonstrative person either. You are going to be amazed when you find out how teachers just love this little tyke that you have had so many problems with. It somehow turns out that your Gemini child is intelligent enough to gain the affection of his teachers. You will be smart enough to realize, however, that your child may use wit to get out of a situation that requires knowledgability.

The Taurus Mother And The Cancer Child

Your Cancer child is likely to get the better of you if you don't take caution in dealing with him. A Cancer child is usually quite adept in getting his own way in any situation, and you are the type who is easily gotten around. You are going to have to reverse this pattern, however, for your child's own good. You may have to turn your back on a pretty miserable sight, and you may feel like a real meanie. But you have got to instill patience and reasonableness into that moon child sometime. If you do it properly, you will have a really wonderful child, one who will give you a minimum of hassle and a maximum of support throughout the years. Your little Cancerion will be the kind of child that everybody fusses over, so if he becomes spoiled, it won't be any great wonder. You'll have to watch over all those doting old aunts.

The Taurus Mother And The Leo Child

Most likely, that Leo child of yours will be the apple of your eye and the light of your heart. The fact that your "fair-haired" child is the envy of practically every other mother around (those with any taste anyway) is just frosting on the cake.

Of course, the foregoing doesn't mean that you will have all smooth sailing, though. In every relationship there is bound to be some turbulence, but this child will bring sunshine into your sometime sombre existence. His joy for life make up for the few misdemeanors. Points on which you and your charming little Leo may differ involve his constantly itchy feet searching for a new and more exciting adventure every single day. It is enough to make a Taurus groan, just thinking about it. You will undoubtedly have to face all those fears that arise when your child is one of the most popular in school.

The Taurus Mother And The Virgo Child

As a Taurus mother, you will be most pleased with your Virgo child, who will more than meet your standards for responsibility and maturity (Virgos grow up earlier than most). You won't have to worry about constant cleaning up after a cluttery child. Your Virgo child won't ask for a real live horse for Christmas when you have got a stuffed animal income and live in an efficiency apartment.

Virgos are basically practical, down-to-earth types whose attitudes and ideas don't differ radically from your own.

You may find yourself forcing and cajoling this hard-working youngster to get out of the house and have some fun for a change. Maybe you would help yourself along too if you suggested an activity that required both of you. Keep your actions extremely noble, and beyond reproach, because that Virgo child has an overly developed sense of what's right and wrong.

The Taurus Mother And The Libra Child

Your Libra child's sensitivity will put a halt to all of your preconceived notions about child-rearing. You can hardly deliver a resounding or threatening "no" to a child, who is likely to be crushed by it. Like yourself, he is ruled by the planet Venus. He will respond to love and harmony. Those innocent eyes can be most disarming and you will eventually have to be won over; bow to the Libran way. This Libra child has an eye and a flair for beauty. You are a basically practical type, who has never had much time for anything that wasn't really necessary. Hopefully, these mutual likes, combined with your earthy common sense, will give your Libran child a true sense of values. Appreciation for the finer things in life cultivates a more responsible and practical attitude towards life.

Your child's choice of life style may dismay you later in life, but you will grow to appreciate the quiet, peace-loving approach, which is his own.

The Taurus Mother And The Scorpio Child

To a basically practical and stable Taurus mother, a Scorpio child can be a real mind-boggler. Just when you think you have everything under control, a new crisis develops, and you are ready to throw up your arms in despair all over again. Scorpios don't take too kindly to supervision, even yours. You are going to have a tough time asserting your superiority in this trying relationship.

Another aspect of the Scorpio personality that may give you a jolt is the apparent lack of inhibition and physical demonstrativeness, two traits that do not find their way to a Taurus' psyche very often. Just grin and bear it, and maybe you will work loose a few of those inhibitions that have been preventing you from enjoying life as easily as you should.

From you the Scorpio child will hopefully gain a more intense feeling of responsibility for the effect that his actions have on others.

The Taurus Mother And The Sagittarius Child

Your Sagittarius child's goals and dreams may seem a bit flimsy and illusory for your taste, but your too frequent intervention in this regard may do more harm than good. At the very least, your little Sagittarius may just stop confiding in you. At worst, you may unwittingly instill a sense of defeatism in this sensitive, idealistic child. Try to find a happy medium and work from there.

You will find it a little hard to tolerate the ants-in-the-pants restlessness of the typical Sagittarius. They are always on the move and have got to commune with nature. No amount of grounding is going to stop that. And if you push things too far, you may be putting an unnecessary strain on your relationship.

Why not let some of that Sagittarius enthusiasm rub off on you and give you something to dream about?

The Taurus Mother And The Capricorn Child

Your little Capricorn may use all the weapons at his disposal to deal the *coup de grace* to your parental authority, but whether or not he is successful depends on how much you value your role as mother. You usually value it to the point that your Capricorn child might as well be beating his head against a brick wall.

One thing that you will really love about this independent and responsible kid is that he is more than willing to give you the attention and concern that deep down you really want, that rock-like exterior notwithstanding. You don't even have to send out any distress signals to your perceptive Capricorn child.

Like the mountain-goat, the Capricorn child will be able to negotiate the sometimes perilous course of life with almost effortless sure-footedness. You can rest easy with this child.

The Taurus Mother And The Aquarius Child

Your relationship with an Aquarius child might be a little sticky at times, and may even be more than you can bear. His frequently mysterious manner and apparent lack of any long-term goals will be so difficult for you to comprehend, bordering on the impossible. The two of you will arrive at an understanding that will allow you both the freedom you need to pursue your individual interests. People might think that you are an odd combination of the practical and mystical, but what matter, as long as you have a relationship that works.

Your Aquarius child will never do the kinds of things that

you value most highly or arrive at the goals *you* desire, but he will be a well-rounded individual with his own brand of success to achieve. You may consider him too passive and uncompetitive, but you will have to admire his generosity and compassion for others. Don't be too demanding, lest you drive him away.

The Taurus Mother And The Pisces Child

Your Pisces child has the uncanny ability to see through the sham of a phony situation. The little fish is intuitive, where you are logical. People have a way of taking advantage of your industriousness and overly developed sense of responsibility, usually without your knowledge that you are being used. They won't fool your Pisces child, however, and he will be none too verbal in letting you and them know it. Trust his instincts and you will find the truth of the matter more often than not.

You may have to work overtime to teach your little Pisces the rudiments of domesticity. His is a mind that transcends such matters, but he is the first to go bananas when the mess starts to pile up. Maybe you could teach him to do some of that characteristic introspective brooding during floor-washing or vacuuming. His desire to talk is honest, but what he feels isn't always what he says.

STAR GUIDE
FOR
TAURUS

Symbol	●	The Bull
Ruling Planet	●	Venus
Element	●	Earth
Gender	●	Feminine
Key Words	●	I Have
Birthstones	●	Emerald, Sapphire
Favorite Flowers	●	Lily Of The Valley
Best Colors	●	Blues, Yellows
Mineral	●	Copper
Favorite Music	●	Symphonies
Favorite Pastime	●	Handcrafts
Lucky Number	●	8
Best Days	●	Monday, Friday
Compatible Signs	●	Pisces, Cancer, Capricorn
Incompatible Signs	●	Leo, Aquarius

FAMOUS PEOPLE BORN UNDER THE SIGN OF THE BULL

PHILIP ARMOUR
FRED ASTAIRE
JOHN J.
 AUDUBON
JAMES BARRIE
LIONEL
 BARRYMORE
IRVING BERLIN
GEORGES
 BRAQUE
JOHANN BRAHMS
JAMES
 BUCHANAN
PERRY COMO
GARY COOPER
BING CROSBY
OLIVER
 CROMWELL
SALVADOR DALI
ELIZABETH II
DUKE
 ELLINGTON
ELLA
 FITZGERALD
ALBERT FINNEY
HENRY FONDA
MARGOT
 FONTEYN

GLENN FORD
SIGMUND FREUD
ULYSSES S.
 GRANT
AUDREY
 HEPBURN
QUEEN JULIANA
HENRY J. KAISER
HENRY CABOT
 LODGE
JOE LOUIS
DOUGLAS
 MacARTHUR
HORACE MANN
GUGLIELMO
 MARCONI
DEAN MARTIN
JAMES MASON
HENRY MATISSE
PAUL
 McCARTNEY
CARSON
 McCULLERS
YEHUDI
 MENUHIN
JOHN STUART
 MILL

JAMES MONROE
HENRY
 MORGENTHAU
SAMUEL
 MORSE
VLADIMIR
 NABOKOV
TYRONE POWER
ROBESPIERRE
BERTRAND
 RUSSELL
TOOTS SCHOR
WILLIAM
 SHAKESPEARE
FULTON J.
 SHEEHAN
KATE SMITH
JAMES STEWART
BARBRA
 STREISAND
NORMA
 TALMADGE
SHIRLEY
 TEMPLE
HARRY TRUMAN
RUDOLPH
 VALENTINO
ORSON WELLES

THE
GEMINI
MOTHER

May 21st — June 21st

THE Gemini does not exactly fit the standards required of the "perfect mother", but you can do an admirable job when duty calls. Your relationship with your children is marked by great friendliness, and is best characterized by long stretches of intense love, short bursts of intense anger, and longer periods of intense remorse and making up. You have a tendency to regard your children as best friends, colleagues, and mentors, who have as much to contribute as anyone from your own age group. Unfortunately, you frequently tend to let your children amass power to the point where they begin to throw their weight around, whereupon you react violently in a manner which suggests that you have been betrayed. You then let your emotions lead you to the other extreme, and you treat your children in a way that makes Simon Legree look like Albert Schweitzer. At least you do until the whole cycle starts over again. Will you ever learn? Of course you will; it's only a matter of practice and experience. In fact, by the time you enter into motherhood you might already have learned this lesson because you've been treating all children and pets in the same manner for years.

Geminians have a reputation for quick minds and mercurial temperaments. These attributes can have both beneficial and detrimental effects upon your abilities as a mother. On the one hand, you will provide many opportunities for rich learning experiences for your children. But, on the other hand, you may fail to give your children, especially in their early and most formative years, the feeling of stability and security that they thrive best on. Your home is in a state of constant turmoil, and you subconsciously

43

wouldn't have it any other way, no matter how much you profess to admire the orderly lives of your friends (although a large percentage of your friends are other Geminis).

Since Geminians have a characteristically quick mind, you may find yourself having difficulty communicating with a child who is slower in thinking than you. Geminians tend to place a high value on wit and persiflage and to judge a person's intelligence on these standards. Therefore, if your child is not quick witted, you may be disappointed to the point that you almost feel ashamed. This is a ridiculous feeling for the simple reason that intelligence takes on many forms and is not synonymous with wittiness alone. Your child may be a slow but logical thinker who arrives at great truths only after careful consideration and measurement of all relevant factors. It may take him time, but he is more likely to be able to wade through complicated problems than you. You tend to get turned off by long involved matters. Your attention span is short to the point of dwarfishness. With methodical thinking of this type around, maybe you'll be able to learn how to cope with problems you previously left unsolved or heaped onto the shoulders of others.

Why is it that Geminians feel that they have the gold cup for intelligence all wrapped up? This attitude toward intelligence is not at all harmful. However, Geminians tend not to be intellectual snobs, nor to care inordinately about whether or not a person went to a prestigious college, or even any college at all. If this person has a basic sense of humor which he expresses in an intelligent witty way, he has the undying respect of a Gemini. This means that Gemini mothers will bring up children to place a realistic value on higher education and not think lowly of a person just because he never had one. It also means that you will not have to spend the rest of your life bowed with shame if your child decides not to go to college, or if he decides to drop out of school in search of an alternative style of life. As a matter of fact, Geminians are noted for their tolerance of other people. This is an admirable quality as long as you don't carry it too far by letting your children develop habits or attitudes that they are better off without. You can do your children a vast disservice by not speaking up soon enough about the things that bother you. Don't expect them to be able to anticipate your concern or to think of your feelings. Man is by nature a selfish animal, and in childhood this selfishness is exaggerated. You have to remind your children of their obligations and responsibilities rather than to feel hurt and disappointed when you find that they haven't taken your feelings or the feelings of others into consideration.

As a rule, Gemini is about as nervous as a rock, but he can fall apart just like everyone else when things start to build up against him. In fact, you don't take too kindly at all to such a build-up of pressure and frequently react in weird and childish ways. You are constantly on the lookout for even the tiniest shred of sympathy and you will go to great lengths to get it. You may feel that you have an unusually large weight on your shoulders and feel that you deserve a medal for your heroics. When you realize that no medal is forthcoming, you start to complain about all sorts of things to drum up sympathy. But even when you do get a rare tidbit, you can't enjoy it because you feel guilty about the manner in which you snared it. This is a trap which hurts you, mainly, but can hurt your children if you inadvertently make them feel that they are responsible for your financial, emotional, and physical collapse. Don't make your children feel like monsters just to satisfy your own ego. If you feel that you are being used, do something positive about it even if you have to exorcise some old ghosts. Otherwise, your children will suffer.

Many will accuse you of being a poor mother for the simple reason that your housekeeping and cooking leave a bit to be desired. Some people are born neat and some are clutterers. You're emphatically among the latter. Your mind is just not arranged in neat little ways like other mothers. You have a lot going for you, so much that you don't have to feel that your whole image is tied up in the quality of your housekeeping. Your children won't suffer from a little clutter, but they will benefit greatly from the results of your sharp mind and curiosity. You'll have them reading at an early age, if possible, and you'll love to drag them off on one expedition after another. Expect your living quarters to be cluttered with books, magazines, puzzles, animals (especially the shaggy variety), creative toys, bedraggled plants, papers of all kinds, and neighbors' kids from a radius of 20 miles. With your relaxed attitude toward neatness and people, you'll be letting yourself in for a life of crowded humanity. Many of your children's friends will remember you with as much affection as they have for their own parents. Your house will be a mecca for the neighborhood children, a fact which may drive you crazy at times and push you into a frenzy of yelling and screaming. But the kids, especially your own children, will understand that you don't really mean it. They'll just quietly disappear until your usual good humor returns in full force. Naturally, the other mothers in the neighborhood may be secretly jealous of your easy relationship with children and subconsciously get even with you, criticizing you, perhaps even to your face, on your less-than-perfect house and your erratic meal schedule. Their remarks may hurt you at the time, but you'll forget them in the long run.

You'll never be able to change these habits of long standing, and why should you want to? Your children love you the way you are, and the way you are is the main reason why they love you so much. If you were a stricter person, you probably wouldn't be nearly so easy going and full of fun. As long as you can draw the line when your children become too lax in facing up to their responsibilities, or start to go astray in some manner or other, you'll be fine going along just as you have been doing. Your children will never feel that they cannot confide in you for fear that you will reject them, and they know that, no matter what they should ever do, you will always be there. You'll never be disappointed in them if they don't live up to your expectations of them because you think of them so completely as individuals that you don't even have a course plotted out for them. That will be their own responsibility and you'll go along, if not wholeheartedly, then at least tactfully, with whatever they plan to do with their lives.

In short, you'll most likely be a mother not completely at ease with the outward aspects of the job, but a smashing success when all the votes are in.

THE GEMINI CHILD

GEMINI is an Air sign and the key word for the twins is "I think."
The symbol is represented by two stars which, in turn, stand for
the hands and the two lungs. Gemini babies are extremely alert,
lively, and inquiring. You will notice, particularly during feeding time, that as soon as the baby's eyes are able to focus, they will
never stop wandering. He will wave and move about, and anything
within his range of vision that does likewise will get a stir out
of him, so much so sometimes, that he may lose the bottle in a Herculean effort to take a look-see around at a moving object. He
is a mover and an inquirer. Think of the air and the movement it
stirs. Picture the leaves that are blown about, things that float and
are moved constantly by a very brisk breeze, and you will have
some insight into the basic nature of your little wonder. Air is
always mobile and never stationary. That's your cue.

The sign rules the mind and it is an alert one. This will mean
lots of activity and restlessness. You'll discover this when it comes
to the sleeping hours, which may be very few at any given time.
The feeding of this child may also be a little frustrating—very little
intake at any one sitting. Don't despair or call for the doctor every
time. Your child is physically fit, but a wound-up, nervous bundle.
His whole psyche is uptight and alert. Have a little patience and
adjust to his schedule for the time being. You'll wear a well-trodden
path to and from his crib at the beginning, and get little sleep
yourself. Things will calm down, but you run little chance of
changing things at this stage of the game. You'll learn to fly at
almost as frantic a pace as he will whizz through life. He is like
a little bird, apt to be easily startled because of his nervous nature.
You must keep your cool and start imposing a routine, beyond a
certain age. Rest is a prerequisite for his health and napping should

be continued for a longer period than is usual with other children. Needless to say, loud noises in and around the household are not to his advantage or yours. Anything that shortens that sleeping time will not help either one of you to calm down.

Your offspring is governed by the planet Mercury which rules the tongue and communications. The Gemini baby will most likely start communicating with you long before he is able to speak. He has a way of his own. Communication and people are important to him. He loves every minute of his life with others. Don't be surprised if he starts to walk and talk before you have your first photos developed. Remember that Mercury is the wing-footed messenger that flits through the air. Alice in Wonderland will take a back seat to your baby once the words start to flow. His own language will be full of jibbity-jibbity and flowing, melodious gurgles. Strange and unusual words or names will be favored, as well as those that produce a tingling sensation to the tongue. The telephone will hold a fantastic fascination for him as soon as he realizes it represents a form of communication. As he grows older, he will be found on or around the phone, frequently getting tangled up in the wires. Be sure to start him on a foreign language as early as possible. Many dialects will fascinate this child, and he will have the ability to master many.

When he starts to toddle about, your stamina will really be tested. Don't lose sight of him for a split second. He won't toddle or creep, but literally dart about just like a little bird up in the sky. It will almost seem as if he believes he is airborne and can float about anywhere that his heart desires, just like a bird might. Keep a weather eye open at all times. Expect many falls and a look of surprise on his face every time it happens. It really is very difficult for him to comprehend how this can happen. The Gemini infant has a basic need for variety. So keep him occupied at all times. If he is left without anything to do or to amuse him, you have no one but yourself to blame for the mischievous consequences. Too much restriction, physical or mental, can lead to the doldrums and an emotional handicap not easily overcome. Squelching the nature of a personality can boomerang back at you— don't create a neurotic personality.

Mercury also rules the conscious mind, and its children are

the learners of the world. They love to learn, and are constantly gathering up knowledge. You'll see it early in your own baby. The mind is as fast as a bat and is surpassed only by the rapid movement of the arms and hands. This combination can be catastrophic in infancy, as he becomes entangled easily. The manipulation of the upper limbs is such that he is very apt to lock himself up and get himself tied up in knots. Keep all appliances out of reach and electric outlets covered, even in remote locations. His alert mind combined with those flying hands means that mechanical gadgets are easily mastered and, consequently, a source of trouble during the wee years. His duality may extend to the point of being ambidextrous. Each of those agile and expressive hands may be capable of performing minor miracles.

The quick mind and flying fingers won't take kindly to regimentation of any sort. Trying to impose routines or restrictions on a Gemini will be of little value to either of you. Repetition has its merits and can prove more successful than the usual tried and true methods. This youngster is an exceptional one in his emotional make-up and one-of-a-kind. In fact, he is purely delightful and never requires real disciplinary action. Rather, subtle motivation will steer him toward success with a gentle puff of air.

Rachel reacts to rules rather negatively. Much as she needs her afternoon naps to fill her with the fuel of energy, the routine of a scheduled sleep-time is not to her liking. After a few harassing weeks of seeking a solution that would be compatible and logical, mother resorted to compromise. Rachel must learn to obey some rules but, in this case, the exact time of the nap could vary a few minutes from day to day. There was not much lost and a lesson gained by mother and child.

A must for the parent of a Gemini is the need to slow the child down somewhat, for his own welfare and yours. You'll be ragged before he's in kindergarten, otherwise. Do remember, though, that your tot has the twins as his sign, and that does mean that he can handle two things at a time just as easily (and sometimes more so), as some children can handle one. Being natural is vital to his well-being even though it may wear you down to a frazzle. Temper the pace a little, but do not try to inhibit his free spirit. He thinks quickly and innately acts quickly. Your child is high-strung and can acquire a multitude of nervous habits such as stumbling, stuttering, and nail-biting. The more calmness and routine that are built into his life, the better off you both will be.

By the time school days roll around he should be well in hand. His mind is alert and agile, and he will learn with great rapidity. The point will come across right away. Rote learning for this youngster may also result in boredom. The repetition involved at school will not hold his interest. His mind is restless, constantly moving from one subject to another. It has been pointed out that you have only yourself to blame if he is not kept occupied and interested. This you should pass along to his teacher.

There is some similarity here to the push-ahead, easily-bored, daring Aries ram. The attention span is limited, and there are always other unknowns to explore. They may all be dead ends or hold little interest, but the Gemini passes on just as surely as time, and just as fluidly. The difference from the Aries youngster is that Gemini innately knows how to procrastinate, ofttimes to his advantage, but sometimes to his detriment.

He will absorb and retain an incredible amount of knowledge. One difficulty here is that he may have a wide scope and yet not delve deeply enough into any one subject to gain a thorough knowledge of it. A Jack-of-all-trades but master of none situation is apt to develop. His approach to most things is daring and bold, but inside he quivers and quakes with shyness, like a bowl full of jelly. This child is a bit of an enigma. He proceeds as he feels he must, paying no heed to advice or experience. The most direct route to helping this child overcome his instability is as transparent as the air that sustains him. Denial is not a dirty tactic when dealing with a child that understands it. With a dullard it would be unfair and downright abusive treatment. With your Gemini, the facile mind recognizes the pot of gold for the reward it represents, and quickly responds (especially if the contents of the pot are a mystery or secret).

Every once in a while you will encounter a situation that requires only intuition to handle masterfully. When you have an instinctive feeling that the time is right, try politely and quietly telling the little twin to cease and desist any future repetition of his wrong-doing. There will be no mess, no fuss, no bother. It won't work often enough to please you, but then discipline is not that great a problem with this child.

Activity in sports is natural to these Geminians, especially those sports that require physical dexterity. Outdoor sports are essential to them, since Gemini rules the lungs, and fresh air in large quantities is vital to his existence. Teach your child to breathe deeply and regularly to expand his lungs. Air will be food to his little system and should be supplanted with the correct foods. Fresh vegetables (principally the green variety) are also essential to his being, as they nourish the nervous system. Your prodigy is hyper-active, as you may have deduced by now.

This may pose some problems with your firefly. Chances are that he will be habitually late for appointments. He came up with an idea that he wished to pursue, or noticed an object that aroused his curiosity. In handling this trait, try to impress upon him that, once again, consideration for others is a prime requisite in communicating with people. You may or may not make headway here.

Most Gemini children must cultivate staying power so that it becomes second nature. What is started must be finished. Ofttimes much of this superior brain power possessed by the twin is wasted because a project or idea is not completed or followed through down the line. The restlessness behind this flitting about is similar, yet dissimilar, to that of an Arian. Aries usually has one goal or purpose in mind. Gemini has a number of objectives. One focal point is missing and, therefore, many purposes are at loose ends or at odds with each other.

Rachel's behavior required that real punitive measures be taken. Her mercurial habits however, had both her parents very worried. She showed about the same lack of concern over an unfinished meal as she did over abandoning yesterday's best friends. They made the mistake of laying down the law with an iron fist, curtailing all activity until each step started in any area was followed through. This only resulted in a completely confused and very insecure little Rachel. To a Gemini (child or adult), love of mental activity is a prime factor in life. For a child, the receiving of mental occupation is security plus; for a Gemini child non-receipt signifies insecurity and confusion. Rachel's parents had not yet fully realized that the strict and severe bring little results.

A taste of honey, spoon-fed with a smile, will turn the trick, followed up by an easily understood explanation of "why not". This would have sufficed and averted a bit of needless trauma.

There are few things this marvel will be unable to master. His ability to adapt readily will find him usually surrounded by a bevy of friends and admirers. As an adolescent he will change his mind a dozen times a day about school, friends, career goals, and romantic interests. He will constantly have you on the go and your home will resemble Grand Central at rush hour. Enjoy it. You may think you are aging a year a minute, but don't be surprised to find that all the hustle and bustle actually keeps your mind and spirit young.

Since your Gemini loves knowledge, he most probably will want to further his education and go on to college. Here your training skills will be put to the test. He will do well if he has calmed down, has adjusted to a routine, and can budget his time. Don't expect to accomplish all this and end up with a Taurean type child who will sit quietly studying for hours on end. Let him set his own study habits. He will absorb for a given period of time and then take a break of sorts to return later to his studies. This pattern parallels that of his feeding habits way back when. You should not interfere with his scheduling. As long as he does his duty, forget about the fact that it may not conform to your ideas about study habits. Despite your doubts about his ability and patience to sit out the college years, keep in mind that his sign rules mentality and you know the capacity there.

Rachel adapted rather well to learning that routine is a part of life, but mother never really learned to accept her habits. Through Rachel's adolescence Mom was more often heard criticizing what she considered to be her daughter's failings than lauding her accomplishments; which were many. Constant harping and too frequently given advice brought back a feeling of insecurity. At this age, it created a schism in the mother-daughter relationship. Only when Rachel finally had a heart-to-heart talk with her mother did the possibility of a sustaining relationship enter the picture. Now, mother of Gemini admires her daughter for the ability to achieve so much in so many areas, and hands out sympathy rather than criticism.

Your child of Mercury is blessed with a charming and beguiling personality that is infectious. He will remain forever young and be very, very sociable and enthusiastic. Communication is his forte, and any form of this medium will have his shining talents on display. Personnel, labor relations, social work are all in his realm. Executive abilities are his as well. On a corporate level he can function, organize, and guide the stratagem of many departments. He'll be on top of every situation and can keep a myriad of detail on tap in many areas. His versatility will allow him the pick of the crop. Success will be his because of that dual nature and that power of concentration that you have instilled.

For babies born between May 21st and May 31st the personal ruling planet is Mercury, which is the symbol of knowledge. This child is the most typical example of a Gemini. Thirsty for learning and problem solving he is, in the same breath, the possessor of a fabulous memory with great powers of expression. More discipline and self-control are required than with other children born under this sign. He can tend to become shiftless at times and flounder about without direction.

Those whose birthdays fall between June 1st and June 10th have Venus, the symbol of love and beauty, as their personal planet. This child will make greater strides than others, and while less flexible, be more sure of himself. Venus injects a sense of beauty which is evident in the desire to share with others. By far the most well-adjusted of the Gemini children, this youngster will be more positive in his outlook and less cautious than some. A true birdlike tendency to dart about prevails here.

Babies that enter the world between June 11th and June 21st are blessed with the personal planet of Uranus. In combination with Mercury, your child's mind will have the potential of genius. As is true with a majority of the super-intellects, he may be a bit eccentric and a little too avant-garde for many people. Idealism is very predominant, and this child is apt to live in an ivory tower, and not deal directly or well in his relations with friends and associates. Nurture the need to develop respect and contact on an emotional level to right his personality.

THE GEMINI
MOTHER
AND HER CHILD

The Gemini Mother And The Aries Child

If you are a Gemini mother, you can well appreciate an Aries child who will stop at nothing to make his dreams come true. You are an unusual combination of generosity, good humor, and intellectual selfishness, the right blend to appreciate just about anything that an Aries child does. With your characteristic success in bending words, both oral and written, you could well add the ultimate weapon to your child's arsenal. Maybe all that's keeping him from his goal is the art of verbal chicanery, which you have gotten down to an art by this time. You two could well be a fatal combination—fatal for all the competition, that is.

Gemini and Aries can have a stimulating, if not wildly exciting, relationship. You will find that you have each other constantly in mind, and can relate well to each other after long separations. Yours is the kind of relationship that is bound to endure and strengthen throughout your lifetime.

The Gemini Mother And The Taurus Child

Your Taurus child will be just the kind of incentive you need to get your mind back on earth where it belongs, at least half of the time. You may have a tendency to let things go, but you can't remain immobile when your own child is trying to be both mother and child at the same time. You will find yourself more involved with the domestic side of life because of a nudge at your conscience.

As someone who values repartee, above all else, you are bound to be disappointed in that steady little Taurus child whose conversation is generally a bit prosaic. A Taurus just isn't much for lightness when there is work to be done. You, on the other hand, seem to shine best when your life is depending on the completion, within five minutes, of fifteen Herculean tasks. Somehow, you always seem to pull through, though, and this can be very aggravating to the Taurus child who has worked twice as hard and has done no better.

The Gemini Mother And The Gemini Child

You two ought to have a whacky time of life if you both display the distinctive traits of your sign. For one thing, the conversation ought to be really great, and maybe you should invest in a tape recorder so that none of the little pearls of witticism be forgotten.

Geminis are born laughing (other babies cry; Gemini laughs). Your home ought to sound like a den of hyenas. Hopefully you will take enough time out of that laughing and jesting to give a thought to some of the more serious sides to life. In particular, start your Gemini child early in regarding the value of money.

Gemini has a tendency to go through money like water and to have this weird belief that his wallet is like a bottomless pit. Now, granted, there is no arguing that Gemini has more than his share of luck, and some windfall usually comes his way before the last penny is spent. But you want your child to be more protected than that, don't you?

The Gemini Mother And The Cancer Child

As a Gemini mother, you may find your relationship with a Cancer child to be rather short of inspiring. In fact, it just might be downright dull. The problem is that you people born under the sign of the Twins tend to rely heavily on verbiage to get what you want, and Cancer is likely to resort to more down-to-earth tactics. Ever see a child having a tantrum? Ask his mother if he is a Cancer child. (Fortunately, Cancer children outgrow this primitive behavior at an early age.)

You can see how hard communication might be under the circumstances. You, serenely cool and giving the impression of unfrazzled reasonableness, are trying to placate a red-faced, pint-sized human dynamo whose mind is effectively blocking out any words except the magical "okay" from your, by now, enervated lips. This is why you will give in, because Gemini cannot stand to think that he cannot get around any situation with his cunning wit.

The Gemini Mother And The Leo Child

Your Leo child will be a source of delight to the Gemini mother. You will just love the way this little devil is always so eager to be off on a new adventure, and you will be only too glad to use this airtight excuse to do some gadding of your own. You just want to please your child, you say with bruised righteousness.

As far as Leo children and itchy feet are concerned, you will never cease being amazed at how your enterprising offspring made the burst for freedom so quickly from diapers and cribs and other annoyances that tend to hold babies back from performing glorious feats and taking world tours. In fact, it wouldn't have surprised you too much to have learned that they had to put a ball and chain on your little roamer in the nursery.

One thing that makes Leo children difficult to bring up is that it is practically impossible to get mad at them. Just try it!

The Gemini Mother And The Virgo Child

A relationship of this kind can be extremely satisfying, although a bit spotty at times. Your Virgo child will have a wisdom beyond his years that you may find frequently unnerving. His instinctive feeling for what is fitting and proper will no doubt put you in awe of his almost flawless intuition. If a Virgo child did slip enough to make a social *faux pas*, he could nevertheless carry the whole thing off, so that people would begin to wonder if perhaps they themselves hadn't been off base.

You, on the other hand, seem to attract accidents and embarrassments like a flower attracts bees. This problem could be alleviated greatly if you would only learn to cast your eyes downward, away from that far horizon, long enough to look where you are going.

The Gemini Mother And The Libra Child

Gemini and Libra can get along very well, indeed, as long as they remain aware (and care enough to remain aware) of each other's needs and aspirations. You, Gemini, are always a little in awe of Libra because of that famous Libra sensitivity and art appreciation. You are getting a little sick of being considered "intellectual", a word which does not connote a modicum of the spirit that lives inside. So you will get along only too well with a Libra child, soaking in all that sensitivity, helping your child to express himself more clearly and cogently in return. You two could very well be a dynamic twosome, enriching not only your own lives but the lives of those around you, as well.

Avoid the tendency to let your child feel that he can do no wrong, however, and be sure that he understands that he has to be responsible, to an ever increasing extent, for his own actions.

The Gemini Mother And The Scorpio Child

This is one relationship that could be really detrimental, if certain severe precautions aren't met and followed. You, Gemini, are easily gotten round, and this doesn't have to be the way it is at all.

A good time to practice your counter measures is just about the time that a new job offer comes up on the horizon. When you have got enough new things keeping you occupied, you'll leave yourself less wide open to the feelings of insecurity that others prey upon. Your Scorpio child is going to expect to have you eating out of his hand in short order, but you can dredge up enough gumption to put him back in his place if you remain alert to any possible confrontations.

Even though your relationship with your Scorpio child might be difficult, you two will still have enough of a union to fend off any trouble from outside forces.

The Gemini Mother And The Sagittarius Child

When a Gemini teams up with a Sagittarius, no matter how the sexes are arranged, there is bound to be some minor quibbling that could lead to who knows where. You, Gemini, are a dreamer to be sure, with visions that can't be discounted, but beneath that visionary exterior beats the heart of a true realist. You know what you want, even if you may not be going about it the right way. The Sagittarius, on the other hand, has dreams that are far more abstract and far more multi-person directed. They may fancy themselves as doctors finding the cure for cancer or missionaries saving an undeveloped nation from mass starvation. They tend to think of themselves as great humanitarians, and they quite often are. So, who cares about motivation as long as the job gets done?

You, on the other hand, feel an unjustified selfishness, which may even cause you to call the cards the way you see them. But try to keep petty emotions out of your dreams, for both of your sakes.

The Gemini Mother And The Capicorn Child

You may spend quite a few uneasy moments throughout your child's growing up years, wondering just what the effects of a lousy mother might be on this lovely child. With a Capricorn child, however, you might as well forget this method of self-recrimination. In the first place, you are definitely a more than adequate mother. In the second place, your resourceful little Capricorn could quickly learn how to cope with life even if his mother were a toadstool. These plucky creatures can find their way through just about any maze or enigma you could throw at them.

They have an uncanny sense of direction and a stamina that is downright discouraging to colleagues. They are fairly short on conversation, however, and this is where you could jump in with your magic bag of wit, spreading some humor dust around those rocky trails.

You ought to adopt some of you Capricorn child's wanderlust and maybe you would have a lot less time to sit around and think how miserable you are.

The Gemini Mother And The Aquarius Child

In all likelihood, you and your Aquarius child will enjoy a relationship that will extend in time and gather intensity with each passing year. He won't make too many demands on you and will give out three times as much as he gets. An adaptable creature, he will fit easily into your haphazard way of life. He will enjoy the variety of experiences and places that your mercurial nature requires.

As your Aquarius child grows older and his individuality begins to assert itself, you two will still be able to maintain a close relationship because he won't feel that you are trying to restrict his growth unfairly. You may feel that he is far too generous with his time, money, and emotions, and usually for no reward other than the sense of satisfaction that generosity brings.

He, on the other hand, may find you just a mite materialistic, but certainly an open-minded and interested parent with whom he can communicate.

The Gemini Mother And The Pisces Child

Gemini and Pisces can have an intensely satisfying relationship if they can bring themselves to talk candidly and openly to each other. You, Gemini, are always pointing out how open and honest you are, but you are not going to be able to fool that Pisces child of yours. He will see through that elaborate red herring in a flash and lose no time in telling you.

Your Pisces child is going to be a disturbing experience for you, make no mistake about that. Your Pisces child has a love of old things, even ancient. Since you don't have any violent objections to antiques that are sturdy and functional, why not develop a common interest? Or your Pisces child may go in for folk music, which has always been one of your loves. Pursue your interests together as much as possible.

STAR GUIDE FOR GEMINI

Symbol	●	The Twins
Ruling Planet	●	Mercury
Element	●	Air
Gender	●	Masculine
Key Words	●	I Think
Birthstones	●	Pearl, Lapis Lazuli
Favorite Flowers	●	Rose, Camellia
Best Colors	●	Light Blue, Grays
Mineral	●	Quicksliver
Favorite Music	●	Modern Jazz
Favorite Pastime	●	Stamp Collecting
Lucky Numbers	●	1, 3, 5
Best Days	●	Sunday, Wednesday
Compatible Signs	●	Aries, Leo, Aquarius
Incompatible Signs	●	Virgo, Pisces

FAMOUS PEOPLE BORN UNDER THE SIGN OF THE TWINS

BENNETT CERF

JEFFERSON
  DAVIS

JOHN DILLINGER

DIONNE
  QUINTUPLETS

ARTHUR CONAN
  DOYLE

ISADORA
  DUNCAN

BOB DYLAN

DUKE OF
  EDINBURGH

ANTHONY EDEN

RALPHY WALDO
  EMERSON

MAURICE EVANS

DOUGLAS
  FAIRBANKS

IAN FLEMING

ERROLL FLYNN

JUDY GARLAND

PAUL GAUGUIN

EDWARD GRIEG

DASHIELL
  HAMMETT

THOMAS HARDY

PATRICK HENRY

BOB HOPE

JULIA WARD
  HOWE

HUBERT
  HUMPHREY

JOHN F.
  KENNEDY

CHARLES
  KINGSLEY

AL JOLSON

PRINCE JUAN OF
  SPAIN

BEATRICE LILLIE

THOMAS MANN

JOHN
  MASEFIELD

MARILYN
  MONROE

BENITO
  MUSSOLINI

JACQUES
  OFFENBACH

SIR LAURENCE
  OLIVIER

NORMAN
  VINCENT
  PEALE

COLE PORTER

PRINCE RAINIER

ROSALIND
  RUSSELL

FRANCOISE
  SAGAN

JEAN PAUL
  SARTRE

ROBERT
  SCHUMANN

IGOR
  STRAVINSKY

QUEEN VICTORIA

RICHARD
  WAGNER

JAMES J.
  WALKER

JOHN WAYNE

WALT WHITMAN

DUCHESS OF
  WINDSOR

FRANK LLOYD
  WRIGHT

WILLIAM
  BUTLER
  YEATS

BRIGHAM YOUNG

THE
CANCER
MOTHER

June 22nd — July 22nd

BEING born a moon child indubitably enhances your capabilities in the area of child-rearing. You are Mother Earth personified and the inspiration for "I Remember Mama" of years gone by.

You thrive on the food of love. Your basic nature has an insatiable need for hour by hour reassurance of your adequacy and importance in the lives of those you love. Here is where you are most apt to run into a stumbling block if you become too overpowering a parent and a smothering lunar mother. In the development of his character, the prime taboo to keep in the front of your mind is one for you to observe—and you alone. Don't be as overprotective of your children as you wish others to be of you.

Since Cancer rules motherhood, holding back is not your forte, and you may feel that you are losing your grip as commander. Brace yourself. Self-discipline in this area will reap rewards. Your offspring can mature without benefit of those knots of insecurity and inadequacy that have plagued you all the days of your life.

From day one, you must provide enough of the primary needs (warmth, love and coddling) but, at all costs, avoid providing too much of a good thing. Tenacity and patience are admirable virtues, but not in this instance. Go all the way to exercise self-restraint, however. Meet your child's needs less than half-way at the beginning to avert a possible coup d'etat in later life.

It is mandatory, too, for you to recognize your status as a moon mother and the variable moods to which you are subject. When you are down, your proclivity will run to lavishing extremes of affection, attention, and adoration to overcompensate for your dewy eyes as the lady of sorrows. You are capable of clinging to your children, not unlike barnacle glue (the first barnacles are rumored to have sprouted forth under the sign of the crab). When the moon dust disappears from your eyes and they come to resemble a darkly clouded lunar planet, you must be on guard against emotional indulgences. Ride out the storm. This can be a titanic task since the time lapse until the clouds move on can take an hour, or a few days if the winds are non-existent. But the rainbow is always there when the atmosphere equalizes itself.

At the same time, when the moon is full, that's another story. Your mood will be ethereal, euphoric, and you will have absolute command. Latent talents for self-discipline and restraint will come to the fore and prevent you from completely smothering your children. Your sensitivity and understanding will be keenly attuned to the rights and wrongs and the "why's and wherefore's" of child-rearing. The one thing to concern yourself with during your high period is a tendency to be just a little inconstant. Keep a weather eye open for the rise and fall of emotions as you undergo a transformation or two even while riding those moonbeams.

Engage your great gifts of intuition and imagination to entertain and educate your child. Give him these gifts that you possess and instill your super-sensitive nature in him as he matures. As you channel this sensitivity, so he will absorb and recognize his needs first, then yours, and eventually be capable of feeling the emotional vibrations in any given environment or situation.

Do not expect your child to mirror your undeniable and unquenchable thirst for displays of affection. Neither should you hold back on do's and don'ts for fear of making him sulk and/or pout. Unless he follows your folly he is not apt to take constructive criticism or punishment any more seriously than any other child. When a youngster is reprimanded, he interprets such action as a sign of rejection. This is only normal in all children (since children are dependent) but should dissipate itself in the natural process of maturation, if he is free of anxieties and insecurities. If your child is also a lunar baby, then he will have to try harder and, more important, you will have to provide the security for him that you do not have yourself. This will require some super-human endeavors. Your instinct and innate understanding should keep you from creating the tie that not just binds, but strangles.

Yes, mood-maiden, it is possible to be devoted and dedicated and yet, not devastating.

Being a mother will present you with untold tests, tried and true, of your Job-like patience. There may be times when you will be surprised to find yourself at an impasse. This will most probably occur between the new and full moons. It is germaine only in that it indicates you may be a bit too saintly and tolerant more often than not. Restrictions must be imposed and upheld at all costs or you will contribute to the care and feeding of a spoiled, rebellious, and unbending monster-child. Good intentions have paved many a road to rack and ruin. Save your patience for the learning processes. Bring your child up to be an emotionally aware adolescent and stable, giving adult. Cushioning and protecting this child from the elements and, in turn, from life itself can be an overnight disaster. He will be unafraid of doing as he pleases (if you allow) and may react to your fluctuating moods in such a way as to wreak havoc with your senses. On the other hand, he may suppress his feelings and simmer silently for fear of slighting you. You must impress upon him that, while you're in charge, his feelings can and should be expressed, lest he become a non-entity and unhealthily dependent.

The apron strings which tie are for you to unbind, sever, and dispose of post haste. Your Mother-earth nature compels you to find new ones every day and the opportunities always present themselves with children. But, if you want your children to develop as individuals devoid of major problems, remember that the strings are for training purposes only—guideposts to love, respect and self-support.

Your warm love, rich humor, and understanding heart will keep his heart with you always. Family ties will mean much to him even if he sometimes prefers to play with a friend rather than with you. While you are gregarious and at home anywhere with anyone, this is not necessarily true of your children. The middle road must be ridden if this is the case, with less dependency upon you and, yet, not so much liberty that it could result in isolationism. You would like to tuck him away in an ivory tower lined wall-to-wall with goose down, but you'll run into trouble the first time someone comes to visit. He may feel that he is Prince Charming, if you don't teach him otherwise and continue to coddle him beyond the cradle. Towers have windows, too, and the sooner he is exposed the less chance of his believing and expecting to be the star at the top of the Christmas tree.

You can still maintain a tower in the house, but let that be you as the tower of strength. Strength and not solicitude, objectivity and not overbearance, cognizance of his flaws and yet compassion for his faults. Since you tend to be a collector, you'll find more warm memories if you are realistic about his talents and abilities, his failings and shortcomings. Allow the good and the bad to intermesh. He is human even when he is no bigger than a minute.

The element associated with Cancer is water and as the waning of the moon affects your moods, so does the ebbing of the tide. Your supersensitivity should tell you that this means you are subject to fluctuations within your lunar cycles. Child-rearing, therefore, presents a greater challenge to you than most mothers because you must do a triple-take before reacting instinctively to the natural demands of nuturing and cultivating a growing child.

One of the major obstacles to overcome as a moon-mother is to not take his misbehavior or refusal as a personal affront or rejection. He is but a child and needs you desperately. Don't retreat and try to climb into your crabshell when he opposes you. Self-pity just won't hold water when the imaginary adversary is a mini-foe. Retain your composure and take satisfaction in the knowledge that your child is his own man and not stifling his feelings. Self-expression is something for which to strive at all times. He has inherited some of your sensitivity and can well sense your aloofness through the soft-shelled crab exterior. The shell can represent a cement wall to the eyes of a child. Alienate him for having such a magnification of your own innate insecurity, and you destroy the love and respect that is the very reason for your motherhood.

Be sure to fully assume the role of parent and present exemplary codes for your child. There is a direct correlation between your mood and your tendency to be hyper-meticulous with your possessions (your child is one of them). Yet, you can be a bit slovenly about your own person. Don't expect your child to do anything but follow your lead and the precedents you set. His toys may be tucked into their playboxes but check behind his ears when he is old enough to perform his own ablutions.

It is more likely than not that you will find it necessary to apply the doctrines of strictness and discipline to yourself more than to your child. Your vivid imagination and flights on gossamer-wing are part of a fantasyland that will enchant any child and at the same time send you slipping away from realityland. Charm him, entertain him, and take him along on your trips, just so long as you know when and where your transportation departs for planet Earth.

Indecisiveness is something else you will have to contend with in the beginning. You will find it incredibly difficult to determine your stand in matters ranging from weaning to waddling. Procrastination will only keep you vascillating along. Learn to be less of a worrier and expedite matters to preclude a mountain taking form while you still contemplate the mole-hill. You sacrifice nothing and gain something more than just self-esteem.

Of all the females in the zodiac, you alone will never feel hampered or restricted by motherhood. This is your life, moonchild, and you may need some prompting to remember that you did not accomplish this feat on your own. Pay attention to your new role as mother, but keep in mind that you were a wife first. Fatherhood, too, is a vital force in the development of your child.

Maintain your interests in the arts, languages, or whatever gives you the most pleasure. Intersperse your individual activity in these same arenas through the gradual education of your child and you will find great fulfillment in the togetherness you come to share. When he is of an age to develop other interests, you will not find yourself left without motivation or mental stimulation.

The greatest problem with which you will have to cope is that of preparing yourself for two milestones in his life and yours. The first is the day he finally leaves home and you, as well (if you have not done your job properly, this will not materialize). Curb your reluctance and tenacity. Console yourself with the knowledge that his heart remains at home. This is the natural evolution towards which you have contributed magnanimously.

The second trauma you will have to endure is the day he chooses a mate. All mothers tend to feel that their children are being short-changed or cheated in the marriage-go-round. As the ruler of motherhood it will be virtually impossible for you to cast a favorable eye on even a high priest or priestess as a suitable lifemate. No one will ever meet the standards you have set but, then again, his standards should be your major concern. Your place in his life will never be usurped. If he has not been smothered, he'll probably walk the primrose path with someone much like you and one who will show you the greatest reverence. Your relationship may be enhanced immensely when you are held up as "the" model to his partner in life.

Understanding, warmth, sensitivity, and patience are all positive traits that make you an endearing and extremely capable mother. Allow your child to reach out for independence and help him learn about his needs, desires, abilities, and talents. As a moon-mother, it is mandatory to compromise your feelings of inadequacy, temper your possessiveness, and exercise moderation rather than permissiveness. Your love and aspirations can be blissfully fulfilled if you follow the guidelines. The more you know about yourself, the better you can help him achieve his goals and make your motherhood an auspicious experience.

THE CANCER CHILD

THE key words for the sign of the Crab are "I feel." It is the first of the Water signs. Water in terms of astrology represents the fluid and the emotional aspects of a personality. The symbol of Cancer pictures a crab or the breasts of a woman. It rules motherhood, home, and the stomach. The children of this sign are extremely sensitive and emotional. How they feel is, at all times, the uppermost consideration. Just as this symbol represents a hard outer shell to the world, your child will try to build an exterior shelter of strength. The crab, however, is all soft and sweet inside—take your cue from this. He loves affection and will respond to it beautifully. The atmosphere in the home for the moon child is the second consideration. You will be kept on your toes, as you can see. He should be loved and made comfortable every minute of every day. Warmth should pervade the air around him and you'll be amazed at just how receptive he can be. Feeding your baby can truly be one of the greatest joys known to motherhood. This baby loves to be held and fondled closely by his mother, the most important person in his life. Since Cancer rules motherhood and the stomach, the combination of being held and fed by mother simultaneously is almost too great a happiness to bear.

You will notice that your infant is really not demanding but is hypersensitive and very moody. His face will mirror those feelings when he is displeased with an overabundance of noise, or upset at being fondled by strangers. You won't have to spend much time guessing what's on his mind. It will register on his face. His eyes will widen and his little chin will quiver if someone gets a bit rough with him. Generally, he will cause few trials and tribulations if the atmosphere is one of relaxation and calmness. His body is equally as sensitive as his psyche, so don't let him sit around wet. He should be changed as quickly as possible to prevent that troublesome diaper rash. Feed him on schedule too, no muss, no fuss if he is kept comfortable. He will be a most satisfying child and can adapt easily to almost any routine you establish. Patience is one of his virtues. There is no need to worry about moving him around or keeping him waiting a bit. He possesses a fantastic knack for keeping himself amused in his own private world.

The ruling planet is the Moon. This planet is the fastest moving of all and the greatest influence upon the earth of any planet in outer space. This should be an indication to you that your baby is not exceptional in his moodiness (which is yet to come), since he is a moon-child. Changes in mood will occur as frequently as feedings, which should not alarm you in the slightest. When a moon-child cries, it is with an endless reserve of tears. Remember the element of Water is involved. Torrents will come pouring down. His power of retention runs little short of being the eighth wonder of the world, especially when it relates to emotional experiences in his life. Be careful not to hurt or slight this sensitive soul. He has a file cabinet for a mind and everything sticks with him through his lifetime. The people around him and their actions and reactions will make or break this child. If he is not favorably treated or received, his little heart will be crushed and this will leave deep and permanent scars. If you are unhappy with something he has done, be sure to follow up diplomatic criticism with an expression of love. Also, see to it that no bickering takes place within earshot. This can be a very unsettling factor in his life. Even when you are taking great lengths to keep a quarrel out of his world, you can bank on the fact that he will detect a strained atmosphere with his sixth sense. Normal household noises do not bother him to any extent. These are perfectly all right. Ugly scenes will stamp themselves indelibly in his mind. They cause tragic trauma and strike fear into his hearing well.

Dear Don is devoted and docile and every inch a moon-child. Every time he hears a raised voice or stony silence, he realizes that all is not well. As one would expect from a Cancer baby, he distorts the picture. He feels himself the cause and the culprit—an unloved one at that. Dutiful son that he is, Don overcompensates to try to ingratiate himself and becomes more addicted to the need for love. Luckily, Don's parents can spot the teardrop he wears on his sleeve and reassure him in time. Without an awareness of what makes Don cry or croon he could have become a Mama's (or Papa's) boy who would never think of leaving the homefires; disastrous for everyone.

His sensitivity is of a dual nature. Not only do his moods fluctuate when he feels slighted (justifiably or not), but he reacts instinctively to variations in the moods of others. Thankfully, this is a redeeming and helpful characteristic. Just as he is sympathetic with his fellow man, so you must be sympathetic to his ups and downs. Very few can be controlled adequately, if any, and you must act as a cushion to help him adjust to his lunar personality, with the difficulties of the unpredictable nature he possesses. It is even possible that once the mystery and fear of the murky moods is relieved, some inner pressure will be released. Don't be dumbstruck if some of the moods are alleviated and less murky or even diminished in frequency.

In the feeding of your baby, you will sense immediately that he is most susceptible to extremes of hot and cold. Never give him a hot bottle. Give one that leans toward the cool side. Weather affects him tremendously where mood and health are concerned. Rain can bring on the blues. Both heat and humidity are bad for his temper and not good for his health. He is, after all, a water sign, and needs enough fluid in his own system.

Much empathy is required for these children. If handled properly, many creative talents can be developed. Cancer children are born actors and actresses, and they love every moment that they are on stage. You'll see this when he is still confined to his crib. The lunar child is given to the dramatic and his imagination will lend itself to staging many exciting and adventurous situations which may exist mainly in his mind. The make-believe will comprise a major portion of his leisure playtime. Imaginary friends will have personalities closely correlated to his own. Your child will be exceptionally well-mannered and docile. Don't be fooled by this. Cancer is a cardinal sign which means that he is not apt to be a disciple. He is more likely a quiet director or dictator.

When the momentous time arrives for those first steps, he will be a little on the timid side, afraid to strike out on his own. Encouragement is needed here and you should start by holding out your hands each time he makes that supreme effort to move forward into an upright position. He needs your help but is a little reticent to ask for it.

Fears are inborn with moon-children, so do not tease him if he is afraid of the dark, dogs, and many other things. The best way to handle this situation is to wait until the child is a bit older and can understand the explanation. If the dark is a problem area, start by turning the light on and off several times to show him that nothing changes. Be patient, the process may take a while to grab hold. As he begins to develop and toddle around, his timidity and shyness will become more apparent. Offer encouragement and take special care to assure him that he is capable of doing things. Girls should be constantly reassured that they are pretty and compliments should be handed out freely whenever a new dress is donned. These fears must be alleviated. Don't taunt your child or accuse him of ever being a cry-baby. Once encouraged and assuaged, your child may easily shock you with some of the things that he will then do. Anyone who is as sensitive as he, must necessarily be competent. He is an observer and aware of details of an operation. Encouragement is your role. Be sure to give him little jobs that will make him feel he is a help to you. It is sometimes difficult to find the right path here. You can be overly protective and smothering, or too harsh and fast with the strap. Either method will leave a mark. Remember that your baby's sign is the crab and he can recoil just as quickly as his counterpart can pull his legs back into his shell. The withdrawal will be immediate and can happen at any time, even when people who are strangers to him stop by for a visit. It will be a complete withdrawal from the world. Love is the panacea and will always bring him around. Mother is the apple of his eye and he will not stray far from the apron strings. You will be a protector and, later on, a friend and confidant. No one can ever replace you.

Even at a tender age your child is endowed with a maternal instinct that can rival yours in intensity. Compassion, obviously, is an integral part of the picture. So, at all times, keep an eagle eye open for the possessive trait that too often is at the center of all that enviable compassion. Strictly as a mother, you should intuitively sense the ulterior motive behind certain forms of empathy. Since he has a proclivity for imaginary slights, a real one (in the form of open punishment) will penetrate the crab's soft shell too quickly and too harshly. Use gentle persuasion always and never a hard hand.

As with the Taurean youngster, those first school days can be very traumatic if the child is not adequately prepared. Careful and logical explanations accompanied by a couple of solid bear hugs should do the trick. Inadequate preparation will bring on fears, tears, and no communication with the teacher that will take time and patience to remedy. You can't blame him, though, can you?

As a student, history and geography will be pet subjects and he will have a favorite president, general, or country at all times. Math can be a sore spot. The moon-child is something of a dreamer and the practicality and coldness of a subject like mathematics will not appeal to him.

Don stands at the head of his class. He always has, and yet he is liked by his peers and teachers. With his photographic mind like a filing cabinet, he has all manner of knowledge stored away. Although teachers like him, they also have had to learn to understand him. Hypersensitivity and a vibrant imagination carry him off on moon tangents once in a while as he embroiders small slights with the colorful threads of a little "rainbow" lie to elicit sympathy. So far, so good! Everyone has understood and been gentle in reminding him of the dichotomy between truth and fiction and he has responded fairly well. Without insight and patience, he would have curled up in his shell, unreachable to human hearts.

Cancerians should have some degree of practicality instilled in their basic personality. Being sensitive and feeling is a marvelous attribute but will not in itself pull one through the realities of life. Your child will adore the magical world of the theatre and, shy as he is, love the opportunities presented in the school plays. Cancerians put themselves right into the role they assume and really feel the part. Music also holds a special attraction for them. Be prepared for music lessons of all kinds and some in diction too. He will excel in all if you are encouraging—do not be harsh. He knows what should be done so do not criticize. Encouragement will spawn self-established routines for practice in these areas.

As the infant begins to develop, you must be forewarned of hidden hurts. If you are busy with some project and don't have time for him this will be taken as a rejection. Some will be imaginary but the crushing effect is the same. He is not the healthiest of children. The best you can expect are fairly good eating and sleeping habits. Do remember that hot foods are not to his liking and will most likely get cold before he has finished his meal. Bland diets are much more beneficial to him since the stomach will be a probable source of difficulty. It is very possible that your child may give vent to his emotional hurts by gorging his little stomach, which we already know is sensitive. If all of these problem areas are under control, then your child can be expected to be an active one. Don't expect that fleeting ball of fire typifying the Arian youngster, but if the interest is there the agility certainly abounds. Skating, skiing, any sport that requires limber muscles, coordination and manipulation is a natural for him. He is sensitive and knows just how the body should be positioned to accomplish a physical feat. His timing is excellent, also. Dancing is another area in which he will excel and find great enjoyment. Activity is good for him. Without encouragement he has a tendency to be somewhat lethargic and may not be inclined to make the first move on his own.

A college education is a yes for him. With his emotions in check, a good set of study habits, and his almost photographic memory, he will do well. Surprisingly, perhaps, teaching is a field in which he himself will shine forth. Actually any field that calls for instruction is in his ken, whether it be dancing, mechanical engineering, or the like. Since the stomach is so sensitive with moon-children and they love to eat, it is not surprising to find that many of the world's greatest chefs are Cancerians. If your child is a boy, it is most possible that in later years he will surpass his wife with his culinary skills. Talent also exists for financial manipulation. The Cancerian has a feeling for the machinations of the business world. The females of the species make good teachers and excellent secretaries, the stabilizing force behind the executive. She will be receptive and have a feel for what should be done and how.

As a dreamy moon-child Don fell in love many times, each time with such great intensity that his parents felt he would become another Tommy Manville or a bigamist. There is none so romantic as a lunar child's heart, and being in love with love is as commonplace as breathing. When Miss Right came along, though, there was little doubt. Never had Don wanted love so much, tried so hard to please, and given so much; never, that is, except with his parents. Yes, he did make one of the most fabulous husbands ever, and today, after many years of marriage, diapers and braces, there is still romance in his marriage, as there will always be.

If mother fails in her duties to supply the necessary amount of emotional security, this child could run into real trouble in his adult years. Feelings of rejection, hurt, and being exploited can be magnified and give birth to a bad seed. Introverted as he is, the child could develop into a cruel adult. All the hurts and slights that are retained in that file cabinet memory will bring out a selfish aspect. He won't allow a repeat performance where he is concerned. Next time it will be someone else who suffers. Bring out his best nature through understanding and interest and you will have a sympathetic Cancerian that is sought out for his advice and counsel.

Because of his feeling nature you have no difficulty in selecting a course of action to follow in bringing him around. If his grades are not what they should be, or he is falling short in the performance of any task, he will readily accept your expression of blighted hopes without question. He will put forth a super-human effort to assure that you will be spared such repeated anguish in the future. It is as simple as that. Love is more vital to his being than any other single factor. If the emotional security it brings is threatened by his misbehavior, laxity, or unawareness, he will remedy the situation in order to bring you pleasure and restore his security blanket. T'would that all mothers were blessed with such potential paradise. Mothering a moon-child is like having the man-in-the-moon all to yourself.

Children born between June 22nd and July 2nd have the double aspect of the moon influence which rules the night. Your child has double strength in the realms of idealism and domesticity. His nature is overly sympathetic and he will be devoted to the problems of mankind. A tendency to be hyper-critical can rear its head once in a while, but generally he will be less moody than the other moon-children who are his peers, but a bit more fearful of the unknown than some others.

Birthdays that fall between July 3rd and July 12th are ruled by the planet Mars, the symbol of energy and war. Your child will be less lethargic than most Cancers, and less fearful of striking out, attempting the uncertain. Organization and practicality are with this child at all times, and he can establish his own inner controls. Diplomacy and discretion are second nature to him and he has many friends and admirers as a result. Powers of judgement are excellent and he does well in the role of a mediator.

Children born between July 13th and July 22nd have Neptune as their personal ruler and this makes your child the fastest-moving of the lunar lot in deed and thought. Little hesitation will be encountered with this individual and he is most flexible and adaptable. He will be caught up in his own life and have little time to become involved in the day-to-day lives of those around him. Self-confidence is great and counteracts the usual caution associated with children of this sign.

THE CANCER
MOTHER
AND HER CHILD

The Cancer Mother And The Aries Child

This can be a volatile combination or the most serene of all
mother-child relationships. You are permissive, indecisive, and
flexible. He is self-centered, impetuous, and assertive.

With this child you must hold the reins, imposing structured
and consistent restrictions. You strive to dominate and he fends
off all manner of restraint. With proper handling you can diminish
some of the fiery spirit, but it must be done on a subliminal level.
He will balk at established routines and try to throw you off-
balance by lashing out at your sensitive nature, knowing full well
that you will retreat. Hold your ground in such instances with
expediency, determination, and just the proper amount of authority
to win your points. It would be a waste of time to try to protect
this child from anything as he continually will forge ahead at his
own speed to uncover as much as possible within his lifetime. He
can be kept in check by withholding those things that give him
pleasure—not in a sadistic manner, but with a rational approach
that he can understand. Guide him with love and he will forget
about trying to dominate you. You will find him quite cooperative
under these circumstances.

Since you both feel that he is greatly gifted and highly superior to other children, your common desire for his achievements
will allow you tremendous pleasures from this relationship.

The Cancer Mother And The Taurus Child

This child will adapt himself rather well to any routines or
regimens imposed. A structured environment is best for him. Your

innate understanding of his basic nature should prevent you from becoming a "monkey on his back".

The Taurus child is deliberate and somewhat methodical. Major problems in his behavior will be at a minimum so long as an outlet exists for both exuberance and the artistic streak kept deep within.

A possible area of conflict can develop if you persist in imposing your opinions. Your child's bullish tendencies will leap to the fore and you must expend twice as much effort to maintain your position without relenting (as strong as the temptation may be). This comes down to the survival of the fittest. Anything but a consistent show of force is an indication of weakness to him and, in his eyes, makes you unsuited for the role of the "fittest".

Exercise your patience and sensitivity but maintain composure for a happy and trouble-free atmosphere.

The Cancer Mother And The Gemini Child

With this child you must concentrate your efforts on establishing a gentle line of discipline which he can understand. His proclivity for seeking variety may unnerve you to a great degree and hold you fearful of a premature departure from the roost.

His curiosity and need for exploration will play upon your insecurities, and in retaliation you resort to rigid discipline which will result in instant catastrophe. Limiting his activity and freedom of movement in a calm, quiet way is the most effective manner for keeping him in check.

Never chide him for being contrary. His symbol is the twins of dual personality and you cannot change this trait. Wrong doing and mischief are obviously punishable but not inconsistent. Encourage his talent for acting a part but be certain he differentiates between his world and that of reality.

Stimulate his feeling for displays of affection and appreciation on a low level as he is inwardly shy even with you. Like parent, like child—if he is exposed to enough tenderness, he will absorb much. Appeal to him by a show of sympathy for his travails, not a gushy, protective show but one that makes sense to him, bolstering his ego.

The Cancer Mother And The Cancer Child

Moon-mother, know thyself and you should have less hurdles to overcome with your child. You recognize his needs, insecurities, and moods. Discipline him as you would yourself, keeping in mind that he is but a child. Remember that you want to prevent the clinging child from developing into a tenacious adult.

He is too capable of imitating, so it is mandatory that you encourage him to be frank, outspoken, and independent. This child is very impressionable, so anything that he finds appealing or interesting will grab his attention. If a soapbox orator is given stature, he will try to duplicate the effort and bring him out of himself. Give him the love he needs. Reassure him constantly, but don't give enough for a brood of children. Be prudent, and sympathize with him over his failures. Make him believe that the greater disappointment is yours and voila! He will make it a point to excel in the particular subject of prior incompetence.

The chore is an easy one. It is easier because you are tuned in to his blessings and deficiencies and because you have a built-in understanding of children. See to it that he is brought up to a more open, more active level, and he will accomplish great things.

The Cancer Mother And The Leo Child

Your Leo child is gregarious, active, full of talent, and vibrant. He is also high strung, dictatorial, and is a ham. Ultimately you will triumph over-all with a devastating combination of charm and diplomacy.

Even during infancy he must be approached with respect and firmness so that he does not find his road to success (as a mature adult) under constant construction. His ego can become quite overbearing and he cannot be allowed to give quarter to his tendency to live a sybaritic life. Use self-restraint. Toss laurels his way only if he has earned them. He is most receptive to the learning process, and will soon realize that he must work to win your admiration and praise. You must also instill in him an awareness that he should gain satisfaction from his endeavors and not your kudos.

Be a woman of few well-chosen words when giving this child direction. His vast quantity of energy leaves him little patience for procrastination, repetition, or redundancy. He will not be a follower, so do not overly concern yourself with his future.

Much genuine love and affection will pour forth from your lion cub. With proper inspiration, his bolder qualities can be tempered, leaving only the advantageous traits of ambition, ingenuity, and vitality.

The Cancer Mother And The Virgo Child

You must realize, from the very moment this child makes his debut, that you have been presented with a perfectionist imbued with obstinancy, perseverance, versatility, an analytical interior, and a somewhat aloof exterior.

It is of the first order that you demonstrate all the warmth befitting a lunar mother to teach your child affection and sociability lest he develop into a cold and selfish adult. The head rules the heart of this being but, with proper exercising and little damage, the heart can learn to function overtime.

You will undoubtedly be looking down at the top of his head most of the time as he studiously perseveres and immerses himself in the pursuit of knowledge and minutia of anything mental. Once started, he will not raise his head until the most picayune detail has been absorbed or worked out. His unfailing memory will occasionally prove a drawback as he reverts to past actions (good and bad) as a matter of rote.

There are no major traumas with this child once he has learned the understanding of love and its demonstrations. With all your charm and sensitivity, though, you must take him out of the world of books and into the people world around him. Be logical and practical. Concern yourself with making him more flexible and loving.

The Cancer Mother And The Libra Child

While your Libra child is shy, clinging, lazy, and absentminded, you will find the personality a tough one to deal with. Many times, clashes may arise that will result in a battle of wills. He also possesses the traits of leadership, self-assertiveness, and mental perspicacity.

He is so inhibited that even his creative talents will suffer from a combination of innate restraining forces and lethargy. The capability is there but the ambition is lacking. Here you must be adroit at administering diplomacy while imbuing self-confidence and enough ambition to drive his limited energies into play for his benefit. Most of his time will be devoted to weighing the pros and cons of possible action; for such a protracted period, that time for action or decision will be long past.

You will enjoy his sense of humor and congenial manner, to say nothing of his considerate attitude toward you and your welfare. His intelligence enables him to grasp things quickly, and disciplining him will not require repeated reminders. Revoking a privilege will suffice. Rarely will there be a time when he does not appreciate life and what it has to offer. He will see to it that he is not denied many pleasures, and will insure his privileges with good behavior.

Your main concern will be in subtly guiding him through the process of decision-making and instilling the confidence which will enable him to eventually do so on his own.

The Cancer Mother And The Scorpio Child

This child can be the most frightening for a Cancer mother to handle. His powers are incredibly strong and his determination equally as overwhelming. Obstinancy, passion, arrogance, and mental agility are all within this intense little being.

As the Scorpion that symbolizes his sign, he is very apt to lash out quickly and without recrimination when he is hurt or pressed too hard. Beware that his flair for the dramatic does not keep you in tears when, in fact, he should be taught fair play and self-discipline. You cannot relax your scrutiny of his actions ever as he is capable of being secretive. As a doting mother, you may take much time to recognize and more to correct this. Do not dissolve when his misbehavior comes to your attention. Instead, do not lose a minute in giving him the proper direction. Never, never send him into an isolation chamber as punishment as you would with other children. This will make him brood beyond belief and only provide him with what he wants most at such a time.

Be precise and blunt in teaching him the control and mastery of a Scorpio to be administered by a Scorpio. You cannot start too soon to keep him from self-indulgence. Here you must be both a scientist and a diplomat with sleight of hand.

The Cancer Mother And The Sagittarius Child

Your Sagittarian child has many gifts such as congeniality, compassion of an inordinate degree, love of fellow-man and activism. Then there are the high and mighty traits that encompass unnecessary truthfulness, a gift of gab, and dull sense of sensitivity. He is as happy as a lark, easy to discipline, and generally well-behaved.

Just about the only concerns you will have are in directing the valuable assets of this child, spelling out the reasons for each and every action or word. He listens well and must be made to understand. You will adore this child because he is so uncomplicated and responds well to your explanations. He is not as self-sufficient as he would like you to believe and you know it all too well. Your guidance in making decisions is of great importance and he will see the rationale behind desire to help.

You may be whisked along with some of his plans and dreams for doing great things as you get to know his capabilities. Hold back and remember that the archer is still trying to hit the bull's eye head on and it will take more than lofty dreams. Plan ahead with him carefully and he may fly you to the moon.

The Cancer Mother And The Capricorn Child

Your Capricorn mountain-goat will be born with all the maturity and wisdom of one who has been around four-score years or more. You have the monumental chore of instilling youthful enthusiasm and vigor in this somber and recalcitrant little thing. He must be taught to laugh and play as the child he is, although you may find it difficult not to ask his advice on your problems.

A tremendous amount of counselling and instruction must emanate from you in order to develop a likeable disposition with trust of those around him. This child is not filled with the milk of human kindness. You can offset the negative aspects of egotism, voluntary exile, and material ambition by eliminating the anxieties that plague him about every facet of life. Summon forth all your moon-mother qualities to coax and coddle him into letting go.

Also watch for tendencies towards ultra-conservatism. He is wise and overly cautious, so tread carefully. Appealing to his heart will be a fruitless maneuver, so play on his powers of observation and display much affection. Flatter his ego at the same time. Do not worry about his capabilities to get ahead. His perseverance and ambition will carry him further than your dreams.

You can find a compatible level of understanding only after he has been somewhat humanized. This project cannot begin early enough.

The Cancer Mother And The Aquarius Child

Since you have been blessed with the most reasonable of all children, you may find yourself with fewer problems than most parents. This child is people-oriented and far from self-centered. His ambition is to improve everyone's lot in life. What you must do is see to it that his background is full enough and his education formal enough for him to accomplish his goals.

Endowed with good nature he is very apt to be a little too easy-going. You must teach him to be less lax, yet trustful of his fellow man. This trait can lead to a major weakness which is the opposite extreme, and not an advantageous one at that.

Your endeavors will be delightfully rewarded. To teach him and guide him is to ask for a *fait accompli* and have it appear before your eyes. Be certain, though, that he does not lapse into a stage of promising the world and delivering nothing. If nipped in the bud, this characteristic will go no further and your problems will be nil. Enjoy this child and what he wants to give you. Don't take too much from him but give an equal measure of yourself and your efforts will be well repaid.

The Cancer Mother And The Pisces Child

You and your Pisces child share many good traits except that he is a bit more of a dreamer than you and must be transplanted back to earth. His sensitivity matches yours and his feeling for hearth and home bring you no end of delight. You must instill self-confidence and an awareness of his capabilities, for he is fearful of failure. Should you not start early enough, he will not bother to make the effort in later years.

Convince him through sincere flattery and a step-by-step outline of "how to" that nothing comes to those who stand and wait. It is of prime importance that you tackle this in a methodical manner. Since he tends to be completely Utopian and would rather be the flying Dutchman, than anyone else, you must proceed with caution. Allow him to start leaving loose ends around and your chances of recouping ground or lost time will be non-existent. His character development hinges entirely upon you and the outline you prescribe for him to follow. Remember that he is symbolized by fish swimming in either direction and so is vague and equivocal in his own mind.

Overcome his apprehensions with good humor and compassion. Discipline him carefully for his sensitive nature will react as does yours. Do not give in or sympathize with his mopishness. This will only make him wallow in self-pity.

Channel outward his spirituality and devotion and he will undoubtedly be a great benefactor to you and many others. The introspective fish is swimming upstream ahead of the current when this occurs.

STAR GUIDE
FOR
CANCER

Symbol	●	The Crab
Ruling Planet	●	Moon
Element	●	Water
Gender	●	Feminine
Key Words	●	I Feel
Birthstones	●	Ruby, Moonstone
Favorite Flowers	●	All Lilies
Best Colors	●	Silver, Sea Green
Mineral	●	Silver
Favorite Music	●	Ballads
Favorite Pastime	●	Entertaining
Lucky Number	●	2
Best Days	●	Thursday, Saturday
Compatible Signs	●	Taurus, Scorpio, Virgo
Incompatible Signs	●	Aries, Libra

FAMOUS PEOPLE BORN UNDER THE SIGN OF THE CRAB

JOHN QUINCY
  ADAMS
LOUIS
  ARMSTRONG
PHINEAS T.
  BARNUM
HENRY WARD
  BEECHER
STEPHEN
  VINCENT
  BENET
INGMAR
  BERGMAN
MILTON BERLE
DAVID BRINKLEY
JULIUS CAESAR
JAMES CAGNEY
MARC CHAGALL
GEORGE M.
  COHAN
CALVIN
  COOLIDGE
EDWARD DEGAS
JACK DEMPSEY
MARY BAKER
  EDDY
NELSON EDDY

STEPHEN
  FOSTER
ERLE
  STANLEY
  GARDNER
CHRISTOLPH
  GLUCK
OSCAR
  HAMMERSTEIN
NATHANIEL
  HAWTHORNE
ERNEST
  HEMINGWAY
LENA HORNE
ELIAS HOWE
HELEN KELLER
WILLEM DE
  KOONIG
CHARLES
  LAUGHTON
GERTRUDE
  LAWRENCE
GINA
  LOLLOBRIGIDA
MAXIMILIAN
MARCEL PROUST
CECIL RHODES
GINGER ROGERS

RICHARD
  RODGERS
JOHN D.
  ROCKEFELLER
NELSON
  ROCKEFELLER
JEAN JACQUES
  ROUSSEAU
J. D. SALINGER
RED SKELTON
MARGARET
  CHASE SMITH
BARBARA
  STANWYCK
RINGO STARR
WILLIAM
  THACKERAY
HENRY THOREAU
VAN CLIBURN
JOHN
  WANAMAKER
JOSIAH
  WEDGEWOOD
JAMES MacNEIL
  WHISTLER
DUKE OF
  WINDSOR
ANDREW WYETH

THE
LEO
MOTHER

July 23rd – August 22nd

SHEENA—queen of the jungle are you, and you will most likely
let everyone know it without hesitation. Fortunately, you can re-
deem yourself with your sparkling personality and exuding charm,
so that you antagonize few people. As a mother, you will not allow
your position to be threatened or usurped by a child, and you will
certainly not concede the spotlight to so mere a mortal.

Your vitality and versatility serve you admirably as you
make the adjustment that imposes on your time. As a lioness you
must preside over the kingdom, and this presents the best possible
opportunity for doing so. A built-in and captive audience is yours
and you love every minute of it. You don't regard motherhood as
demeaning, or taking a back seat to your little cub.

In rearing and housebreaking your child, you will find it
necessary to see beyond the trees through to the forest while understanding the very real possibility that your child may have his
faults, too. Your arrogance and optimisim have validity and merit,
but your qualities of leadership are of much more value in this
long-run, record-breaking role of motherhood.

Authority must be exercised by you over your child and, to a
large degree, yourself. Since you are gifted with so many strong
and admirable traits, you may find it difficult to accept the possibility that a member of the royal family is not as well-endowed
with natural charm and precociousness. You also cannot expect
him to assume a regal stance before he takes his first steps.

As royalty, it should be quite simple for you to issue a restraining order against yourself, to keep you from indulging him with
all the luxuries befitting his position. There will be ample reason

to justifiably treat him to goodies as his behavior merits them (and it will). Recognize the endless wonders of childhood and all it can bring to your credit, if handled properly.

You must plod past the palm trees in your jungle and out in the open air, reassessing your position in relation to that of your child's. There is no need for him to be placed center stage on a silver throne because you thrive on the ostentacious and opulent. Your cub is an infant and must be treated as such, and not as a possession.

You have a propensity for extremes. The most dangerous one for you to null and void is that of giving too much materially and emotionally. Once you realize that your child is not an extension of yourself, and hence to be revered, you will be able to see the folly of such an approach. Better let the grandparents dote on him than you. It will do much less harm.

Lord help those who are foolish enough to criticize his behavior or your child-rearing policies. Once a lioness has been wounded, she will not rest until the injury has been righted. The dignity of the feline is at stake and, once the wrath has been incurred, let those who have been bold run for cover. It wouldn't hurt a bit for you to at least listen to the opinion of someone you respect. An outsider's objectivity could be invaluable as an aid to you. It will help make the little prince a better developed full-grown king.

You should follow through with your penchant for spit and polish, and require your cub to heed the voice of authority, learn etiquette from A to Z, and respect his elders and others in command. Just be certain that this isn't your program for completion within sixty days or less. This cannot even be achieved by a ninety day wonder (full-grown). Give him time and a small handicap befitting his size and years. This must be a long-range plan so that it will become second nature and not rote just to pass the test of the day.

Unlike the Cancer mother, your love and devotion for your child is highly unlikely to featherbed him from the realities of life, except that you may make him believe that a snap of his fingers will bring everyone to attention. It is mandatory that he learn the meaning of the word "no"; what comes to him is because it has been earned. Here again, your self-restraint is required. Flattery should not be bandied about except for real accomplishments that warrant praise (or as encouragement to an insecure ego).

It is doubtful that you will go so far as to smother your child, for then he would not be lordly in his own right. If you have foresight and use your analytical mind you will be able to decipher the possibility of your child being a might more insecure than you are. The chances are at least fifty-fifty and, seeing this, you will summon forth your remarkable talent for showing compassion, without the maudlin sentimentality that will do nothing but confuse the issue and waste your highly valued time.

You will take precautions to maintain your dignity as an individual and mother by seeing to it that you do not place yourself in a position where you can be taken for granted under any circumstances. The fierce leonine pride that is innately yours will let itself be seen without hesitation. Please temper it though, with a child a strong display of this pride can be overpowering and debilitating.

See your way clear to an awareness of your child's shortcomings. Then implement and expedite a routine for him to follow that will allow for human frailties and yet be strict enough to be effective. It will please you when he exercises the strength to follow through. If he is unable to do so under the terms you have chosen, reassess your standards to see if you have asked for the moon when the stars will suffice.

Playing mother will delight you under any circumstances. It adds dimension to your personality and places you in a new spotlight. This pleasurable feeling will only be heightened when you spend time frolicking and gamboling with him. A myriad of possibilities is open to you in terms of introducing your child to all the good things in life that you enjoy so very much. Hours upon hours will be spent developing his talents, testing his skills, and just talking over ideas. His promise is as bright as sunshine and you will bask in it (never in the shadows—fear not)!

With all the gusto and gladness to be reaped from this relationship, take care not to cloud the skies with your inflatable ego. Should your little prince not bow to you, the queen, the way you feel he should, don't retreat into a corner to pout. Do not react with a mighty roar either, and toss him out of the palace. He is not to blame, for what you consider due you.

As you lavish affection and attention on this child, be cautious about lavishing luxuries that would spoil a well-to-do adult. There will be a tendency to shower him with sweetmeats and whatever else you can find that is expensive or out of the ordinary. As a matter of fact, it is perfectly plausible that you will find it necessary to be less self-indulgent, depending on financial circumstances (yes, Leo, even money trees wither away).

It is gratifying to know that your lion cub will emerge from the royal chamber as his own man. Your independence will allow and encourage his to flourish. Thankfully, you are not about to abdicate from your private realm, since many of you have important positions outside of the home. No one is more capable of coping with two separate lives with greater ease and still have time left over for new experiments. Through all this, your child will remain far from neglected, and one eye will always be turned in his direction.

A flair (or rather, dogged dedication) for the dramatic is a vital part of your personality and will provide you with many a supreme moment in the role of motherhood. First, a real talent for being a public person does exist within you. This can assume the place of a teacher, lecturer, drama coach, or soap box orator. Second, as a guide and tutor for your child, you will excel in stimulating him and carrying his interest in any subject to an all-time high. You will dazzle him with your enthusiasm and prove to be the most exciting and adventuresome companion he could ever wish to find. Playmates will pale by comparison, and that is when you must urge him into sociability with his peers no matter how he protests. In the end you will have gained more respect for this than many other deeds. "The pains of love are sweeter far, than all other pleasures are", some Italian fortune cookie writer once said.

Dignity and pride are almost synonymous in your life, and it is essential that you realize the difference before an attack of hubris is your downfall. You are entitled to a certain degree of adoration for being yourself and not as your royal right. Alienation of affection does exist, and just such a persistent, inflexible

trait as pride can most easily bring it about. Spurred on by smid-
geons of jealousy sprinkled hither and yon, you may be heading
for a fall. Protect yourself wisely in advance for this possibility.
It is even beyond your ken to retain the same posture with a child,
any child, that you present to adults. Toss your head and flip your
mane to the rear for an unobstructed view of what's up front that
counts.

Since you have a like for gambling, keep it restricted to areas
far and away from the nursery. Being liberal in allowing your
child to develop his own personality and express his own will is
marvelous. Chancing it that he will be able to handle all obstacles
in his path is reverting to extremes and trusting to luck. Neither
of these will do when the stakes are so high. What is good for *you*
will not hold true for your child. Be meticulous in setting examples
and a structured framework within which he can feasibly operate.

Keeping the blue-blood line pure is something *not* to try.
Checking into his interests and choice of companions is something
that bears investigation. Independence should be encouraged, but
allowing a child to roam completely free is never advisable no
matter what his sun-sign or inherited super-traits. It is not stultify-
ing but structurizing and never versa vice.

Just as you cannot abide being taken for granted, be certain
that you do not respond flippantly to his achievements and accomplishments. Every child needs encouragement and praise for a
job well-done, even members of the royal family.

Pet him, adore him, and genuinely love him for himself. As
long as you recognize his royal right, the two of you will be fine.
Remove your crown during the formative years and pretend you
are common folk. You will have more fun and perhaps win greater
respect from him as a real person than as his monarch.

THE
LEO
CHILD

THE lion of the jungle has the words "I will" as its key and it is represented by a symbol that depicts the sun with a mane of hair over it, or the heart which has one valve leading in and one leading out. In other words, it is the center of activity and that is the basic nature of your little lion. Like Aries, he is a Fire sign but there is a difference. Aries impulsively dashes towards his goal and the activity being dispersed from a central point. Leo pulls everything into a point of convergence and the activity is searching for a central point. Your baby expects a lot of attention and feels that the world does, indeed, revolve around him and his needs. He can be patient and not overly active at times, but he leaves small room for doubt when it comes to who's in charge. Your Leo will take to routine nicely and not cause problems at feeding time if you are not late. Not too much and not too little at one sitting in the way of food—his capacity is limited.

Leo is the largest member of the feline family and, as such, it should not be surprising that he needs his cat-naps often and quite late into life. Also his fondness for adoration will resemble the same feline nature. Nothing pleases him more than having many people bustling about and making a commotion over him. This youngster has an innate sense of what is to be done by you and others in his behalf. He is certain of your role and the needs you are to fill in his life. At times he will be extremely active, and then there will be prolonged periods of lethargy when he is not apt to make a move. In all these instances you must let him know that he is not really a king and no one is his slave. When he is a little older teach him that if he wants something he is perfectly capable of getting it himself. In infancy, when he wants changing, he knows this is your job. You will have to answer to his urgent wails when you do not perform quickly enough. Not quite the same as the Arian child, he will not begin to bellow for you before he has finished wetting his diaper, but you will feel a sense of urgency, nonetheless. You can almost picture his little brain thinking about your whereabouts and, when you do not show, saying to himself, "Well, I guess it's time to start letting off steam." He starts that bellow slowly but it will gather momentum as it continues.

Your baby will prefer a nice warm bottle. He is a Fire sign that can stand the heat; the flame is a steady one. A typical Leo is rather radiant, cheerful, and playful but he enjoys being entertained. Funny little games that you play with him are a delight; when they are lacking he will roar like that lion. There is another type of Leo, however, the withdrawn and quiet one that retreats into the lion's den when he is unhappy. This is not done in the Cancerian manner of pulling back into a shell. The air will be thick and strained with the Leo's brand of quiet, and at times you will feel that you'd rather hear that roar than deafening silence. You must teach him that to be fair is the right way, and always being first is not fair. His pride will not react well to reprimands and never try it in front of an audience.

Suzy was to the throne born and she feels she is a perfect Leo princess-in-waiting to assume her proper station in life. She displays all the egocentric qualities, but every once in a while will slink (even babies slink) off into a corner for no apparent reason, except that with typical leonine pride Suzy occasionally mistook a quick shake of the head or tap on the bottom as an indication that she is unloved and unwanted. Dark depression was often confused with sulking, and Suzy was further reprimanded and denied both attention and affection. Even egocentric lion cubs cannot withstand such punishment when it is unjust, and conversely need a little sunshine and love just like the moon-child. Suzy's parents discovered this proclivity early, in time to prevent further incidents and possible permanent damage.

When a Leo baby starts to walk he is very sure of himself and self-confident. He likes to have his wits about him and sure-footing under him. He won't dart out or be overly cautious. Here he strikes a happy medium. You won't have to hold his hand for long. Amazingly enough he will do very well, no hasty moves or any without thought, and his efforts will be praiseworthy. His sense of balance is excellent. Be sure that you do offer that praise. The more he receives the more he will respond, and the greater his confidence will grow.

With all his haughtiness and regal airs, self-confidence is not as strong as it appears to be within this child. You will be a vital factor in teaching him the why's of his arrogance and egotism and the necessity of learning to curb and control it to some degree— any degree. The more favorable aspects of his dominant qualities can lead to great paths of glory, if he is not allowed to run rampant and use the talent adversely to push his weaker brethren around. Although a feline, Leos are big bullies but generally will not tolerate like treatment on any level, even a justifiable voice of authority.

As a youngster, your child will be a leader. At his first encounter with other children you will see that regal streak come to the fore. The other children will watch his actions, crowd around, and emulate him. He will not be too selfish, but does like to have things done his way. In games, he always wants to be first. If that doesn't work out, once he learns the rules you won't have any monumental repercussions. Usually, with these cubs it is all or nothing. He can have a quick temper in addition to a desire to rule over others. Here you must mold the child and, if the job is well done, no more problems. He has a sympathetic and forgiving nature. The emotional make-up can lead to rivalry and an urge to dominate or become all-powerful. You must train him to the forest around him and play up to that innate sense of dignity. This is your key to the problem of aggression when he starts to exhibit "know-it-all" tendencies. Love and discipline should be blended subtly, and the proper amounts of each should be carefully calculated. Whether your lion is the timid or tyrannical type, he needs to be in the limelight and needs to hear the sound of praise to nurture his ego. If it is not provided at home early enough, he may attempt to get it later in life in an offensive manner, or withdraw so completely that he will be totally repressed and frustrated.

With her playmates Suzy is the vital cog and directing force from "once upon a time" on. She patronizes favorites and doles out favors like a fast-fingered card shark that wins a blue ribbon for his underhanded dealings. Suzy handed out rewards to those friends who best followed her lead and that set the regal family's flowing names on end. They scolded, punished, and ignored, all of little consequence in such an instance. Finally, in desperation, mother voiced her disappointment and wounded pride in Suzy's behavior and, SHAZAM, the magic court jester created a smoke screen. The little princess's bad habit vanished almost before her very eyes. Her feline nature must have familial approval.

At home with mother he should be introduced to the arts— good music, paintings, and the like. He will never have his fill of entertainment. When no one is entertaining him, he will take to the stage himself with an air that bespeaks of having been to the manor born. Leo rules the theatre but in a different sense than the emoting Cancerian. He has a love of laughter and the essence of entertainment in his bag. The smile that a Leo flashes is dazzling and rivals the sun for intensity and radiation. Many are born comedians, too. Being a little stage-struck, he will enjoy impressing other people with himself and his talent (he usually is talented, so have no fears of having an embarassment on your hands). This is a real ham.

There is no such thing as status quo with a Leo. With the common people there is a swing of the pendulum, a spread between progression and regression. With a Leo it is straight on— ahead, up, and away. He may occasionally live in the present but that is a rarity. It is always tomorrow, and yesterday never existed. This is one great failing that you must dutifully and doggedly aim to change. In a world with no yesterdays, past experience is of no value—nothing learned and nothing at all gained. No greater waste could exist in the life of a Leo. His interests are so varied, his opportunities so numerous that few people are ever exposed to such offerings. Some do not even court such dreams.

When school time arrives there will be little trouble on a scholastic basis. Routine is something to which he adapts easily and only praise is required to keep him on an even keel in the classroom. A fierce pride is inherent to the character of a lion (as is true with most royalty), and your little tot wants recognition for his accomplishments. Nobility demands recognition and the spirit of a nobleman should not be crushed. Always keep the words "I will" in your mind. Applause from an audience means as much to your youngster as acceptance does to a king in his court. Praise, however, should not be confused with encouragement. He will do things on his own without your goading but must have these feats admired. Teachers will enjoy working with your child because he is very creative and full of good ideas on how to do things. Imagination runs rampant with this child and he is always an asset when it comes to a need for original thinking. Teaching others will be a delight to him because this brings the focal point of attention back to him. There will be no trouble spots with the speed with which he learns things; the only hurdle may be that lethargy that crops up once in a while. His marks will undoubtedly not suffer, though. That beguiling smile and enchanting personality will let him twirl his teachers round his minute little finger.

Supreme Suzy has always been aware of the princes within her sovereignty as well as the common boys. She has always known how to manipulate men and knew about the "birds and bees" years before mother got around to telling her. Naturally, this has been a matter of much concern to her parents as she reached adolescence and became the Queen of the May, tossing out acceptance of dates like a patron saint, all the while playing games and seeking male attention. In Suzy's case worry is of no avail. Whatever will be, will be. Setting an early curfew or forbidding lone dates (rather than with a crowd) will not turn the trick. Whatever Suzy wants or wants to do, Suzy gets and does do. Her parents have learned that the third degree only arches that cat's back and will spur her on to more daredevil activity. Suzy is a woman before her years and a warm one at that. Anything can happen and only reliance on her sense of dignity will matter. These days though, dignity can accompany almost anything a liberated female does. The more proud the female, the more dignity can be carried along with each and every act.

Just as the Leo youngster needs your encouragement and support (when he levels with himself) he is more than willing to reciprocate in demonstrations of affection and a willingness to accept familial obligations. Since he does need your love the most effective way to reach him is through a lack of attention. Force yourself to hold back and be apathetic toward him. No Leo child can tolerate being ignored and will not be made to survive without

pleading for a truce in his own inimitable style. He recognizes your
tactics but will still acquiesce to regain his place in your good
graces.

You can expect his leadership qualities will come into play
early in every realm. He will hold an office or some position of
importance within his class or school group. This may not come
about, though, if he has been thwarted in any way at home. If his
pride has been injured or he has been downed too often, he will
recoil and retreat to lick his wounds. The danger here is that he
may well stay that way. This is an unnatural state for a Leo, and
at the first symptom of the disease bring out the laurels and make
sure you have an adequate supply to last through the battle. One
of the main things that should be instilled in childhood is that all-
important tolerance; without this he will blossom into an obnoxious
adolescent and an equally unappealing adult. Patience with other
people is essential and cannot be stressed enough. Your child has
the vim and vigor, the courage and ability to do great things, but
he must not expect others to cater to his whims or operate on his
wave length. As a for instance: when you are tying his shoe and
fumble or not work as quickly as he would like, you will be the
object of his volatile criticism. He probably could have done it
better and faster. He will expect you to be as capable as he is and
here you do not stand alone. Remember that the sun revolves
around the heavens giving off heat and warmth and this closely
parallels your child's psyche. He will not be very interested personally or involved with the troubles of others. At the same time
he is extremely generous, always the defender and protector of
the underdog. Many a bloody nose may result from his coming
to the aid of a peer who is being bullied by a larger or older
child. He will step right in and try to right the matter. It will
offend his nature to see someone at a disadvantage being abused.
His personality shuns the mean and unjust, and he feels strongly
on this subject as he does on most. If, however, he feels that someone is capable of holding his own or handling his difficulties, he
will let things lie and not interfere. Go paddle your own canoe.

There will be some moments when it may appear that your
pride and joy is being pushy and spiteful. This is not really true
as a general rule. It's just that natural leadership taking hold
again. He is quite capable of taking the lead and usually will.

Those few occasions at school when he starts pulling pranks will usually be when he finds a class somewhat dull. This is the time for mischief making. Generally, as it has been noted, he will cause no more trouble than the average alert and rambunctious child can be expected to get into.

Cooperation does not come naturally to your little cub and you must instill it at all costs, especially if he has been even slightly spoiled. Those times when you feel your service to the king will carry over to others, not a particularly desirable or endearing trait, see to it that he has chores to do around the house. They should be his job alone to carry out. Catnaps will recharge his battery, and they are necessary. Don't let that be an out that he can use to avoid his tasks, or it will never be possible to have him perform any type of work that he considers menial.

Where health is concerned Leos are generally in the pink of condition and healthier than the average child of the same age. Leo rules the heart and activity is a prerequisite for the stimulation that the heart requires, no problem if you don't allow that old lethargic tendency to set in. His backbone is exceptionally strong and he walks beautifully in a regal and stately manner. But then, what would you expect?

Higher education is recommended, and chances are that your natural born leader can earn a scholastic or athletic scholarship. Energy abounds and athletics are good for him. This child will be the well-rounded individual that colleges are interested in enrolling and are always on the look-out for. Once there, he may again be found in a position of authority as a class officer or captain of the football team. His pride will almost demand of him that he attend college, and the required degrees of endurance and capability are not lacking.

Just about anything is in the realm of possibility when it comes to a career or profession for this leader of men. He will excel at whatever he decides to do. Dominant spirit prevails. If you have pointed him in a certain direction with lessons or interests, there he will go. Any field to which he has had exposure is a possibility. Whether as a vocation or not, all his knowledge will be put to good use within his lifetime. The arts, of course, are a natural—particularly the theatre. He is executive material and will gather followers in any field.

For lions born between July 23rd and August 2nd the personal and ruling planet is the Sun, generator of heat and activity. This is the optimum of beneficial influences in the entire zodiac. Your child will be somewhat more open to suggestions and less constricted by convention than most Leos. He knows his capabilities, and at times they may go to his head, and not unjustly so. His spirit may be more enthusiastic than with other children, and his self-confidence as well. He will have many followers and loyal friends who will prize his friendship.

Jupiter is the personal planet of babies born between August 3rd and 13th. This is the planet of supreme wisdom and controls the mental and moral aspects of the personality. Success will come to him, and it will be well appreciated because it has been gained through personal effort and brain power. He will guide others well but should take care not to become too easily bored with the mechanics of a job. Unrest and ambition can lead to taking risks which are not advisable for those born during this period.

Children whose birthdays fall between August 14th and 22nd have Mars as their personal planet. This planet will influence the constructive and creative streaks in your child's character and aid in offsetting some of the negative factors such as possible lethargy or a tendency to rule the roost with too strong a hand. Continuity of actions and a desire to delve into the new should be developed to prevent this child from falling into a rut and deciding to stay there. Artistic talents should be pursued and perfected.

THE LEO MOTHER AND HER CHILD

The Leo Mother And The Aries Child

When your personalities are not smoldering as an aftermath of a fiery encounter you will be vying with each other for supremacy over the homefires. Both are volatile characters, determined and unwavering in the desire to become an achiever.

The powers that be are evenly matched, and you, as the voice of authority, must exert your right to might in order to establish and maintain order and discipline. Once the battle has declared you the victor, deal with a reflection of your own traits as you would; exercise self-control. Do not be condescending but rather try to be a companion.

Kindred spirits provide a basis for a mutual admiration society that is one of the best going. You each respect the drives of the other just as you share the excitement and adventure of exploring ideas and itineraries. Be earthy and truthful in handling this child to earn his cooperation and respect. The bond between you is enhanced by what each of you has to offer and the traits which complement each other. A deep and long-lasting life together is most likely if you eradicate his stubborn streak at its inception. Your persevering nature should cope with this negativism, post haste, and then they live happily ever after.

The Leo Mother And The Taurus Child

The little bull will win your heart with his resistance to your views. If not, then there is much travail ahead unless you are prudent enough to be patient and tender. As you try to imbue him with sufficient security to make his own decisions (and more quickly, at that) you may find yourself going halfway to match his slower speed. This is not necessarily such a bad thing and perhaps a measure of your own ability to deal with situations on a realistic level for a change.

Just as you are headstrong and inflexible, so is he stubborn in his own manner. While his habit of procrastination can be ultimately injurious in terms of turning into lethargy it has its merits. Do not try to impose your solutions rather than allowing him to reach his own. To do so is to run the risk of raising a half-hearted, half-witted imitation of yourself without the fire and steam to propel himself anywhere.

Use all your charm to bring the bull in to pasture but never prod or harass him lest he turn and head straight on for the bull's eye—your heart. Much damage can be inflicted if you try to corral this child against his will. Moderation and understanding will bring cooperation and a deep love for your relationship.

The Leo Mother And The Gemini Child

This child is as fond of change and diversity as are you, and will incessantly plague you with questions that could drive you to distraction. His is so nervous and high strung that you must bear with him as he dissipates his pent-up energies. You must curb this tendency while relaxing him enough to capture serenity for his mental and physical health.

When he starts to unwind it will be wise to watch the mercurial thermometer for a complete about-face. He adapts easily and has the gift of creativity which should be developed within a real framework and not an imaginary one.

Since his spirit is so restless he becomes bored easily and consequently has little regard or appreciation for tangible possessions. You must carefully explain the value of both human and material property rights.

Now you see a bold child, now a timid one. The dual personality emerges as he matures and you must learn to discipline each of them. Stimulate him adequately so that he will find compassion within himself and an appreciation for sensitivity and affection. Insist that he picks up his own loose ends so that he may learn the meaning of completion, physical and spiritual.

Learn to love and live with both twins and consider the raising of the child to be an endurance test. Once you have acclimated yourself to this idea you will enjoy some of the traits from column A and some from column B.

The Leo Mother And The Cancer Child

Be gentle with your caress and care of the little moon-child. He is as sensitive a soul as you are vital and the imagined slights he feels would build a wall of protection in one day. There is no adequate way to help him except through unfettered understanding and a great display of affection.

His need for love and reassurance even surpasses yours for praise and adulation. Give him a world of intrigue and he will return the gift with undying devotion. Compromise is not a dirty word, and you would do well to let some of his warmth and sunshine enter your heart. Consider it to be spiritual therapy.

When you must reprimand the crab, *never* ostracize him or send him to his room. A wink of your eye can be misinterpreted as rejection, and isolation will represent the construction of a remote moat. Think at least three times before criticizing or punishing a crab in order to deter the urge to crawl back into his shell to shield himself.

You need not concern yourself with driving him away from home. It would take a batallion of tanks to remove this child from the home fires. He pledged alliance to you and domesticity, come what may. Please treat him gingerly as a Humpty Dumpty; he is as fragile and a mite smaller.

You will derive much happiness from the man in the moon as he sprinkles you with stardust and moonbeams. Don't toss your mane to shake them loose.

The Leo Mother And The Leo Child

"No greater love hath man . . ." to try and cope with the royal lion cub is useless until you know thyself. Only then will it be possible for you to see the faults in this heir to the throne. He is the genuine article.

This is a highly favorable combination as long as you prepare yourself for a maelstrom of constant activity—good and bad. But then, your expectations should be real and accurate and your insight profound. You cannot beleaguer his failings without chastising yourself and that is not exactly an adverse development. There will be times when you are incited to violence by something that you would say or do mechanically.

A formidable amount of time should be spent in teaching the heir apparent the formalities of education and etiquette that you so dearly love. This should also extend to teaching him the proprieties of the court, keeping him in line with the rules firmly set down.

When he throws a tantrum or sulks dramatically, do *not* react instinctively. That wounded pride will heal itself. There is no need to deepen the intensity of either. At the same time do not retaliate in a like fashion—two preening, proud cubs in one household are more than anyone can bear.

Hopefully, many hours should be devoted to common hobbies, a dissemination of ideas, and just plain unregal frolicking and rollicking. You can lapse into fits of unconscious earthiness and cajole him into doing the same without damage to your position of authority. The happy times together should be worth their weight in gold and you will be a very rich woman (which does not go against your grain). Actually, you'll need every penny in sight and then some, to afford the luxuries you regard as staples and those you feel inclined to shower upon your child. Now is the hour for all good Leo mothers to come to the aid of the household budget.

Little effort need be expended in order for you to gain the lifelong pleasures this child will bring into your life.

The Leo Mother And The Virgo Child

Handling a Virgo child will require that you re-evaluate your innate capabilities in administering charm. Little else will be highly effective in combatting the cool interior nature of a Virgo child. Affection must be displayed first without the physical touch or caress which all Virgos find annoying. Gradually, a tender expression of love will be tolerated and finally welcomed if your timing is right.

You are a superb hostess and love to entertain. It will be of little consequence to you to keep your house filled with the patter of many little feet in order to encourage a social streak in this child. Once friendships are developed, you can relax. They will be long-standing and solid.

Another area which must be given attention is the lackadaisical rut into which they can fall. Since the child is intellectually motivated, he can lapse into a state of complete lethargy all too easily. You must inject him with several shots of your vibrance and vitality to prevent the possibility of a totally passive personality.

Your senses must be as sharp as your claws in uncovering those likes for which your child is eminently suited. Every attribute should be drawn out and developed to enhance the future of the child. His attitude will be basically negative and he can become a fully ordained worry-wart by age five.

Charm and understanding are the secrets of success with this introverted and reluctant child. Imbue him with your sunny side to life and overcome his fuss-budget ways. Only you can manage to turn the tide. Only then will a real and warm relationship come to fruition.

The Leo Mother And The Libra Child

No "ifs, ands or buts" about this relationship—your leonine nature reigns supreme. The combination can be disastrous if you do not recognize his right to the pursuit of happiness. Make your position on the throne known only as a mother and not queen of the realm.

You may create chaos if you let your frenetic pace infringe or impose itself on your child. More than with children of other sun-signs you must temper your lifestyle and increase your capacity for patience. Toss off the facades that are part of the regal you, and learn to enjoy the simple things in life. The best things are free and the Libra child will introduce you to most of them, given the chance.

Allow yourself the pleasures of giving and you will receive much. The scales will have a soothing effect that will turn the ruler of the jungle into a domesticated and, yes—purring with pride—mother.

The Leo Mother And The Scorpio Child

This is a bombastic combination and will be hell's-a-poppin all the time, as well as a mutual admiration society. The relationship will be born with respect, and it will grow in intensity almost faster than junior sprouts out of his clothes. The driving force behind the two of you will bring and keep you together although, very often, you will be set on different courses and into separate worlds.

It is not unlikely for one of you to rub the other the wrong way and cause surface abrasion. Two such potentates in one household must send sparks shooting in all directions. The struggle for power will be on a subliminal level, but there is an underlying and strong undertow to the current. All men are created equal and the powers are quite evenly divided in this relationship. It can go either way and often weight will shift from one to the other. It is the most ideal set-up to maintain if you also alternate in letting off steam and keeping your cool.

Your biggest challenge will be in keeping the Scorpion from retreating into his shell in a blue funk. There is that special something about a Scorpio that keeps him beyond reach at times; the reach of reason, or humor, or a mother's reins. As a lioness, you will understand and forgive. Just be sure to raise his spirits when required, and the two of you will be the first to place a neon sign on the moon.

The Leo Mother And The Sagittarius Child

This archer will be born with a bow and arrow awaiting him back in the nursery. You will be tempted to push and prod and plod along with this child since he has the dreams and visions that delight you endlessly.

As with other offspring (other than those fire-signs) patience is your most important secret weapon that you must first locate before it can serve you well. The relationship will be strong and cemented through your mutual ideas and goals. He should neither be expected to attain your record of success nor chided for failure. Rather, charm and delight him and he will be enchanted and motivated to please you even more.

This child will revel in the glory of belonging to a royal family. He will be your Merlin, court, advisor, and lady in waiting all in one bundle. You will benefit him most by a gentle prodding of royal sceptre so that dreams become realities instead of pastimes.

Infinite pleasure will be derived from this relationship by both of you only if the queen mother is munificent and magnanimous. Stay put long enough to learn about dreaming and he will want to parallel your activity and achievement. You must give a little to get a lot.

The Leo Mother And The Capricorn Child

Your mountain goat is no match for you and it is an indisputable fact that you are the sovereign in this relationship. This is your child who will fit in with your scheme of things when it comes to soaring high, but he may often have one foot on the ground.

You must teach him that good faith alone will not remove obstacles or bring the good fairy to his aid. Your Peter Pan personality and Mary Poppins supercalifragilisticexpealidocious facility for doing great things will most likely move this climber to the top of Everest on the heels of your determination.

Don't intimidate or suppress him lest he become overly withdrawn and introspective to the point that you will have an untouchable on your hands.

The relationship is fraught with potential pitfalls but if you stay tuned in long enough at any one time it will be a beautiful one.

The Leo Mother And The Aquarius Child

Speaking of beautiful relationships this is almost Utopian. You will imbue this child with enough of your restlessness and dynamo spirit to charge up his philosophical pace. In turn he will teach you much about loving and seeking wisdom and truth and not just adventure and limelight.

He will rarely be a problem in any sense and, in fact, when one arises, it will probably result from your inherent regal airs that rise occasionally to seek reassurance and support. Recognize and give audience to your lineage and then shelve it again so that you and the water bearer level off on a plateau somewhere that combines insight with inciting to action.

Once you are there the relationship will be keen and bonded together with admiration and sensitivity.

The Leo Mother And The Pisces Child

You will be hard put at times to cope with the blend of personalities. The Pisces child swims hither and thither as the jungle queen roars. The need of a child must be met as he requires coddling and purring, rather than roaring sounds.

Remember, you are the one he should emulate, and your usual non-conformist ways can make both fish absolutely frantic in a search for stability and security. On the other hand, mother is the only one that can turn that frenetic swim into a smooth gliding motion. Charm and enchantment are on your side and it is not an impossible dream to feel that self-confidence in a capricious child can be instilled by you with little effort.

He will be more than fair in tolerating your seemingly erratic behavior. So exercise your feminine wiles and there will be happiness in your relationship somewhere between the jungle bush and the ocean floor.

STAR GUIDE
FOR
LEO

Symbol	●	The Lion
Ruling Planet	●	Sun
Element	●	Fire
Gender	●	Masculine
Key Words	●	I Will
Birthstones	●	Coral, Sardonyx
Favorite Flowers	●	Poppy, Tiger Lily
Best Colors	●	Red, Orange, Yellow
Mineral	●	Gold
Favorite Music	●	Grand Opera
Favorite Pastime	●	Collecting Medals
Lucky Number	●	1
Best Day	●	Sunday
Compatible Signs	●	Cancer, Libra, Sagittarius
Incompatible Signs	●	Taurus, Scorpio

FAMOUS PEOPLE BORN UNDER THE SIGN OF THE LION

ETHEL BARRYMORE
BERNARD BARUCH
HILAIRE BELLOC
INGRID BERGMAN
SIMON BOLIVAR
NAPOLEON BONAPARTE
CAESAR BORGIA
RALPH BUNCHE
LUTHER BURBANK
FIDEL CASTRO
LE CORBUSIER
CLAUDE DEBUSSY
CECIL B. DEMILLE
MADAME DUBARRY
ALEXANDER DUMAS
EDNA FERBER
HENRY FORD

SAMUEL GOLDWYN
EYDIE GORME
DAG HAMMARSJOLD
ALFRED HITCHCOCK
HERBERT HOOVER
ALDOUS HUXLEY
ROBERT INGERSOLL
CARL JUNG
FRANCIS SCOTT KEY
HARRY LAUDER
EDGAR LEE MASTERS
GUY DE MAUPASSANT
CHARLES MAYO
HERMAN MELVILLE
ROBERT MITCHUM
MAUREEN O'HARA

PETER O'TOOLE
ERNIE PYLE
SIR WALTER SCOTT
GEORGE BERNARD SHAW
PERCY B. SHELLEY
FRANK SINATRA
ED SULLIVAN
HERMAN TALMADGE
BOOTH TARKINGTON
ROBERT TAYLOR
LORD TENNYSON
LEO TOLSTOI
RUDY VALLEE
SIR ISAAC WALTON
MAE WEST
MONTY WOOLEY
ORVILLE WRIGHT

THE VIRGO MOTHER

August 23rd — September 22nd

THE Virgo maiden is strictly a mental sign with little or no emotional leanings that amount to much. As a mother you will have to develop many traits that are non-existent, or so latent it will take a full nine months to uncover them.

Your exterior facade is one of cool, concise, practicality; the inner core is cool, concise, and practical—hardly the most auspicious traits for the demands of motherhood. Seldom does a Virgo female find complete and real love. Under these circumstances you behave as if there truly is blood flowing in your veins, but the odds are a hundred to one.

It is hardly necessary to iterate that you will encounter double trouble as a mother. If you care to introduce a well-adjusted and stable child to the planet earth, very probably you will succeed, somehow, since you demand a perfection of others that you aspire to possess. You are without question a perfectionist, but that does not mean that you practice what you would preach (if that were your proclivity).

No one is more thoroughly convinced than you that you are the model of efficiency and orderliness. Unfortunately you have a point. This fanatical penchant will serve you well as a mother half of the time. That time devoted to the mundane chores of tending to a child's needs will equal one dewdrop of water rolling off your back. The job is mastered with one hand while the other is straightening out your personal closets.

The other half of the time you will be hard put to provide your child with the understanding, affection, and warmth required by all children. It is not that these traits are truly non-existent, but they are so controlled that you may not even know of their existence. Underneath the top dozen or so layers of the onion pulsates a heart that is generous and giving and that manages to surface just enough to lend a mystical appearance to your otherwise cool facade. If need be, use your child as an implement to arouse this hidden side of your personality. He should toy with your feminine nature sufficiently to bring warmth to the surface. If not, seek outside assistance by all means rather than assuming an attitude of resignation. No single factor is as important or necessary for your success.

While your meticulous nature is indeed an asset more often than not (this could be a moot point) it can be a permanently crippling trait in relation to your child. Naturally a neat, orderly, well-organized child will become a highly efficient adult. The restrictive and limited framework in which your child must try to function is one that few adults could handle. It is vital that your standards relax, adjust, and be relegated to a back seat before they impede the total maturation process of your offspring. Once again, you must give more than an equal share to exert the controls over yourself and not the child.

Once motherhood becomes your lot in life you will function well even though you could have done nicely without children. He will want for nothing tangible or material. His education will lack little in any area not associated with the heart or emotions. If you have to, take time for a reassessment of your ledger sheet. As soon as you recognize all the credits on your side you will feel appreciated enough to relax your stringent ways. You will allow a little of the putty below to rise above it all to provide the love that must be lavished on your starving youngster. Tenderness and discipline can cohabit without your losing a firm grip. Give enough to let him know he is wanted and loved. Secure the basic essentials for him before you stop to think of what you believe you are sacrificing. Upon closer examination you will realize that there is no sacrifice in the world of child-rearing and be pleased with your versatility and capacity for giving. Your love potential will stagger you with its enormity.

You have a lean for being a constant critic that would inhibit even an Aries or Leo (if they don't use violence). As I have mentioned, this trait must be shelved to shield your child so he does not become neurotic and compulsive. At the same time, you are your own severest critic, since you are so perceptive, and consequently are very resentful of your critics—more resentful than is customary because you feel that these critics do not possess your keen powers of discrimination. Usually, you are more right than wrong. Do not react with indignation, however, if the critic is your own offspring. Try to understand his viewpoint. It may apply only to the interaction of your two personalities and nothing else. If it is a general censure then pay heed. He lives with you and sees all facets of your Virgo nature. He qualifies as your second most severe critic and rightly so.

When troubled with strong or multiple anxieties the efficient mechanical robot is afflicted with some exotic malaise. This can also occur when you hear of a friend's illness or read of a new epidemic of a hitherto rare disease. We each have our defense mechanisms and escape hatches, your easy out is a common route—hypochondria. This is not to say that you are not physically ill at any such time, but a history of repeated sicknesses would lead one to conclude that this is a concrete possibility. Try confronting this fact head on and reach your own decision. In the meantime, exercise every conceivable sang-froid to keep your child healthy and free from following suit by developing sympathetic aches and pains.

Virgo mothers are happiest and most campatible when they pursue a career or part-time interest. Most likely it will be a detailed profession or artistic hobby. It is of major importance that you have an outlet that provides you with a certain amount of freedom and inner satisfaction. Your child will benefit by self-satisfaction as you unwind and allow yourself a measure of repose.

A wise Virgo mother will keep herself busy for another reason too. Your thinking processes are so precise and clear-cut that they must have food for thought to keep them from floundering a bit when your mind is not occupied. Acumen is best retained when exercised often and well.

Your natural bent is to reverberate instinctively in most situations and you fare well much of the time. With a child, however, it is often necessary to reconsider your initial reaction and devote a little thought to the reason for his behavior, weighing the possibilities cautiously. Your practical and acute mind will check every detail. Only then should you respond in a crisis situation or one fraught with traumatic potential.

Virgo females generally exhibit more patience with children than with adults. When you stop to think about it you realize that all children are impatient from the sheer exurberance of youth and you work extremely well with children. Despite your orderly nature, you recognize on occasion that a perfectly disciplined model child is no longer a youngster—mischief has its merits, too. However, you are a strict taskmaster regardless of your child's age. He must learn harder early and work longer.

That analytical mind is quite capable of becoming too involved in a myriad of details. Your powers are keen and you can find the rationale behind almost any logical word or deed with a frightening accuracy. This is not always called for to such an extreme since children are not always logical. There is a happy medium between instinctive reaction and steely analysis. Resolve the problem into its elements before taking action in either direction. Both can inhibit your children's social and mental maturity if applied incorrectly.

Another source of danger to the literate and studious Virgo mother revolves around too much research into the proper way to rear a child. You can become so embroiled in boning up on how to best handle your child that he will graduate high school before your bookwormishness has run its course. Being the stickler you are for details you also run the risk of taking hourly checks to see if your child's performance is up to par or charting each and every yawn or tear. This may well satisfy one of your needs but will scarcely comfort you when you realize your child is an adult and you have missed the best years of life together.

Should you catch yourself in time to watch the growing process, be conscientious and helpful in the areas mentioned. Never be so helpful and accommodating that you leave little for him to do on his own. Venus imbues you with an extrasensory awareness of what comprises true beauty, and watching your child learn to function on his own is truly beautiful. Unfortunately, earth injects the practical aspect too often. There are times when your appreciation of beauty is marred if the deed or object does not serve a function or purpose. You may want or need a car and are appreciative of its trim body lines and complex construction. At the same time you will most likely not buy the car of your choice since you would consider it to be impractical and uneconomical to drive a car unless every seat is always occupied. It is precisely this perverse type of "logical" thinking that could become as dangerously insidious as a black widow spider and make you miss out on the more beautiful and natural aspects of childhood. Keep your eyes and ears open. Let your mind rest while you absorb with your heart.

Since the psyche does rarely rest and your nymphet body is efficiently dispensing with household and other chores you are very apt to push yourself beyond endurance into utter and complete exhaustion. This will be strictly a physiological hazard and not associated with the ills mentioned earlier. Even you, Virgo, can see the folly of spending your vacation bedded down and reclining (despite your preoccupation with preventive medicine).

Your nature appreciates the useful and the established and you do not anticipate acclaim or thunders of applause. As a consequence you find it virtually contrary to reason for anyone to expect praise from you for deeds well done or good behavior. Up until now anyone was of no import. Now your offspring is someone deserving and standing in need of your praise. Give him this along with all the love you have found within your once placid and now palpitating heart.

THE VIRGO CHILD

VIRGO'S key words are "I discriminate" and the symbol resembles the reproductive organs of a female, closed at the bottom like a virgin. Virgo babies are liable to be a little nervous, finicky, and somewhat fussy. The natives of this sign are seekers of the perfect and reject what they consider to be faulty or imperfect. Your child is destined to be an idealist. He expects to find his ideals within this world and will not have inner peace until that ideal is discovered. These people are the most discontented of all because true ideals are so rarely uncovered in this world. The Virgos of the world are our greatest asset. Without them nothing would take form or shape. They are the molders and the organizers of details.

The digestive system and the intestines are ruled by this sign, so ofttimes you will run into trouble with the first feeding. The little one's formula must be just so for his individual system. You may have to go through several trials and errors before the correct combination is hit upon. Once you find the magic secret things will be just fine. Some do fuss when changing time rolls around, but there are few exceptions on this subject with babies born under any sign of the zodiac. Virgo children are basically peaceful but have very defined likes and dislikes in food. They may cause you a wee bit of difficulty on this score. As foods are introduced to him he may refuse some and have some trouble spots in the digestive tract. Hold off and try it again in a couple of weeks. Most likely he will accept it then and you'll puzzle over the reason for the initial refusal. There is no bellowing or wailing with this kid when he is hungry—just ordinary crying. The period of infancy should be an easy one for you as your child is every mother's dream. What a pleasant experience! He will laugh easily and be curious about his surroundings. The comforts of mother and close family members are relished and appreciated. Being fondled by strangers is another matter but not one to be really concerned about. As soon as he establishes some identity with the outsiders the situation will become more relaxed and he will accept the hand-to-hand treatment without fuss.

When he starts to toddle around he will exhibit great agility. Those first real steps, once taken, will be followed by good, swift motions, but not dangerous ones. He is alert and just has a natural knack for getting around pretty well. Your child will be holding a broom (or trying to) shortly after those first steps. He is a helper and you are the one he wishes to aid and imitate. Here is the original great impersonator; he will parrot your every word and emulate your every move. Watch out that you behave yourself in his presence. You will be amazed at the extent to which he apes your actions and will be certain that these are all inherited traits. Look a little more closely and watch the baby watching you. He sees things in great detail and his mind is sharp and retentive.

This child is the essence of practicality and can attack any project known to man. Mentally he is quick and little escapes his mind. He will sometimes allow himself to slip into a rut since he wants to take things slow and easy every once in a while. Virgo children seem to be possessed with X-ray vision and two or three extra pairs of eyes. Little escapes his observation, and mental notes are filed away in a warehouse lodged somewhere within that minute body. He will never lose track of a memory, a name or souvenir. During his teens you will need an extension to your home or apartment to house all the memorabilia. He will collect and cherish each and every momento. Never be concerned that this child will be too loose with a dollar. Money is almost as precious to him as a souvenir, and is stashed away with tender feeling. Virgo ears perk up at hearing the sage advise of the millionaire who said, "neither a borrower nor a lender be".

Malcolm is a model of decorum and behavior—meticulous and mindful. Even before he could talk he had a memory bank brimming over with observations. The Virgo formation took hold as he emerged from the playpen. During his first play group session, he started to grunt and grumble and finally wrenched a toy away from another infant. After all, he was made to understand that the group was to share and Suzy had been playing with the walking dog for at least a minute or two longer than he had. Mind you, the message comes through loud and very clear with no verbalization. At least mother knew enough not to let loose in front of the kiddies. A warning sufficed in this instance. Lucky Mom, the Virgo stubborn streak did not make Malcolm stomp his feet this time.

Virgo is ruled by Mercury—you remember, that fleet-footed messenger. This means that your baby will speak at an early age quite fluently in the home with his nearest and dearest. Do not try to push him into performing before strangers; he is timid and, as you have learned, must warm up to outsiders. Even those with whom he feels comfortable before he has uttered his first words now take on a different light when it comes to a new situation or appraisal. He is most capable of doing many things and has some of the versatility of the Gemini child but lacks the positive nature of a Gemini. Your baby was born under an Earth sign which injects practicality into the personality but there is still that innate shyness. Encouragement is needed here for the most favorable development. Capability is inherent and all that is done will be done well, but it may take some coaxing and goading to get the ball rolling.

In school you may find yourself with a teacher's pet on your hands. This is very logical. Your child is cooperative, easy to discipline, and agreeable. Not only all that, but he will study carefully and enjoy doing things to perfection. Now, tell me, what teacher isn't going to melt at this combination. Meticulous attention will be paid to detail and where neatness counts your child will win the prize hands down. The only possibility for a disruptive force on this scene is a hypercritical or brash teacher who cannot handle the shyness of the child diplomatically. There will be some reticence when the time comes for this youngster to recite before the class. This will require super-human effort for him and rote learning. The latter will assure him that all his energy can be concentrated on keeping his nerves in check during the recital. Having to follow a script, too, would be beyond his scope at this age. This is where you step in. Start by having the child perform for the immediate family from time to time and then increase the frequency a bit. From there you can lead into close relatives and finally performances for close friends who are regular visitors in the household. Praise much and encourage more. This should counteract some of the timidity if you start early enough.

His mental make-up is such that he delves into and savors details (picayune) and analyses on a computer level. The intricacies of almost anything hold intrigue for him but this is one child who can reassemble your watch and whatever other things have been dismembered in the name of education. In all probability he can author a "do-it-yourself" book for reassembling the follies of other children and some adults as well.

Virgo children will be fuss budgets about their clothes. Your child will want his pants neatly creased and the girls will demand crisp, freshly ironed dresses. This follows through in the constant combing of the hair. Details are of the utmost importance to your progeny. Do not frustrate him by not having everything just as expected, particularly if it is for a first encounter with any situation. To him, facing the world and all its strangers is tough enough, but to do so without being assured that his appearance is flawless only increases his insecurity and emphasizes his shyness. Talking to and mingling with people is a major obstacle to be overcome. If his thinking processes have to be cluttered with doubts about his physical image it is just too much for this tot.

Compulsive is an apt description of Malcolm. He insists on being bathed after each play period, indoors or out. This sounds a little neurotic, but if you had to cope with the fits induced by a refusal to cleanse Malcolm of the world's pollution and bacteria you might give in, too. The danger in not doing so would be to allow the infesters to enter Malcolm's precious mind and, imagined or not, the mind becomes cluttered. It is better to have a semi-paranoid Mr. Clean than a boggled thinker.

This child is a natural for educational toys. His mind is alert and geared to the detailed and the mechanical. Toys that will jog the brain a little will make him happy and content. He will spend many, many hours of pleasure with such playthings.

In terms of physical health, the digestive tract and intestines (which are ruled by Virgo) are the most susceptible and likely sources of danger in your baby. His system is a delicate one and he will be among the first to pick up the latest in bugs and viruses. Be most careful of his diet and everything that is ingested into his stomach. Even medications could be a potential source of trouble.

Too many rich foods, too much food, or anything that deviates from the norm can be unhealthy for your delicate doll. Eating habits are of great importance to over-all health.

Virgo children have the potential for becoming perpetual hypochondriacs. It is up to the parents to instill an interest in personal health and a desire for fun and frolic. Without the mind being occupied, your tot can slip into a state of flux. Exercise, both mental and physical, is the cure-all for most of the ailments that can beset him (other than digestive). The vitality is, at best, moderate; so, take care. This child is a difficult one to spoil, so don't fret about that aspect. Emotional stability and health can best be insured by an organized household and everything in its right place. Routine is important. Physical affection is the best medicine and preventative for this child. Oodles of kisses and hugs will be satisfying and rewarding, especially before going out to face the world. Take care to note the habits he establishes and the routine to which he adheres. He will not appreciate your cleaning his room while he is away at school. He has a proper place for all his belongings, and should you misplace an item that he will have difficulty in locating, you will hear a complaint voiced. You may not approve of his filing system and wish to arrange things more logically. Please don't! This can be most upsetting and unnerving to a Virgo child.

The field of medicine seems to hold a fascinating interest for Virgo children. When the time comes for college or further education don't be surprised to hear of plans for a career as a doctor, nurse, or dentist. On a lesser level, lab technicians and hygienists are commonly found to be Virgos by birth. Large institutions hold appeal since they involve specific routine and teamwork. Oftentimes the job itself is immaterial as long as he feels that he is being of use and helping someone, directly or indirectly. He enjoys feeling needed and serving the needs of others no matter what the capacity.

Another characteristic that borders on the negative is that he can be very critical of people, despite his own fear of criticism and need for praise. Try not to overly criticize when he is young, since your child is always the imitator. This can stick with him just like one of his routines. If frustration sets in there will be real trouble. This can give birth to a dyed-in-the-wool nagger.

Imagine what could transpire should your child marry another Virgo and the encounters that could ensue when one or both of them were slightly frustrated or irritable. This can come about all too naturally with a Virgo child and must be wiped out completely. Start trying early in his life and you may avert a hazardous and encumbering drawback to his personality. Teach him that this is just not the way to get anything accomplished. When approached correctly, he can be reasoned with on this level.

As time goes on, you will notice that when you ask this child to be open and quite honest with regard to his feelings or in terms of a judgement, he can be extremely harsh and sometimes even cruel. When he finds fault in others he is not reticent to point them out. That earlier timidity will seem like a vague dream when your Virgo becomes hypercritical and your severest critic. Everything must be in its place, and that carries to a single extra grain of salt or a quick vacuuming that doesn't quite make the grade in his estimation.

No greater helpmate hath any man, woman, or child than a dutiful and conscientious Virgo youngster. As much as you adore this quality and are delighted with his giving nature you must force him to enjoy socializing with his peers and acting just plain childlike. Even pry a book out of his tight little fists to do so. He will heed you just so long as you ease his fears of sticking to the grindstone. Your child was born worrying about getting the first cry out in proper fashion. Assure and soothe him throughout his life. Eventually that keen mind may learn to put two and two together the hard way. Do your job well; it is such an undemanding one to handle.

Malcolm went the whole route and became a greater terror to his parents than a top-notch reviewer on opening night. His compulsive behavior inspired mother to be a bit too stern in her reprimands. She followed it all up with a hug or kiss, heedless of Malcolm's need for a logical explanation and his Virgo nature (basically impervious to the warmth of demonstrative love). Since he was born a wise man, by his teens Malcolm was a seer and a stuffy one at that. Now it was twice the job to defret and defrown a young old man. Patience, encouragement, and a unique approach to the worry-free world of fun are required but, at this age, Malcolm's parents may not be able to handle the burden alone. Well-meaning but not prudent or precise parents created much of this problem. They even find Malcolm a bore. This child is a smart one and will go out of his way to help you if he is sure of something that will make you happy. His sense of moral obligation is strong and will develop far in advance of the usual time. Many days of delight are in store for you with your child of Virgo. You will be the envy of your friends who undergo major traumas and up-heavals with their offspring. Count your blessings and shower him with the love he so deserves.

Those children born between August 23rd and September 2nd have the swift-footed messenger of truth, Mercury, on their side. This rules the mental agility and perception which will bring your child immeasurable knowledge. Make sure that the advantage is put to good use. It can also result in a curious, busybody, and imitative personality if not handled correctly from birth. The power of expression is favored here and few of the Virgo children have this benefit with which to counteract their shyness.

Babies born between September 3rd and 13th have Saturn, the ruler of time, as their personal planet. This influence will make your child methodical, precise, and set in his ways. Perseverance and stability are forerunners of this child. He is more sensitive than most to the needs of others and anxious to help fulfill these needs. There will be some inclination toward a tightening of the purse-strings with this child and the importance of generosity should be stressed from birth.

Venus is the personal planet of babies born between September 14th and 22nd. This child lacks the degree of shyness that is so prevalent in other Virgo children. He is a seeker of truth and cannot tolerate pretensions or frills. His mind is well-ordered and artistically inclined. He is by far the most generous of his Virgo brothers. Venus allows him to judge clearly and well. He is critical only when it is warranted and hands out praise as magnanimously as he does his friendship.

THE VIRGO
MOTHER
AND HER CHILD

The Virgo Mother And The Aries Child

A Virgo mother with an Aries child has her work cut out for her if she wants to help along a beneficial and mutually rewarding relationship between herself and her Aries offspring. She will have to reconcile herself to the strong possibility that her Aries child may fly the coop at a fairly early age, more than likely due to the vast differences in temperament that are likely to occur here.

The Aries personality has a tendency to dominate a relationship of this nature, and signs would point to an eventual breakup on grounds that Aries are generally looking (whether they realize it or not) for someone to dominate them. There is no telling what might happen later on, however, when both parties have gotten their separate worlds together—perhaps a super merger and reunion of kindred spirits.

A stable Virgo mother is a wonderful touchstone for a volatile Aries child to get a strong foothold in the complex world.

The Virgo Mother And The Taurus Child

A Taurus child is likely to have the upper hand in a relationship of this kind for the simple reason that a Taurus has the kind of obstinacy that can outlast all challengers. A Virgo can put up a good display of stubbornness, but practicality will win out in the end and the Virgo will start to see the consequences of her adamance. No one can match the Taurus for sheer strength of will.

As the Taurus child grows older, however, his actions will be based upon increasingly more mature and logical attitudes and reasonings, and the incidence of quarrelling will start to wane.

If the Virgo mother can force herself to shrug her shoulders and wait for this later period, everyone concerned will benefit.

This is a relationship that could use a shot of creativity, even though the mother may not feel so inclined. She should try to encourage her Taurus child to develop his artistic sense.

The Virgo Mother And The Gemini Child

This particular relationship can be highly beneficial to both parties for the simple reason that each can find comfort in (and perhaps imitate) the nicest qualities of the other.

The Virgo mother will find that her Gemini child is a constant delight but a constant headache. Geminis have notoriously short attention spans and can be exasperating to an intolerable degree. But no one can remain immune to their charms, even such a practical creature as our hardworking Virgo.

The Virgo mother can be a rather shy creature, depending upon comfort and amusement, to an unusual degree, from her children. With the Gemini child, she'll be highly gratified and entertained, since Geminis are always full of surprises and get-rich-quick schemes from the age two. In a relationship of this kind, the Virgo mother will be required to exert a moderating influence upon her child to prevent any possible waywardness.

The Virgo Mother And The Cancer Child

This relationship can be a wonderfully harmonious one as long as you do not let the Cancer's stronger will dictate in all matters. You should make an extra effort to exert a strong influence over your child to prevent him from getting the upper hand.

The Cancer child has a tendency to react peevishly whenever he feels his power eroding; he may even revert to childish tactics in order to get his way. It's up to you to prevent him from this kind of behavior by showing him that these tactics are fruitless.

This is a relationship that will reflect much stability and domesticity rather than action and adventure. The Cancer child can be hopelessly lazy at times and may require a little prodding. You are not the epitome of restlessness either, so this relationship won't be trying for either of you. Perhaps you can work each other out of the feelings that keep you in the house.

The Virgo Mother And The Leo Child

You can heave a sigh of relief if you are fortunate enough to have a Leo child. They seem to mesh nearly perfectly with Virgos, and the relationship features no serious power plays on the part of either member.

Your dramatic, handsome child will provide a perfect contrast for your own less adventuresome temperament. Your child will receive a measure of stability and practicality from you by the process of osmosis; and hopefully, your child can drive you out of the house in search of adventures you never thought possible.

You can expect this relationship to continue favorably over the years because you will both be able to lead happy lives without drawing too much upon the resources and energies of the other. You, especially, will not be disappointed if your Leo child does not follow the course you would have liked.

The Leo child is such a likeable creature that you'll feel comfort in just being around him.

The Virgo Mother And The Virgo Child

You and your Virgo child will experience a relationship successful in almost every way. Since your attitudes and goals are nearly identical, you will have very few major arguments over anything at all. Even if you should have what seems to be a serious disagreement, you cannot remain angry or hurt for long because your lives are so entwined with each other that you're almost lost when you're apart.

You'll find yourselves doing thoughtful favors for each other without even looking for any praise for yourself. You'll just enjoy doing nice things for each other.

There is a tendency for a Virgo mother and child to develop too intense a relationship, almost to the point of shutting out others. Don't let yourself do things that will make your child too dependent on you, and don't let yourself get so wrapped up in your child that you feel a stab of rejection whenever your child takes a step on his own.

The Virgo Mother And The Libra Child

Your Libra child will give you some aggravating moments unless you work overtime to come up with an extra amount of love and understanding. Your handling of this relationship in its early stages will set the tone for years to come.

The problem here arises from the fact that you are a lover of practicality and logic, and Libra's are most often idealistic dream seekers and lovers of beauty and harmony, who are turned off by what they unfairly label your "crass materialism". Your differences will come to a head during your Libra's adolescence and early adulthood when differences and attitudes seem to acquire a lion edge.

If both of you aren't careful to think before you act or speak, you each may contribute to a final and complete breakup. On the other hand, if you can both control your emotions, your relationship can be mutually beneficial by having certain characteristics rub off on each other.

The Virgo Mother And The Scorpio Child

In a relationship of this kind, you may find the power you come by naturally in your role as mother seems to be slipping through your fingers. This is a very strong-willed, passionate, and demanding child you have and you'll be required to expend a great deal of yourself in bringing up this child to a happy and productive adulthood.

Don't look for too much sentiment in this relationship. Your Scorpio child takes these things for granted and doesn't feel the need to prove his love by mere displays of sentiment. You'll be all right as long as you remember this basic fact.

Your Scorpio child will do you a few unintentional favors as far as your own personality is concerned. He won't be able to understand your seeming preference for the life of a loner and will force you into many more interpersonal relationships.

The Virgo Mother And The Sagittarius Child

You will have a great deal of influence over your Sagittarius child, due to the tendency of Virgos to dominate Sagittarians in personal relationships.

Try not to take advantage of this natural phenomenon to the point that you inhibit your child's mental and emotional development. Left to his own devices your child will perhaps be carried away by those idealistic, even quixotic, dreams of his. But he will have to learn some important lessons on his own in order to have a successful life later on when you cannot always be there.

Right now you can be a wonderfully supportive influence if you watch yourself so as not to step too far over the limit of motherly concern.

Your Sagittarius child can help to overcome your image of sheer cool practicality that sometimes prevents you from enjoying life by involving you with just a few of those dreams and some of the enthusiasm for a better future.

The Virgo Mother And The Capricorn Child

This particular relationship will take a great deal of effort on the part of both mother and child. If both of you just let things ride without expending the extra effort you can practically kiss this relationship goodbye.

Although the signs point to a lot of problems here, you can use astrology to your advantage by being prepared for certain problems that are bound to occur and using some preventative strategy to ward them off. Since your Capricorn child is born with a maturity far beyond his years, you can perhaps sit down and discuss your difficulties honestly and constructively. You will feel at many times that your child is trying to usurp your role, trying to place you in an inferior position. Perhaps another mother could take this, but your Virgo backbone arches at the very thought.

Make your desires known and just hope for the best.

The Virgo Mother And The Aquarius Child

Your Aquarius child will be a source of delight to you as soon as you have weathered the storms of a tempestuous childhood.

Aquarius children can be a bit trying in their early years, but they are more successful than people born under other signs in ridding themselves of the petty feelings of jealousy and hostility that hinder true human relationships. Perhaps their stormy childhood allowed them an opportunity to work out their frustrations at an age where brashness is not quite so harmful.

At any rate, you will find great solace and happiness when around your loving Aquarius child of teenage or early adulthood. The wait is certainly worth the aggravation of a few years.

Because Aquarius children seem to have all of their problems worked out, they are reasonably free of worry or frustrations, exerting a cooling effect on those around them. They sometimes have a tendency not to worry even when they should, however, and this is where you can help them.

The Virgo Mother And The Pisces Child

A Pisces child can have the most annoying habit of uncovering your most unattractive traits and holding them up to the light for all to see. This could be a good thing, however, if it's the only way that you would ever do something about them.

With his razor-sharp mind, your Pisces child can usually get to the bottom of things and to the truth in important issues much more quickly than you can with your slower form of logic. This will give him an advantage in a relationship that he is overly trying to dominate. You'll have to put him in his place firmly and often if you're serious about retaining control.

When you two have everything out in the open, you'll be able to carve out a satisfying life for yourselves, with certain responsibilities delegated to your child so that his desire for control is at least partially satisfied.

STAR GUIDE
FOR
VIRGO

Symbol	●	The Virgin
Ruling Planet	●	Mercury
Element	●	Earth
Gender	●	Feminine
Key Words	●	I Discriminate
Birthstones	●	Sapphire, Lapis Lazuli
Favorite Flowers	●	Aster, Morning Glory, Petunia
Best Colors	●	Yellows, Blues
Mineral	●	Quicksilver
Favorite Music	●	Old Tunes
Favorite Pastime	●	Making Charts
Lucky Number	●	4
Best Days	●	Wednesday, Friday
Compatible Signs	●	Cancer, Capricorn, Scorpio
Incompatible Signs	●	Gemini, Sagittarius

FAMOUS PEOPLE BORN UNDER THE SIGN OF THE VIRGIN

ALBERT,
  PRINCE
  CONSORT
ALEXANDER
  THE GREAT
LAUREN BACALL
ROBERT
  BENCHLEY
LEONARD
  BERNSTEIN
ROSANNO
  BRAZZI
SID CAESAR
MARGE
  CHAMPION
MAURICE
  CHEVALIER
CLAUDETTE
  COLBERT
SEAN CONNERY
JAMES
  FENIMORE
  COOPER
PIERRE CURIE
CARL VAN
  DOREN
THEODORE
  DREISER

ANTON DVORAK
ELIZABETH I
MICHAEL
  FARRADAY
HENRY FORD II
GRETA GARBO
HENRY GEORGE
JOHANN GOETHE
JOHN GUNTHER
FRANCIS BRET
  HARTE
OLIVER
  WENDELL
  HOLMES
CHRISTOPHER
  ISHERWOOD
LYNDON
  JOHNSON
SAMUEL
  JOHNSON
MARQUIS DE
  LAFAYETTE
D. H. LAWRENCE
ALAN JAY
  LERNER
SOPHIA LOREN
MAURICE
  MAETERLINCK

H. L. MENCKEN
GRANDMA
  MOSES
FRIEDRICH
  NIETZSCHE
FRANCIS
  PARKMAN
JOHN PERSHING
WALTER REED
WALTER
  REUTHER
MARGARET
  SANGER
WILLIAM
  SAROYAN
PETER SELLERS
UPTON SINCLAIR
WILLIAM H. TAFT
LEO TOLSTOI
CORNELIUS
  VANDERBILT
GEORGE
  WALLACE
H. G. WELLS
QUEEN
  WILHEMINA
ROY WILKINS
DARRYL ZANUCK

THE LIBRA MOTHER

September 23rd — October 22nd

AS a Libra mother you possess the desirable traits of intuition, diplomacy and brain power. These, in combination with your inherent charm, will serve you well in providing the necessary fundamentals that all children require, and you will dispense them wisely.

Since it is not generally difficult to motivate the sign of the scales and you are both appreciative and responsive to the offerings of life, you should approach motherhood with a wholesome attitude. More often than not, however, Librans find themselves mothers for the wrong reason. It is not always your desire for offspring that results in the arrival of a bundle of joy. Too much of the time children enter the picture because you feel that this will bring great pleasure to your better half and not because of an overwhelming maternal instinct on your part.

Before you can adequately proceed with the tedious and time-consuming task of child-rearing you must first learn to want your child for your own selfish reasons and not as a disinterested third party. This is not to say that you are lax in your duties or resent the child's presence, but it is essential to your general outlook that your desire be at least as strong as that of your husband so that the child is a product of a mutual wish.

First, you must dispose of any subconscious feeling that your child is an intrusion upon the blissful state of union that existed prior to his birth. *You* may believe it is possible to live on one-to-one love happily ever after, but, by now, you should have realized the fallacy of the fairly tale. If not, you are not being fair to anyone. As a Libran you should fight for the might that is right.

131

If your attitude is not what it should be then you are indubitably wrong.

Once you get into the swim of things all your positive qualities are put into immediate action, You probably make the best mother of any in the zodiac. The scales are evenly balanced as you exhibit all of the desirable female aspects and the mental alertness and wit that match that of any male. The masculine strength is there as well to see you through some of the rough spots along the way of life. Fear not, you never lose your femininity since you are far too shrewd for such folly. You may assume the vested rights of the opposite sex but never long enough for anyone to notice before you strike home with your point and revert to being all woman.

The scales aptly symbolize your sun-sign. You are compelled to weigh and counterweigh everything before you reach a conclusion or issue a decision. So powerful is your sense of justice that you must preclude all possibilities of making a mistake. You are both a listening machine and an oracle. So great is your desire to be impartial and right that you often find you are arguing against yourself. There are times when you skirt the issue and relegate the decision-making to someone else, and that usually occurs most often in your role as mother.

Your innate fear of erring is so forceful that you lapse into a habit of leaving decisions relating to your child to your husband. This is not only unfair (heaven forbid) but an escape hatch for you. Of course, you feel it is for the good of the child since you have little confidence in yourself to do the right thing. It is also because the child must give happiness to his father, first and foremost, with you running second or even third in the race.

Your mental acumen is clever enough for you to see the irrationality and inconsistency of such a stand. To begin with, you are more than adequately equipped to reach the right decision and the one best for your child. No one will take more into consideration than you yourself to insure success.

Second, you often take such an interminably long time to weigh every ounce of pertinent data that you must learn to pick up some speed. How else can this be achieved if not through practice? Most situations revolving around a child require rapid, if not hasty, moves and action. The child and the crisis can sink or swim while you debate yourself. Experience in paring down to the essential factors to be considered is something you must learn quickly. It need not be said that it will be done well, you can't fail once you have brought yourself to repeat the process time and time again. There is little doubt that your intuition will apprise you of which occasion calls for immediate action as opposed to methodical deliberation. This is not to be taken lightly since it is really your only major drawback in becoming an excellent and much-loved mother.

Children of any age must be made to feel secure by being given generous doses of love, affection, and attention. During the formative years warmth is something that they must sense in the environment around them, also. You will provide your child with all of these requirements, but on a restricted level which can be dangerous and castastrophic. He will be educated, tidy, well-behaved, never abandoned or ignored *totally*. It is the partial attention that will cause havoc as he grows. He will instinctively sense that you are reserved and holding back, because nothing or no one comes before Daddy and that little fact will grow and grow and grow at a faster rate of speed than he changes sizes.

Motherhood is not a part-time occupation, and, while you feel that your child infringes on your marriage, you must also realize that he is now part and parcel of a family, not an intruder into your personal relationship. Don't stifle a child's playful spirit because your husband has an aversion to noisy activity; don't send him to his room so you can enjoy a candlelight dinner. You are perfectly capable of finding a middle ground that will allow your child to develop naturally and to be a participant in that process. Exert extreme pressures to bear upon yourself until your pretty little head has completely absorbed the necessity for an about face in this area.

You should encounter few problems in the discipline and motivation of your child if you take note and resolve your conflicts. Most children will respond well to a logical explanation of "do's and don'ts", especially when you flash a smile and kiss a cheek. When the occasion calls for a firm hand you are there. You combine gentleness with fairly strict regulations or rules and pull it off beautifully. Only you can charm a child so totally while instructing him in proprieties and amenities of life. Only you can lift him out of the doldrums with cheerfulness and good humor.

Every so often when you feel that he is not loving or respectful enough of his father, you will react too strongly—just as you may when he has been disobedient of one of those decisions handed down by dad. You must not vacillate in the punishment of your offspring. What is construed as misbehavior is wrong whether it is in contradiction of his father's wishes or of yours. You have a tendency to use the rod when he disobeys his father and save the rod if he disobeys the same instruction emanating from you. This does not just upset the equilibrium of justice but confuses and befuddles the child beyond his comprehension. He will be hard put to understand exactly what you want, and he (or she) can end up either nurturing an Oedipal complex or becoming a misogynist.

You strive so incessantly to keep a perfect balance and maintain peace, yet exhibit impatience in the process of doing so. The world and its inhabitants are not as concerned with parity. Therefore, everything cannot always go smoothly and you must bear this cross as a Libran female and mother. Your efforts to get things back on an even keel will not consistently be successful, and this, too, you must learn to bear.

You are endowed with sweetness and strength that in turn make you soft and yet tough. In educating your child you will approach each and every lesson equipped with a balance sheet. There will be periods when you imagine yourself seated at a conference table as you expound on the advantages and disadvantages of a point as minute as why Washington tossed a silver dollar across the Potomac. Most of the time you spend debating with yourself since no one else (certainly not your child) is as well-versed in both sides of the issue. Monologues are your specialty so you must remember that the attention span of a child is limited. Save the long dissertations for adult companions who will provide you with an opposite viewpoint and stimulation.

As your child matures and develops his own ideas you should devote just as much time to lending an ear as you would to proselytizing. Not only does he have certain inalienable rights but you hold the key to his self-expression as well as his future mental and emotional expansion. What better means is there to establishing a truly individual personality? You should delight in the prospect of such an opportunity.

Naturally, there will be times when your emotional scales are tipped a bit and you will tend to be a little domineering, irritable, or very verbose. You are entitled—everyone else has their ups and downs. During these periods take care to remain as constant as possible in disciplining your child so you will not upset the harmonious environment you have worked so hard to maintain. Besides, it won't take long for the scales to regain their evenness. All the while you are off balance exude an extra measure of attention and affection on your little one.

The most reassuring fact about a Libra mother is that you are intuitive and concerned. A natural proclivity for practicality usually prevents you from resorting to extremes. Your child is fortunate to have you dole out wise guidance that will make him emerge as an extraordinarily well-balanced adult. Your rewards could not be greater—respect and love from one who realizes the full value of each.

THE LIBRA CHILD

LIBRA is an air sign and babies born under this sign have "I balance" as their key words. The symbol for this sign resembles a rising or setting sun on the horizon which is half-hidden. Your little tot's personality will closely parallel this illustration of the sun. Venus is your child's ruling planet which injects beauty and peace into the soul. You are the lucky one with beauty, contentment, and sensitivity all rolled into one bundle. You will see all of this at first sight and be as pleased as punch. Don't then be tempted to complain at the first display of crankiness. Your baby is still a human being; not just another human being but a Libra being. The scales should tip you off to his dual nature and the sun above should complete the picture for you.

A small screech or whimper does not mean that there is serious trouble such as an open pin sticking into him or wet diapers. This will just be his way of letting you know that things are not exactly perfect in his world. He may not even know himself just what's gotten under his skin. He will fuss a bit on occasion just for a change of pace. It will be a mystery most often to both of you. Once you have checked all the possibilities and come up with no source for the grievance, then resort to the physical touch. Coddle him, caress him, and make the cooing sounds that make him feel secure emotionally. Once he has responded a little, plop him right back into that crib post-haste. He'll quiet down and most likely be back in dreamland before you are out of the room. If not, then let him fuss a bit more by himself without comfort from you. Libra is an Air sign and your baby is as alert as can be. You can almost see his mind at work or in deep thought as he lies quietly in his crib. Some difficulty may be encountered with feedings and the establishment of routines with your up-and-down baby. When feeding time necessitates waking baby up, you will probably get upset by his mood. For a few minutes he will irritate you as he tries to decide whether or not he can be bothered to wake up enough for just a feeding. Make some of the usual efforts and he will come around. Seldom will he cry for food with rage in his voice. Rather expect a constant and persistent cry that will wear you down if you are slow to act.

Your baby will respond to the Venus touch which includes billing, cooing, and gentle caresses. He adores being fondled, revelling in the glow of your affection and attention. Expect the same type of cry when he needs a changing. Being wet is a hang-up with him. It offends his sense of refinement. This child is another one that can be kept happy and content most easily. Just listening to music will satisfy him most of the time. There are those periods of crankiness, however. He manages to convey the impression that he is of porcelain delicacy and quite helpless. You will notice as time goes on that he does manage to keep you near him for a good portion of the day. He sees to it that someone close is around him during almost all his waking hours. Some helpless infant! His facility for keeping you around continues along with his growth. Cute childish tricks, pranks, or games such as hide-and-seek will ensure your interest and presence.

He will resent the lack of your presence or any other change in the routine to which he has become accustomed. Here is one of the few real trouble spots you will encounter with this youngster. Never surprise him with a change of plans. Making any adjustment tips his delicate balance and you will hear about it noisily.

Stepping on the light fantastic is an apt description of how your child will approach those first steps. His manner will be dainty and hesitant, but don't let that fool you. He intends to succeed and he will, cautiously. He will wear a smile all the while, giving those dimples some exercise. Pre-school Librans are delightful company and in turn enjoy having company around. Your offspring will try to speak at an early age and, again, succeed. His sweet and loving nature will endear him to all. He is just plain fun to be with most often. Do remember that hidden side of his personality that is so mysterious. You will never be quite sure why he is fussy or irritable now and then.

Toys that stimulate the mind are those that will be his favorites. Also toys that are beautiful to behold will appeal to his Venus personality. Color will be a determining factor in his own selection of toys. You will notice that harmonious colors and not the clashing ones draw his eye and a creative toy with eye appeal is one that will be well-worn.

Librans are not unlike Geminis in that the personality is dual by nature. Two roads are open for action most of the time for each. With a Gemini it's simple—he will make a choice and stick with it. Not so with a Libran. The scales are delicately balanced and it may take forever for him to reach a conclusion on anything. Basically he wants to reach for and retain both ideas, actions, etc. Far from being wishy-washy, this clever child is firm in what he wants today and just as firm in his opposite desire tomorrow. The inner scales will never allow him to go to extremes in any matter and sometimes he may appear to be insensitive as a result. Please do not topple the scales by urging him into a decision too quickly. Many neurotics have developed from exasperated parents who insisted that immediate choices be made in childhood. Suggest, don't insist. Help in a subtle manner rather than hinder. He is bright and will soon see the light if his inner tranquility is maintained. Should something be out of kilter, however, it will take much time, patience, and understanding to right it.

The duality in his nature will cause some indecision as to what he would like to undertake next. When he does make the choice, however, expect that he will be determined and persistent in following through. Since your child is one of exceptional refinement and manners he will ask for approval from you before proceeding with his activity. A little anger may accompany a refusal, so be prepared. He can adopt an attitude of strong silence following a refusal, and you can expect him to turn you down when you make your next request. You come into play at this point and should handle the situation with velvet gloves. If you were to tell him to dress himself, the immediate problem he has to face is which piece of clothing he should attempt to don first. It is not laziness on his part. This will crop up in instances where he has not sufficiently watched the procedure in question, and he will be stumped as to where to begin something. Where mealtime is concerned you and he will benefit if you do not present him with the problem of deciding between pudding and pie for dessert. Just serve one or the other and eliminate some stress. If dad wants to take him to the store, he will be caught up in a tizzy trying to choose between that and perhaps staying home with mother to bake cookies. As time goes on, your help will be more valuable in showing him how to solve the little problems he has to handle. He should also be given to understand that some decisions just aren't all that important and don't warrant all that anguish. If he decides to go to the store with Dad instead of staying home, mother will not be upset.

Sumner is a determined little fellow and just can't be budged, so mother has started to employ counter-bullish tactics. Little does she realize that he is far from determined, just frightened; not stubborn, but so indecisive. As he becomes constantly exposed to new things each day he becomes more confused. He needs time and a helping hand, not prodding and punishment. Some of Sumner's sense of balance rubbed off on Mom and she reassessed the cherub with Taurus tendencies, and, indeed, he turned out to be just a floundering little boy after all.

Librans are born seekers of wisdom and truth. Keep in mind that anyone concerned enough about making the right decision obviously does not want to make an error that will have unpleasant repercussions for him or those near and dear. Better, no, than the impulsive headstrong type whose lack of thought and conscience makes life one disaster after another. Just keep harmony in and around him. Beware of loud noises, sharp voices, and even clashing colors. This child is a peacenik and the forerunner of the Love not War movement. Occasionally, what may appear to you as lethargy is simply a child with a run-down battery. He plays hard and, when he doesn't watch out, pent-up energy is dangerous.

His personality is so charming and so magnetic that friends, relatives, and especially teachers will adore him and marvel at his sense of propriety of consideration. The teachers will oftentimes forget those traumatic moments of indecision and escapism when the Libran instinct to preserve balance tells them that the time is right for a wise and endearing move.

Charm will ooze from this cherub's every pore—even when his moods vacillate and you are subjected to fluxes of highs and lows. You will find it difficult to reprimand or punish this one. He seems to have found Aladdin's lamp and not only can melt away your determination but make you wonder why you ever considered the possibility of wrongdoing on his part.

All this may give you the impression that your child stands a good chance of needing his wings clipped a bit. It just could be, but attack this problem slowly. Do not set up irrevocable rules and do not set up any that are impractical or illogical. This child has an intricate mind and he will go along with your disciplinary tactics only if they make sense. He may often be one step beyond you in planning ahead. Be affectionate but don't smother him with stifling, coddlesome love. Keep everything neat and orderly in routine, rules, and regime and he will reciprocate.

Your lord or lady will be a model for the entire neighborhood to follow. Every parent will be envious of the genteel way in which your offspring behaves. Plenty of zeal and ardor will be thrown into any activity that interests him, but you'll never see the slightest hint of a ruffian at any time. He has his own sense of values that are sacred and being well-mannered is way out front, rivaled only by respect (yes, even at this tender age) for individuals and their privacy. It is no wonder that he will draw admiration for himself as the years go by.

Naturally, not all Libra children are one hundred percent perfect nor are model children one hundred percent Librans. Now and again, the charm that follows chaos cannot atone for improper behavior. Indecision, change of interest, or restlessness combine with ingenuity or secrecy. Your little love will play with people to get something that strikes his fancy, or just be downright frustrating to handle. Disciplining him is a fairly mechanical process, though. He readily understands anything that produces static or disrupts his orderly routine. Talk to him, deprive him of something he enjoys doing. He will then cooperate very quickly without much fuss—he hates arguments.

Since he is accustomed to attracting people with just a smile or cute act he will not take kindly to the loss of attention. Whether it be another child to whom he loses or an unknown quantity, it will upset him. Libra children can be as possessive as over-protective mothers and almost as overbearing. Avoid spoiling him in this manner as he must first learn that you are not all his around-the-clock (even if you secretly want the same thing). No one can remain center stage through life and he will soon learn this from others if not from you. Playmates, relatives and teachers will not continually look to him and the sooner he is forced to make the adjustment the less it will hurt you both.

Sumner is always the center of attraction with family and friends, not just strictly by chance. It seems the Libran magnet is always pointed in the most advantageous direction that assures Sumner of doting attention and a few extras for good measure. Uncanny talent, as Sumner's parents discovered, was not latent. Mother did realize him to be a bit possessive of her time and attention but neglected to make note of this propensity with other people. By the time she caught on to Sumner he had piled up quite a few loyal fans and an even greater treasury of toys and much good and plenty. To say that the child was spoiled is an untruth. He was more like an egocentric, selfish Leo than just a heavyweight Libra tipping the scales. Strangely, balance here does not matter to Sumner. This situation will right itself with a little help from the folks at home. Time, exposure to more people, and real situations will learn him.

His health, and his nerves, as well, can be tremendously affected by his vacillating moods. Massive doses of rest are mandatory to his vitality which is not really stupendous, at all. Always remember the magic wonders of quiet, peace, and solitude and all will be well.

Libra is such a delicate sensitive child that the world he lives in is esoteric and filled with beauty. A rare gift is that of seeing and appreciating the positive and exquisite side of everything—a little unreal at times if not tempered with a looksee sans rose-colored glasses. But do not become overly concerned. Leave him be and he will eventually bring this beauty into the lives of others.

Your little genius is capable of many great things, particularly in the arts. He is strong of mind, refined in nature, and will love the higher arts, of them, excelling in at least one. In school he will be a model student if his background is stable and you have helped him along with the decisions he has had to face through this point in his life. His mind can soar way up in that air and follow the progression of any lesson with little difficulty. He will be an avid reader and will be a source of delight to his teachers. Don't be surprised if he becomes captain of the debating team. This will be his forte since he finds it necessary to weigh both sides of every issue. Some of the foremost debaters in history have been Librans because they see and argue both sides in their own minds before the debate begins. This prepares him for any and all challenges.

Higher education will mean a lot to your master of balance and college will provide no obstacles. With all these inherent traits you can see that Librans have the potential to become great attorneys. Also any position that requires an alert mind is within his grasp. The arts may hold appeal as well. Music, art, or interior design will make the best use of creative and artistic talents.

Little ones born between September 23rd and October 3rd have Venus, the symbol of peace and beauty, as their personal planet. A child born during this time will be more constant and well-balanced than most Libran children. Success in professional and personal life will be of great importance to him and pride assures this success. A magnanimous and happy disposition facilitate the fulfillment of goals and make the best of innate potential. The positive aspects of the typical Libran personality will be emphasized with this child.

If your child's date of birth falls between October 4th and October 13th Uranus is the personal ruling planet. Stamina and endurance are the prevalent characteristics. These are interspersed with occasional attacks of emotional tension or ragged nerves. Flair and vibrancy will enter all routine activity and make the enjoyment of life a prerequisite. A marvelous ability to mingle and deal with all people sets this Libran apart from the madding crowd and injects an infectious element of charm into his personality.

Mercury is the personal planet of those born between October 14th and October 22nd. This planet gives insight into truth and imparts knowledge to the rational mind. This personality will be alert, level-headed, and astute. Less coaxing will be required with this child as vigor and initiative abound in large degrees. The temperament will lean toward the genteel and artistic and great gobs of affection will exist for family and close friends. Keep an eye open for the possible development of a haughty and arrogant attitude.

THE LIBRA
MOTHER
AND HER CHILD

The Libra Mother And The Aries Child

You, as a typically sensitive Libra, may be discouraged by this child of yours who is so completely different from you.

Whereas you have always contented yourself with peace and harmony, perhaps at the expense of something you value highly or desire. Your Aries child is never content unless all of his demands have been met.

In addition to demanding a lot from others, sometimes he sets impossible goals for himself and drives himself almost into the ground in order to achieve them. He will feel that you, left to your own devices, are too lethargic and ask too little of life. He may even start to talk you into setting some high goals for yourself.

Naturally, this is a desirable situation, but you must be careful not to give your child the impression that you have relinquished your roles as mother. You must still be in charge.

The Libra Mother And The Taurus Child

You as a Libra mother can have a very satisfying relationship with a Taurus child even if your relationship may not appear to be quite so successful to others around you.

What matters is not what others think but rather what you and your child get out of the relationship. It would appear that your stubborn Taurus child would be able to thwart your efforts of control at every turn. But this is most definitely not the case. He may try to get the upper hand but will resort to sullenness or childishness when not successful.

Eventually your Taurus child will learn that his actions are

143

to no avail because he will realize that rather than give in to his demands to bring about peace, you'll just try to seek peace elsewhere. You two will be able to develop a mutually satisfying relationship based on recognition of each other's needs.

The Libra Mother And The Gemini Child

You may quite possibly find that your Gemini child has inherited an intelligence that you cannot quite account for, and this will be a source of great pride for you and for your child, as well. But you would be doing your child a great favor if you could help him to develop some of the sensitivity and love of beauty and harmony that are your most distinctive traits.

Your Gemini child seems to be in a constant state of chaos. This will dismay you greatly, even if your child seems to lap it up. He will always seem to be searching for something and waiting for something that never quite materializes. He will look to you for guidance when things go wrong. You should never turn him away no matter how much you may hold him accountable.

Your Gemini child may be thoughtless or neglectful at times, but his heart is in the right place.

The Libra Mother And The Cancer Child

A Libra mother and a Cancer child set the stage for a heated relationship in which each party is always trying to gain the upper hand.

You Libra mothers ought to be forewarned of this in the unlikely hope that major battles can be prevented. You're going to have a difficult time convincing this strong-willed youngster that your way is the correct way and that you really only have his best interests at heart. Not only will he constantly be demanding an equal, if not louder, voice in his own affairs, he won't be satisfied until he is running your life, as well.

Now, these battles could have a fine constructive purpose by helping to develop those leadership qualities that make Cancer, but they're going to have a telling effect on you. Maybe you would be wiser if you gave in on some important matters. You'll be surprised at the results.

The Libra Mother And The Leo Child

In a relationship of this kind, your Leo child will quickly grab the upper hand for the simple reason that you will feel that he so justly deserves it. Your Libra temperament will be enthralled with this charmingly demonstrative creature and you won't have the willpower to frustrate him in any but the most crucial matters.

You'll have a healthy, mutually satisfying relationship that ought to continue just as smoothly for all time. Since you'll view your child (without reservation) as an individual at such an early age, you'll never have any of the problems with teenagers that strike other parents with such intensity.

From you, your Leo child will learn consideration for others as well as a love and appreciation for the beauty of which he is an effortless part. Your influence will prevent him from losing some of his appeal through false pride or vanity.

The Libra Mother And The Virgo Child

A Libra mother and Virgo child can find a happy life together if they try to identify each other's needs and do their best to fulfill them.

As stable, almost staid, the Virgo child will exert a calming effect on a Libra mother's dismissal of practical matters. On the other hand, the Libra mother can help her unemotional child fill his life with the kind of beauty and awareness that makes life worthwhile.

In a relationship of this nature, the Libra will always have the upper hand for the simple reason that the Virgo is not interested in personal power. But no amount of power in the Libra's hand can hope to dissipate the over-whelming practicality so common to Virgos. And it would not be the Libra mother's intention to do so because Librans are only interested in power as a way to force people to enjoy themselves.

The Libra Mother And The Libra Child

If you are a Libra mother with a Libra child, you can expect to have a mutually satisfying relationship based on common goals, attitudes and likes. You will fit together almost perfectly, and the kind of lifestyle you choose will not hold any sources of dissatisfaction for your child.

A mutual love of art and natural beauty will give you a common interest capable of binding you together through even the most difficult periods.

You will probably have less difficulty raising a Libra child than a child born under another sign, and every Libra mother should be born with at least one Libra child.

Your apparent lack of difficulty, however, should not let you fool yourself into believing that everything is all peaches and cream. You will have to work hard to make this relationship a lasting one since the faults in your child may be easy to overlook as you will no doubt have the same faults. Give your child's welfare some thought.

The Libra Mother And The Scorpio Child

If you are a Libra mother with a Scorpio child, you may find yourself in for some rough sailing right from the outset.

Scorpios are passionate little things and are difficult for even the most dedicated and accomplished mother to handle. After the initial blow, you'll grow to love your unaffected and willful child for the completely natural person that he is. But you'll have to accept the fact that Scorpios are out to conquer the whole world and they won't be happy if they've left one stone unturned, even if that one stone is you.

You're intelligent enough to realize this, but almost powerless to prevent it. Why not use your famed Libra diplomacy to see you through? Let your Scorpio dynamo delude himself into believing that he's got you eating right out of his hand while at the same time exerting subtle influences to modify his insatiable appetites.

The Libra Mother And The Sagittarius Child

Your Libra nature can mesh very well, indeed, with that of your Sagittarius child. He will even accept the mother/child relationship with little or no complaint.

Sagittarius children are basically agreeable people like yourself and your relationship should reflect good humor and consideration.

You'll find that your Sagittarius child is constantly on the lookout for something that always seems to be just out of his reach. In most cases this constant yearning is good for him and may even be good for you. You must not let him get carried away by his dreams, however, as he will probably only be disillusioned in the end.

Try to let a little of your characteristic patience and acceptance of things rub off on him. You'll have the authority to keep him from forever charging forth on some new venture, and it will be necessary for you to use this authority from time to time as you see fit.

The Libra Mother And The Capricorn Child

In a relationship of this sort you may find that you are often delegating responsibilities to your child that you should be taking care of yourself. The eagerness of your child to accept responsibility and your frequent laxity in this area may combine to produce a harmful situation wherein your child gains sufficient power to achieve a dominating role.

This would be detrimental to you in that you would begin to shy away from responsibility more and more, and to your child in that he would develop the unhealthy attitude that he could get away with usurping power in other situations and relationships throughout his life.

You can achieve a healthy relationship by buckling down to the duties of motherhood yourself and by delegating just enough responsibility to your child to satisfy his desire to play a leading role.

The Libra Mother And The Aquarius Child

You'll enjoy a satisfying relationship with an Aquarius child because of your mutual love of harmony and beauty. You will have much to teach each other, and the lessons will not cease with your child's adulthood.

The Aquarius' natural bent toward peace and understanding makes him a wonderful child to raise, and one who will give you a minimum of trouble throughout his entire life, although he may not live up to your hopes in the area of career.

His personality will win you over forever, despite the apparent difficulties he may have adjusting to society. You'll feel a great responsibility to protect him from the harsher aspects of life, but you must not let this desire corrupt itself into a killing, stifling over-protectiveness. He will have to learn about life himself in the end, so it would be better if you were there during the rough times to lend a supportive hand.

Don't gloss over the world's inequities so that he will have to face them alone in the future.

The Libra Mother And The Pisces Child

Your Pisces child may be a bit disturbing at times, but you appreciate his habit of laying the truth bare, even if that truth may not be a bit pleasant. He may be overly brash at times and maybe even insensitive (especially to one as sensitive as you) but don't be fooled by that rough exterior. Scratch a crusty Pisces and you'll find a heart of pure gold.

Pisces are maneuverable types who seem to be able to find their way out of any dilemma with a minimum of thought. Instead of avoiding issues, as you do, they fend to meet them head on, usually with amazing success. They could use a little of your tact, however. Perhaps you could trade some of your tact for some of your child's competence in a crisis. You'd both benefit.

Your Pisces child will be easily manageable and respectful as long as you hold up your end of the bargain. If you shirk your motherly responsibilities, however, don't expect him to stay around too long.

STAR GUIDE
FOR
LIBRA

Symbol	●	The Scales
Ruling Planet	●	Venus
Element	●	Air
Gender	●	Masculine
Key Words	●	I Balance
Birthstones	●	Opal, Pink Jade, Marble
Favorite Flowers	●	Pink Rose, Dahlia
Best Colors	●	Pink, Blue, Mauve
Mineral	●	Rose Quartz
Favorite Music	●	Operettas
Favorite Pastime	●	Memorabilia
Lucky Number	●	6
Best Day	●	Friday
Compatible Signs	●	Leo, Libra, Sagittarius
Incompatible Signs	●	Cancer, Capricorn

FAMOUS PEOPLE
BORN UNDER
THE SIGN OF THE SCALES

CHESTER A.
 ARTHUR
BRIGITTE
 BARDOT
DAVID
 BEN-GURION
SARAH
 BERNHARDT
ANNIE BESANT
CHARLES BOYER
CHARLIE BROWN
TRUMAN CAPOTE
SIR AUSTIN
 CHAMBERLAIN
GEORGES
 CLEMENCEAU
SAMUEL TAYLOR
 COLERIDGE
ISADORA
 DUNCAN
DWIGHT D.
 EISENHOWER
T. S. ELIOT
WILLIAM
 FAULKNER
GREER GARSON
MAHATMA
 GANDHI

GEORGE
 GERSHWIN
LILLIAN GISH
GRAHAM
 GREENE
JOHN HAY
HELEN HAYES
RUTHERFORD B.
 HAYES
RITA HAYWORTH
CLAUDE HENRI
CHARLTON
 HESTON
VLADIMIR
 HOROWITZ
VAN JOHNSON
DEBORAH KERR
JOHN LENNON
JENNY LIND
WALTER
 LIPPMAN
FRANZ LISZT
MICKEY MANTLE
JOHN MARSHALL
GROUCHO MARX
MARCELLO
 MASTROIANNI
LOUIS MENARD

ARTHUR MILLER
YVES MONTAND
HORATIO
 NELSON
ANTHONY
 NEWLEY
EUGENE O'NEILL
GEORGE
 PEPPARD
CHARLES PERCY
POPE PAUL VI
EMILY POST
EDWARD
 RICKENBACKER
ELEANOR
 ROOSEVELT
C. P. SNOW
ED SULLIVAN
MICHAEL TODD
GUISSEPPI
 VERDI
GORE VIDAL
VIRGIL
HENRY WALLACE
JEAN WATTEAU
OSCAR WILDE
P. G. WODEHOUSE
THOMAS WOLFE

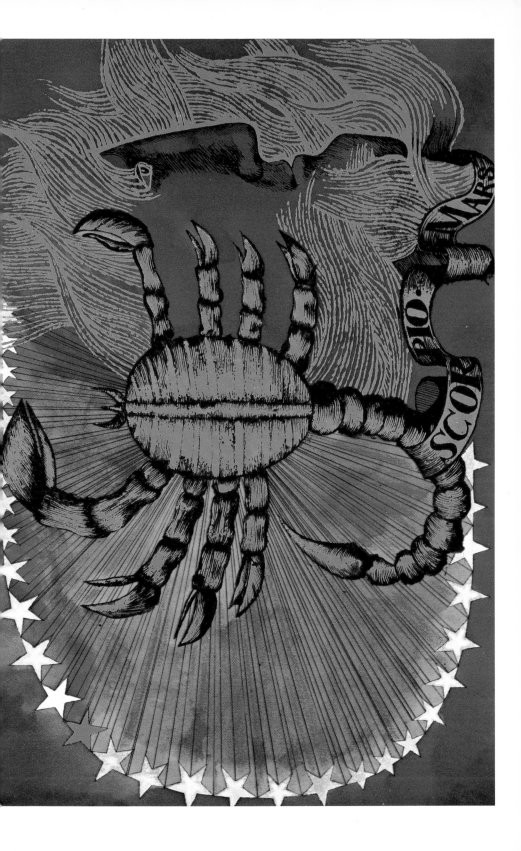

THE SCORPIO MOTHER

October 23rd — November 21st

THE Scorpio female is first a woman and then a mother. As a woman you wield enough determination, intelligence, and ingenuity to frighten most men and almost all women, save Arians and Leos. As a mother you brandish enough emotion, independence, and animation to make your child a Superman. These are, of course, only the positive characteristics of your nature.

Occupying yourself with motherhood will please you and provide yet another activity for your boundless energy and superhuman capacity for work. You are always reaching into the future. Rearing a child is a constant search and challenge for improving many tomorrows. You are so dynamic a personality that you act as a catalyst for the early maturation of your child, good or bad.

Since it is a recognized fact that you possess superhuman capacities, then it is not incomprehensible that you must direct much energy toward instilling a tremendous amount of self-restraint and evolving a gray area of compromise in your character. Instinctive actions and extremes of any nature must be quelled and almost banished when dealing with your child. Forget about tossing caution to the wind and concentrate on developing tolerance.

To begin with you must lay down some ground rules that will eventually be embraced and become part of you, discipline and firmness are of the first order for *you* and not your child. You must demand cooperation from your steely spirit and persist in your own obstinate way until you have incorporated these traits. Tackle the project with the attitude that it is something a man could easily do and you should graduate overnight. The old line holds true— anything you can do I can do better. You'll rarely let a male get the best of you and certainly not in a contest of wills. This can-not be emphasized enough. Repeat it to yourself in your sleep if necessary. You know that you are capable of making the best out of a situation and this is one that is not about to change. Resign yourself and accept the restraining measures stoically, as only you can do.

You must immediately recognize that a world which includes a child cannot consist of blacks and whites. Compromise for you does mean half-way measures many times. This is just something else you must live with to prevent your home from becoming the Old Faithful of erupting volcanoes. It has been rumored that you tend to be argumentative and downright nasty, especially when things do not go your way. This would lead one to believe that, if your child should misbehave or disobey you, the wrath of Pluto will be incurred and the very foundation of your home will quiver under your fury. That just won't do under any circumstances.

Your basic nature is very tempermental and you fluctuate from one degree of emotional unsteadiness to another. One minute you are domineering, sarcastic and vindictive; the next, obstinate, dramatic, and overly possessive. There are those times when you are tender, very passionate, unafraid to show your warmth, but very few are they and far between. Now, it is necessary that those moments become many and frequent. Subjected to an over-abun-dance of your more volatile and venomous moods your child could grow into a distrustful, inhibited, but detestable adult. His senses are keen and a hostile atmosphere will be felt by him before he learns how to talk.

Being secretive is one of your greatest passions. It is really not such a contemptible trait. Mystery and intrigue enhance your appeal to both men and women and enable you to cast a spell over both. Remaining secretive, however, in the presence of your child must be forsaken. Children are so in need of support and security that this could undermine all your efforts and void some achievements.

If one were to interpret patience as the citing of a goal and relentlessly struggling to attain that goal, then no one is more patient than a Scorpio female. You'll try one approach and, if that doesn't work, you have a reserve of alternate strategies to choose from. Nothing can deter you. It is just this quality that charges ahead (I hope) to insure you that you will do right by your child. Please use this definition of your patience with your offspring and not the garden variety type of which you have little. Precisely because you are a planner and thinker, children could make you impatient. The chatter and activity of a normal, healthy youngster can grate your nerves enormously. Don't selfishly raise your child to be quiet and abnormally inactive. Whatever would you do with such a bore anyhow?

Exercise your sixth sense and X-ray eyes in uncovering the faults of your child. For some strange reason, you seem to have distorted vision in this area, which can obviously create tidal waves later if the first ripples are not carefully checked. Mischief and misconduct are part of every child (hopefully). It is only when this behavior is gently controlled that it can be checked. Any child will take advantage of parental weakness, and here again you are apt to go to the extreme of non-action and excessive permissiveness. Don't! Look to split the difference between too much and too little discipline. You can be just as stern with yourself as as with your child.

Once you have learned to openly demonstrate love for your child, the bond between will be cemented with emotional glue. Your passion will unleash itself and be unmatched in its expression. Every possible avenue will be explored to find areas of talent and interest for your youngster. No cost is too great or time-consuming when in pursuit of cultivating skills of expertise.

When advice is sought, adolescent problems encountered, or a need for conversation arises, you have the strength and where-with-all to be the wisest of counselors. You revel in solving problems and cut through to the core immediately. This is a superb way to burn off some additional energy too.

There is little chance that you will display the possessiveness of the Cancer mother—nothing quite that mild for you. Your hold will be so great and strong that you use the sting of the scorpion to keep people at bay. This does not mean that your child is held captive and thwarted from achieving independence. It just means he is part of you forever.

In typical Scorpio fashion you will repel any overtures that could be remotely interpreted as an attempt to gain possession of you. The remote overture coming from a child is not a stab at possession but a need for protection and security. He must know that he can come running when he seeks reassurance or sympathy after a disappointment. This is sincere, redolent flattery and sometimes difficult for him to show you. Please take it as a beautiful expression of love that will not restrict you in the least.

You have the courage to face any foe, seek any prize, and spur your child on to seemingly impossible accomplishments. This same courage can lead you to be brutally frank in assessing these accomplishments or criticizing the failures. Since your nature sometimes is unpredictable, it is difficult, even for you, to know when you will encourage or exert your own brand of courage. Forget about private labels and stick with the known brands of fodder for your child.

Many Scorpio mothers hold down jobs, preside over the PTA and head up some charity drive or function; there is no such thing as too much activity for you. You make time to engage in limitless activities and none suffer from a lack of your time. If anything, the activities almost seem to stimulate you and give you more energy. You are an idol for any child to adore and an inspiration to emulate if he happens to be on the lethargic side. Your combined drive and discipline provide the best possible framework for child-rearing despite your fierce independence.

There are one or two negative aspects that must be mentioned here. As a Scorpio woman you are a potentially dangerous female and can be a holy terror to those who cross or antagonize you. Some astrologers have even said that you are underhanded and deceitful. This could be the case in instances where you cannot achieve your goals through fair play and your determination is such that it leads you to employ unjust means to obtain whatever you want. Generally, you would not resort to such action within your own family but, if practiced often enough, for whatever reason, it could eventually creep up on you unconsciously and sting with scorpion fury. Even being underhanded in checking up on your child's activities could lead you down the thorny path. Realize that this will completely dissipate and destroy your relationship possibly forever. Since adults cannot condone such dealings, how can a child be expected to understand and forgive. Expressions of mock sorrow will be transparent and it will certainly not solve the underlying problem.

Also prevalent in Scorpio females is a tendency toward self-indulgence and a driblet of selfishness. These traits may be dormant from now to infinity, but then again, maybe not. You will dislike living with these characteristics if they are not dormant, but not dislike it enough to refrain from acting up once in a while. Face the evils head on in the open and they can be exiled from within. Do not and you risk causing a rift between you and your child sooner or later.

After expending so much effort, exercising so much self-control and restraint, your alliance is a beautiful and healthy one. Take all the precautions necessary to keep it that way. If you feel that you have made sacrifices, the relationship has been strengthened. Respect that is hard to come by should be yours.

THE
SCORPIO
CHILD

SCORPIO is the second of the Water signs and has the key words "I desire" as a clue to the personality of the tots born under this sign. The symbol is represented by the scorpion with a stinger or the male reproductive system. Your baby will be a fascinating one from the moment of birth. He can be so quiet, in an intense manner, that you will be constantly wondering what's going on in that little head. You are almost positive that he is actually thinking of something, and chances are that you are right. This child has an intensely sensitive nature, but it concerns itself with others and is not as ego-sensitive as is the Cancer child. His nature is highly emotional and psychic, as you will find out. Here again he differs from the moon-children. Cancer babies can never hide their emotions; with Scorpios one never knows that emotion exists until it is released with driving force. The desires and wills of this bundle of joy are strong and defined. You will never feel that he would like something. Rather, it will be that he must have something then and there. His emotions are deep-seated, and he is one of those people who appears to be born wise and far advanced in years. Little will escape his eyes or ears. An awareness of everything within his world is his. With all of this, it is most likely that his personality will remain a mystery, possibly even to you, throughout his lifetime. He may well be a lovely, calm baby enjoying the pleasures of being held and fed. Who wouldn't enjoy such emotional comforts?

The imposition of strict routines will help enable a Scorpio child to get his emotions in order at an early stage in life. If he should feel neglected or need help, in any way at all, expect that he will cry and sob with persistent strength. He knows just what he wants and will expect it from you, along with love and kisses. You will see very soon how enthusiastic a baby you have. He will perk up his ears and thrash about with delight when he knows you are on the way to him. Excitement will be in the air when you arrive, and sadness when you, or someone else that he loves, makes an exit. Those little extras in the display of affection are really necessary to keep him content and sweet as an infant.

This child's health will be generally good and you may be somewhat surprised to find that his diet should be watched (no highly seasoned foods), and that his body requires tremendous amounts of sleep and fresh air. He will rarely be in a hurry to do anything. Yet he will manage to develop most of his faculties without even noticing that he has done so. The first time you see him doing something in quite an efficient manner you will be tempted to ask yourself if he knew how all along and just didn't feel the need to perform before.

He has a third seeing eye and a sponge-like memory that makes for complete comprehension. Once he has decided that it is time to walk, he will be up and at it without any ado. He is Captain Courageous with the steely determination of hurricane proportions. In some other child this would be admirable and cute, but Scorpio has the added benefit of intelligence with a self-program computer built in. There will be few moves that are not carefully calculated, and less that are unsuccessful.

He will be a sturdy walker and not in much of a rush. But do not make the mistake of laughing at him if he should fall when taking those first steps. The look you will get will positively singe you. His pride is overwhelming and he will not tolerate being made fun of, unless, of course, he is playing the clown for your benefit. These disapproving glares are apt to come long before he starts to toddle. It may sound a bit ridiculous that a pint-sized bundle like this is capable of such doing, but you will not remain a doubting Thomas for long. The first time he manages to wither you with one of those looks you will know his power. Mother beware! If you do not have a strong will, remember that he does, and you may find yourself being ruled by this infant.

His introverted personality will make it more difficult for you, gain the upper hand and keep it. Even so he makes his feelings silently known to you and it is a blessing for which you give thanks on many occasions. There is none so violent or tempermental, nor so attentive when interested or abusive when in the mood.

The deep, piercing look in Richard's eye should have tipped off his mother that the scorpion was running true to character in his desires. Even though he was quiet and went about his business, few Scorpio children are born without stingers. Richard is a poor loser and he had been made something of an "also-ran" recently in a play group. Just like the "Bad Seed" child, he harbored a grudge and planned for the day when he could seek revenge. That day came when he glued together all the pages in Don's coloring book and spread silly putty on Sylvia's blocks, all at the age of four. Discipline was meted out justly but Richard felt no guilt or remorse. Verbalizing the problem made a slight dent but not enough to satisfy his parents. The Scorpio nature is such that the intensity of any feeling becomes omnipotent, and little can dissuade the vengeful child. A few more incidents of this nature and Richard was taught to bring some of his feelings out into the open to alleviate the degree and risk involved by allowing them to fester within.

Never forget that his memory is long and his heart not truly forgiving. Be firm and completely inflexible in setting down disciplinary platform. Be just as firm as he is. Please don't be the first to give in or he becomes permanent lord and master the first and only time you waiver. Think not, that a mere child is above using your weakness to his advantage. So don't turn your back or be inconsistant in your strategy. Accustom the Scorpio to acquiesce to your demands and you will achieve success. It is impossible to be premature enough in implementing your rules and regulations. You must have a sufficient amount of strength, also, to court the thought of success, or you will be worn to a frazzle after the first or second round.

Rearing a Scorpio child successfully necessitates employing his tactics. The day of birth is not too soon to start. It is possible to have these children develop according to the way they are trained and, since he will be open and above-board in demands and feelings, you can take these extremes of behavior by the reins and instill an attitude of tolerance. Scorpions also have temperamental streaks. Here again the firm and loving hand can prevent the development of a nasty temper and vindictive nature. His desires will be demanding and devastating. Never show the slightest sign of knuckling under. Once he suspects that an iron will is not yours, you may be out of the catbird seat. Expect to be challenged on every issue. He loves an argument, but compromise is not within his ken. He expects to win each and every time. You must win in a way that will demonstrate your strength and your love and affection for him simultaneously. Be sure to train him to be considerate of those less strong than he and particularly to be a good loser. His bright mind will understand that he must be forgiving and recognize authority, and his honor should keep him from over-inflating his ego. Once he has seen that you will not bend, he will respect you for your ability to resist him. He is more receptive to accepting discipline and training from someone whose strength he can admire.

He is a lover and keeper of secrets. You would be wise to let him have his own way here at the beginning and not pry into his own little world. His true personality is veiled by secrecy and off limits to you for good reason. It keeps you and others at a distance, and from getting to know him well enough to be forewarned of his private thoughts, suspicious of his machinations. As a result, he can silently harbor ill feelings and allow them to multiply within to some day emerge with the uncontrollable passion for which Scorpios are known. Entrust him with your secrets, and he will carry them locked within forever and a day. Sharing your private thoughts with him will seldom make him change his ways, but it is certainly worth a concerted effort since you have little to lose.

It cannot be emphasized enough that all of this must be accompanied with adequate portions of love and affection, or you may end up with a dark, secretive, and gloomy baby on your hands who lashes out almost without provocation. Be alert and perceptive at all times and follow the Boy Scout motto—be prepared. Use common sense in all matters and season everything with tenderness.

Your baby is a bright one but will sense things rather than know them with his mind. He will be an early talker if encouraged, and you will notice an immediate tendency to be sarcastic even at the start. Do try to nip this in the bud. As he grows older, he may surprise you with some of the biting and caustic remarks he can make, but then you were forewarned about the scorpion's stinger. Try to reason with him once again. Tell him that words can hurt and that he should take care when talking to people, especially when he is angry. You yourself will often be the target of that sting as he lashes out verbally at those closest to him.

He is great at concealing his own thoughts but makes an excellent detective when it comes to ferreting out the thoughts of others. A keen mind is his and with it comes the uncanny ability to zero in on your feelings. If the relationship is a good one, he will be an invaluable aid and comfort to you in times of crisis or with just an ordinary problem. When your mind is troubled he will almost always sense it and be very cooperative and kind during this time. His family ties mean much to him.

See to it that his mind and body are kept active. His make-up contains an enormous amount of pent-up energy that must be worked off somehow. Remember that it is difficult to ascertain when this child is overwrought since he appears to be more calm than he really is most of the time.

He has the facility for remaining cool and apathetic through the roughest of times, especially, when he is being chastised or severely punished. There is never a grimace, cry, or certainly not a tear. The most you catch on a rare occasion is a biting of the lip or gritting of those pearly whites. The strange phenomena here is that, as passionate and volatile as he is, he still understands the need for corrective and punitive measures and hence the St. Joan bravery. Never try to put him down or deal with an outburst without employing logic and love. This is the magic panacea for most problems that you will encounter with him.

When school time rolls around he will have a desire to achieve and a strong will behind that desire. If he is disturbed emotionally he may have a proclivity to daydream rather than pay attention to what is going on in the classroom. Chances are that you will have done your job well and have prepared him to meet the world. Under these conditions little difficulty will be encountered. Sometimes he will unnerve his teacher with one of those Scorpio looks if he should be caught daydreaming or unaware. Many teachers feel a general sense of discomfort around Scorpio children and justly so. Here again, strict routine must be imposed as soon as possible when it comes to homework and study habits. Few deviations should be allowed. Check on him every so often when he is in his room working on home studies. Since this child loves so intensely and loyally his close friends will be numbered. Don't expect throngs of children around. It is not possible to love a great many when one loves so passionately.

With all his innate perception and intelligence it is surprising that Richard does so poorly in school. At first his parents were alarmed, especially when his teacher concurred that his mind was as sharp as a needle. Her complaints about his inattentiveness in certain classes and unfinished homework provided the answers. While his average grade was a B-, he was doing A work in some classes and not doing passable work in others. It was determined that Richard's performance was strictly contingent on his interest in any subject at any given time. Once reassured that he was not dull or lazy, remedial action was tried. Instilling a modicum of moderation into his interests and making those subjects he regarded as useless somewhat intriguing, Richard slowly delved into some of the secret aspects of history or science. He still does not give his all, but at least he isn't sitting in class making effigies of his teacher that he stabs with his penpoint either.

Speaking of passion, and its vices or virtues, it has more of the former. The underlying vigor is so highly energized that it should be given proper direction. This is the type of force that changes men and sometimes worlds in the mature years. In childhood the love and anger, the hate and joy, are much too intense to be at all healthy, physically or emotionally. It is almost better to have him bat a ball, beat a rug, or chop trees to release some of that tension from the power-house of dynamo numero uno.

Should your little Scorpion indicate any interest in music or the arts be sure to allow him to take lessons in his field of interest. With the added benefit of your encouragement his own natural talents in this area will take him far. His potential in this realm far surpasses that of children born under another sign. The arts will also be wonderful for him from the standpoint of acting as a release for some of those meteroric inner emotions that don't come to the surface as often as they should.

His health will usually be strong as his will and his recuperative powers (when he does fall prey to illness) are phenomenal. It is possible for him to be too ill to move his little head one day, and to be up and toddling about the next. He will have accidents and spills, as all children do, but very often will not cry, unlike many children. His threshold of pain is high and his pride great. If the accident is a serious one and blood is shed he will be even more inclined to remain quiet, brave, and strong. His self-control will amaze you.

The idea of higher education will appeal to him tremendously if those study habits have taken hold. He is intelligent and intensely curious about many things in life and he will want to pursue this curiosity. Research is a natural for Scorpions, and a career as a researcher would be most rewarding and illustrious. Any type of profession in the medical field, whether as a general practitioner, surgeon, or lab technician would make excellent use of his abilities. Psychiatry is the epitome for Scorpio child because it combines the details of medicine with the facility for probing and digging things out. Whatever you do, please do not try using your influence or imposing your ideas of a career on your child. Don't forget that he always knows what he wants. Give him a shoulder to lean on, if necessary, but let it go at that.

He will bring you much delight and happiness. You will always be in his thoughts and part of his life.

Scorpios born between October 23rd and November 1st have Pluto as their personal ruling planet. This influence will bring out the more positive side of the nature such as patience and determination, the aggressive, and the critical. He will be more cautious than the average child and possess far better judgement. Achievements are not for personal satisfaction only, but often for the development of competition in others. A deep understanding of the psychic is his, and time should be devoted to tempering the outbreak of tantrums and verbal attacks, both of which will be more profuse than those born later on in the sign.

Children that come into this world between November 2nd and November 11th have Neptune as their personal planet which injects unpredictability into an already changeable personality. This child will know how to make the most of everything that comes his way and has the capacity for doing so. The ideals he has established cannot demand too much from him. Self-sacrifice will be common but can create inner turmoils that can be harmful. The long-range and permanent in life will hold great meaning but the daily stepping stones to this permanence will be of little consequence.

Birthdays that fall between November 12th and November 21st are ruled by the all-powerful Moon which molds character. The emotional, creative, and proud parts of a Scorpio's personality are enhanced by the grace of the Moon. This child will undoubtedly be a champion of causes. He will have the knack for instilling self-confidence in others and receive their esteem in return. His personality will be magnetic, very, very mysterious, and most romantic. Strength will be channeled into balancing the inequities of life and making it more free for many.

THE SCORPIO
MOTHER
AND HER CHILD

The Scorpio Mother And The Aries Child

A Scorpio mother with an Aries child has an interesting relationship to look forward to, one that isn't likely to become stagnant or tedious by any means. You will exert approximately equal powers with your child in the long run, but each of you will have his moments of glory. You can expect a great deal of friction here, but fortunately your battles are of the short-lived and soon forgotten variety.

Most of the friction between you and your child arises from the fact that you both would like the reins of command. If you can accept the underlying motivations of your child's rebellion and lay your cards out on the table, you two will be unbeatable.

You'll constantly be amazed by that little Aries child's need for competition. It seems like he can enter no activity or game without the single-minded desire to come out on top. Make sure he doesn't take defeat too much to heart, though. No one can hope to escape defeat forever.

The Scorpio Mother And The Taurus Child

As a Scorpio mother you may be dismayed by your little Taurus child's lack of demonstrative affection. You, after all, are the hot blooded type with a healthily uninhibited attitude toward emotional display. Your little Taurus, on the other hand, is a rigidly controlled armadillo when a display of emotions is called for. This is not to say that a Taurus child does not feel great emotion because he most emphatically does, but he just doesn't allow himself the freedom to express this emotion verbally or physically. Instead, he goes to great lengths to do thoughtful things for his loved ones, such as ironing sheets or washing cars by hand. Before you begin to wish that your child were more open and responsive, stop a moment to think of how hard it must be for your child to co-exist with such a passionate dynamo as yourself.

When you stop to think of this hardship for your child, you'll learn to appreciate your child's efforts to please you, even if they may fall short of your expectations. Be extra careful not to inhibit your child even more by making him feel inadequate or that he has let you down in some way. There are those who feel that you need to modify your own personality.

The Scorpio Mother And The Gemini Child

You can expect a lot of rough going in a relationship of this kind. Your child may well become so frustrated with not being able to get his own way that he may develop into a classic whiner. You as a Scorpio will have the driving need to dominate everyone and everything in sight, and this driving need could be the worst thing imaginable for your child. Now, Gemini needs a *bit* of supervision because they tend to let their living habits get way out of line with their income. But too much supervision is worse than none at all when dealing with a potentially neurotic Gemini.

You must have heard about the Gemini susceptibility to martyr complexes, taking a lot of abuse just so they can feel noble themselves and get the sympathy of their friends. This technique works for a while, but ultimately drives away the Gemini's friends as he becomes more and more bitter. Don't let this happen to your little Gemini child still in the formative stages.

The Scorpio Mother And The Cancer Child

You and your Cancer child can have a satisfying and rewarding relationship if you can be willing to sacrifice a bit of that forward drive in order to think of your child's welfare. He will have his own ideas on how to go ahead with his life and they most likely won't agree with yours one hundred per cent; but you'll manage to get through the rough times somehow because of the special feeling between you.

Your Cancer child will want to spend a good portion of his time talking things out before, during, and after their occurance. You aren't much for talking things out, especially when there is so much to be done; but when you do make time for yarn spinning, you can't be beat as a master story-teller. Your child will be overwhelmed, susceptible to a good yarn as Cancer is, and you'll take pleasure in making your child's eyes so full of sparkle.

The Scorpio Mother And The Leo Child

Your Leo child will be everything that you have dreamed of, a child whose good looks will satisfy your desire for beauty and sensuality, and whose love of adventure will promote a restless energy that will rival your own. Leo children are anything but brooders and are able to work out any problems they may have in physical ways, like shooting rapids on a raging white river or pushing their McLaren racing cars to new and seemingly impossible feats.

You, Scorpio, on the other hand, have the wanderlust because you are always trying to escape something that is never completely shakable. You can even brood on the run, it seems.

Even a championship performance cannot lift you from the doldrums for a great length of time. But at least with a Leo child you will have constant adventures to look forward to, adventures extending far beyond your child's maturity.

The Scorpio Mother And The Virgo Child

You, Scorpio, frequently have problems with your children, arising basically from the fact that you do not usually take too well to the idea of motherhood and often act toward your children in a way that reflects an undercurrent of resentment. You will very likely have a mother/child relationship with a Virgo child that will be as free from trouble and problems as any relationship could be under the circumstances.

Your Virgo child is a well of maturity and domestic responsibility, even at a tender age. Your frequent sudden flights to far off places will hardly be cut back at all. At a relatively young age, your child can be entrusted with almost as much responsibility as an adult. However, you want to be sure not to take advantage of this to the extent that your child doesn't have a chance to enjoy the carefree and fun-filled days of childhood just to give you a chance for more leisurely time. Your child should come first.

The Scorpio Mother And The Libra Child

Your sensitive, loving Libra child will be an almost perfect complement to your own passionate self. You will have a relationship with this child that can be ultimately pleasing in all ways, as long as you keep in mind one important condition. Granted, you have an eye for beauty that rivals that of your child, and an open and honest attitude toward life that makes a great deal of love possible. Still, you have a much more realistic and pragmatic view of life than your Libra child and about 1/100 as much of that thin-skinned sensitivity. Be extremely careful not to stab through this thin skin or you may wound your child unnecessarily. Try to temper your usually headlong actions with a little thought as to what effect your actions may have on those you love. You feel a special responsibility toward this child, so don't throw everything out the window inadvertently by forgetting your Libra child's limitations.

The Scorpio Mother And The Scorpio Child

You may have a few problems with your Scorpio child when your two specific desires are antithetical, but on the whole you can expect a full life because your desires and goals are basically identical.

You may encounter some problems with communication because each of you is so concerned with his own needs that you frequently forget to consider the needs of the other. In this case, it would be best to have a long talk with your child from time to time to make sure that both of you have no thwarted or frustrated goals that could be easily solved by your working in concert. Your life and that of your child will be filled to overflowing, if the influences of your sign have a say in the matter.

You two may present such a united and formidable front to the outside world that you may put people off. Your best relationships will be as separate units, not as mother/child. Together you would seem so overpowering to others.

The Scorpio Mother And The Sagittarius Child

Your Sagittarius child's idealistic dreams may aggravate you to the point of distraction, since you are a doer not a dreamer. Whereas the Sagittarius spends a great deal of time dreaming about his future, the Scorpio just goes ahead and does things intuitively.

Since you have the knack for making quick, on-the-spot decisions that almost invaluably augur well, you'll have little patience for one who devotes and unusually long time to long-range planning and vaguary for mere pleasure's sake.

You must be careful not to destroy your little Sagittarius child's dreams completely, however. Sagittarius has a fragile ego and is easily crushed by heavy handed actions and harsh words, especially those provoked by your impatience. Find a happy median from which to work, you'll have a satisfying relationship with your Sagittarius child. You will gain a partner on your spur-of-the-moment escapades if you can amuse your child out of his reverie without destroying his visions.

The Scorpio Mother And The Capricorn Child

You and your Capricorn child will have a rewarding life together if you are willing to bend a little to make the uneasy times a little less sticky. Most of your difficulties will arise from the fact that once in a while you will notice that your little Capricorn seems to have taken on a great deal of the family responsibilities—and therefore authority. You can see how easily this could have happened because you were never too fond of domesticity in the first place. You are only too glad to let things slide, knowing that your eager child will be glad to take up the slack.

But during the moments when you do give some thought to the situation, you can't help being incensed and regretful, both at yourself and at that restless Scorpio nature that must be obeyed. Take special pains not to lose too much of your control over this family situation.

The Scorpio Mother And The Aquarius Child

You'll have a most difficult time understanding this quiet, loving, passive Aquarius child whose serene nature seems to be the direct opposite of your own inflamed, passionate one. It will be hard for you and others to accept the fact that this child is indeed yours. Many times you'll feel like climbing the walls—or Mt. McKinley—while your child will be happily lying down reading a book of hardus.

Frequently, you'll find that philosophical attitude of acceptance and adaptability almost too much to bear. You'll want to scream and throw things, and your little Aquarius will just smile and come to you with a loving hug. And, wonder of wonders, this child will have a soothing effect on you, although you would never have thought it possible. Don't look a gift horse in the mouth. Just be thankful for what you have got and look forward to a wonderful life with this startling mature child.

The Scorpio Mother And The Pisces Child

You and your Pisces child could have a wonderful relationship, but more than likely there will be some major problems here. This little Pisces of yours has an unnerving perspicacity that is able with frightful ease to cut through all of the nonsense in a situation to the core of truth beneath. He is very likely to be put off completely by your frequent carryings-on and ravings and to make a penetrating remark that will stop you dead in your tracks. This one little remark will hit you like a ton of bricks and make you feel like cancelling your activities until you have got your confidence back.

Now this little brain child of yours can do you some valuable favors if you ask for them. Before leading up to every challenge, find out what your Pisces child thinks of the situation. You might very well be spared some unfortunate moments if you follow this sound advice.

STAR GUIDE
FOR
SCORPIO

Symbol	●	The Scorpion
Ruling Planet	●	Mars
Element	●	Water
Gender	●	Feminine
Key Words	●	I Desire
Birthstones	●	Bloodstone, Black Pearl
Favorite Flower	●	Chrysanthemum
Best Colors	●	Scarlet, Blue, Green
Mineral	●	Iron
Favorite Music	●	Military Tunes
Favorite Pastime	●	Antiques
Lucky Numbers	●	8, 3
Best Day	●	Tuesday
Compatible Signs	●	Cancer, Virgo, Capricorn
Incompatible Signs	●	Leo, Aquarius

FAMOUS PEOPLE BORN UNDER THE SIGN OF THE SCORPION

JOHN ADAMS
MARIE
    ANTOINETTE
SHOLEM ASCH
GEORGES BIZET
ADMIRAL BYRD
EDWIN BOOTH
JAMES BOSWELL
RICHARD
    BÜRTON
ROY
    CAMPANELLA
BENITO CELLINI
THOMAS
    CHATTERTON
AARON
    COPELAND
SAMUEL CUNARD
MARIE CURIE
FYODOR
    DOSTOYEVSKY
MARIE
    DRESSLER
GEORGE ELIOT
GEORGE GALLUP
JAMES GARFIELD
W. S. GILBERT

BILLY GRAHAM
INDIRA GANDHI
WARREN G.
    HARDING
AVERELL
    HARRIMAN
JUNE HAVOC
KATHERINE
    HEPBURN
WILLIAM
    HERSCHEL
SAMUEL
    GRIDLEY
    HOWE
ROCK HUDSON
BARBARA
    HUTTON
SHAH OF IRAN
JAMES JONES
JOHN KEATS
GRACE KELLY
ROBERT
    KENNEDY
BURT
    LANCASTER
VIVIAN LEIGH
LEOPOLD III,
    BELGIUM

MARGARET
    MEAD
MARIANNE
    MOORE
NEHRU
GEORGE S.
    PATTON
PABLO PICASSO
JAMES K. POLK
CLAUDE RAINES
AUGUST RODIN
WILL ROGERS
THEODORE
    ROOSEVELT
ERIC SEVAREID
ROBERT LOUIS
    STEVENSON
JONAS SALK
FREDERIC
    SCHILLER
NORMAN
    THOMAS
JEAN VERMEER
VOLTAIRE
ETHEL WATERS
OSCAR WERNER
ELLA W. WILCOX

THE SAGITTARIUS MOTHER

November 22nd — December 21st

BORN under the sign of Sagittarius you are: as an individual, curious and philosophical; as a female, charming and disarming; as a mother, a potential cornucopia of love and tenderness.

In making the transition from protaganist in the marriage to Mother Superior of the family you may encounter a hurdle or two. Initially you may regard the road to motherhood as an obstacle course paved with boredom and restrictions. Too often the Sagittarius approach to child-rearing is yet another step in the climb to success rather than recognition that it is one of the most gratifying achievements any being can experience, a great challenge.

You know you care enough to do the very best so first things first—resolve to overcome your anxieties and apprehensions of taking on another responsibility. Once you reassess the role of motherhood in your innate determination to make the most of this "venture", you will contend with the routine of it all as though you were born guardian of the nursery. Nine months should suffice for even the most stubborn of expectant matriarchs—with your ubiquitous sense of logic and inflatable pride it will take a reflection no bigger than a minute. Allow your naturally blithe disposition to carry you through the feedings and diaper changes and you soon will be feeding baby with one hand while you strive to become the gold-medal winning one-armed archer with the other. But then you usually master the hurdles one way or another—occasionally with a superficial abrasion but always on the right side of your target.

More often than not you aim well with your practicality and great cool. For this reason you and those around you are thoroughly convinced that you are a homogenized blend of Wonderwoman and Germaine Greer. With little speculation you will admit that there are rare instances when you do need a helping hand (or, at least a few fingers). You cannot perpetually keep yourself out of trouble. Even you need doses of care and guidance to maintain your foothold along the winding path. Take someone's hand, (preferably your husband's) when you feel less sure-footed before you brave the elements alone. Learning to seek and accept assistance is mandatory if the "blessed event" is to have a happy start.

The other half of your character development course should be to zero in on the advocacy and advantages of dispersing just discipline. A deficiency in this area, when combined with possible isolationist tendencies, will result in a dreadful and dangerous duo —the dynamic potential is an aside. No mother can be more of a super-hero to her children, none a greater ally and friend than the palsy-walsy Sagittarius. However, you are just as capable of being a damaging and destructive influence by abstaining from the exercise of behavioral guidance.

Spoiling your offspring is one of the lesser concerns to be dealt with but not to be dismissed. Don't promise him everything but give him what you do promise. Left to your own devices he will have his first car before he is ten and she will be swaddled in furs and jewels at twelve. Self-restraint and awareness are needed on your part (well, everything is relative).

You have a bent for being lax in meting out chastisement. The tendency to criticize or correct appears to arise only when you are harassed or irritable, overtired, or ovulating and not at all in keeping with the actual behavior of the Lilliputian to whom you are waitress, washer and yes, warden. Jupiter's influence has made you a protector of the weak. However don't short-change your child by developing a weakness in your laissez-faire philosophy to spare the vanquished. Neither a dictator nor a hireling be; your friendship will not suffer, but your authority as a guiding light could be severely and permanently dimmed if discipline is consistently disregarded by you. Chances are that he has inherited some of your traits and, if a dislike of authority is one, better to suppress it than support it in the vital developing years. This is not a search-and-destroy mission, but rather a learn-and-employ one with a myriad of implications. Learn to decipher whims from wrong doing. Employ a dash of discipline where necessary.

"Where necessary" usually begins at home. Imagine the little one tossing things about sloppily leaving clothes and toys strewn around and you see your child as an instant litterbug. Train him properly now and have a mother's helper later when you are off and running on one of your sprees or to a meeting. Little Mr. (or Miss) Clean will clear away the dinner dishes without mishap. In most cases, a glimmer of sunshine should be coming through if you expend a little effort in self-discipline, and you will have a lesser job training your child.

It should begin to look as if materfamilias is not such a great confinement. Yes, you will lose some mobility and liberty, but from a rational point of view no one duped you into believing joys were all for taking without any giving. That could hardly come as a staggering discovery to you.

Your natural propensity to aloofness toward family ties should dissolve before your child appears on the scene. Generally the arm's length between you and family is not attributed to disinterest but simply to a profusion of activities and to an intense wanderlust. Perhaps you should consider curtailing some of your projects and curb the traveling lust just enough to include the little one—for real or in fantasyland. Both of you can fly on a magic carpet in perfect harmony to visit with fairies, gremlins and trolls.

Once you have learned to live with the advantages and disadvantages of child-rearing, there is a strong possibility for you to become the Model Mother of the Year. The odds are all in your favor; your warmth, love, kindness and devotion. The "glasses" you wear are rosier, the stars you see are brighter, and the tales you weave are more magical than most mothers. You are your best audience and believer. Your little tot is more fortunate in having you around than most other children.

The happiest hours for you may well be those you spend frolicking and gamboling with your youngster. He will worship you and be president of your fan club with all his little chums as members. Other mothers will cast a green eye your way and wonder what is your private brew of super-sorcery. Even when your babe comes of age you will remain his most loyal and favorite friend, probably to the end of time.

Early in his life he will be imbued with your great love for the wide open spaces and your passionate dislike for indoor confinement. Depending on his degree of awareness of your claustrophobic bent, he may start to kick up his heels in the playpen, and most likely when he seeks his first job, he will back off from a nine-to-five in a paneled office. Of course, if you deeply desire him to be a draftsman or investment counsellor then play with him before the homefire and not the campfire.

The original Nature Boy undoubtedly must have been a Sagittarian or the offspring of one. The ecology movement and *The Last Whole Earth Catalogue* were contrived by and for all you archers, the forecasters of bio-degradables, ski-mobiles and re-cycling in the wide-open spaces. He will probably share your enthusiasm for sports, which would please you immensely.

Exude and effervesce to your heart's content. Just do not boil and bubble in his presence. Your attitude is changeable and the sarcasm, rage, or bolts of thunder that accompany the flackfits should be closeted. To a child whose senses are not fully developed, outbreaks of temper are scarey and become scarring traumas for such a little mite. Hold back your tongue lashings and release your hostile aggressions by weeding the garden, a hard serve on the tennis courts or an extra bull's eye or two. Keep those golden slippers on your feet or you stand a chance of losing your throne.

As a Sagittarius female, you are without question most congenial and loving when following a star—any star. When your child comes of age it would be best for you to return to your calling or interest of the moment. Since you always catch that star, the gratification it affords makes for a more delightful and well-rounded you. A happier you creates a happier household. You will set a good example if your targets are within reach, although applications are now open for the first female astronaut.

Fortunately, you are not cut from the cloth of over-protective mothers. The only risk you run is in not checking on his growing pains frequently enough. Just as you dislike domination and interference you do appreciate being watched over and looked after. During the years leading to maturation, your child must have gentle guidance along with romantic and spiritual exposure in order that he matriculate into a free-thinking, functional adult. This is his life, which is strongly influenced by you.

Charisma and coquetry are an integral part of your basic personality and second nature to your soul. You use them well with the adult population and they will serve you as well in beguiling your child. That practical and analytical head on your shoulders should hold you in good stead in making him an uncommonly care-free and rewarding ally. Some day in years to come take the time to contemplate, meditate and put your logical mind to work. Conjure up a balance sheet. It just might prove to you that motherhood was the greatest and most gratifying challenge.

THE SAGITTARIUS CHILD

THE last of the Fire signs has "I perceive" as its key words. The Archer is its symbol. An arrow being shot into the air is commonly used for the symbol as is a side view of the thighs or upper legs which Sagittarius rules. The arrow denotes the directness that is so much a part of the archer's make-up. This child will be as active as his fiery brethren with tremendous energy and drive. He will converse more readily than the Arian and be more gullible and easy-going than the Leo. His interest in law parallels that of Libra; the distinction is that Librans are concerned with the justice of law for individuals while the Sagittarians are more involved with the science of law.

Here you have the happiest baby of all. This one is really all smiles. Jupiter rules this sign and makes the personality a jovial one. This child wants to be where it's at. Wherever he hears the sound of voices and activity is where he wants to be. When you are entertaining plan to include him so that he can enjoy, then, with no fuss or trouble, he will probably fall asleep right in the midst of the party without your even noticing. He loves the companionship that goes along with feeding and it is all marvelous fun to him.

This same little cherub is apt to be restless and wavering at times and become unsteady and puzzled. You'll have a hard time keeping up with his wandering nature. Rearing this child may keep you haggard and toilworn. Forming his character is in your hands. Mold carefully and painstakingly. The archer has been born with aspiration and the primary years will be the enlightening ones for the realization of his ambitions.

At a very early age (possibly in a few weeks) his little mouth will contort in an attempt to form words. If you should talk to him quietly and slowly and then stop as if waiting for an answer, his effort to make a reply will start. The gibberish baby sounds will start earlier with your Sagittarian than with other children of the same age. He will communicate to the extent that you are positive he seems to understand what is being said. Needless to say, he will be an early and verbose speaker. He will adapt to routines very easily. He really doesn't want to give you any trouble or have any problems himself. He is as pliable as Plasticman. Expect loud cries when he wants attention. As soon as you arrive on the scene, however, he will start to smile through the tears, showing gums and a happy face. Some part of every day should be devoted to your playtime with him. This will mean that you love him and he will feel secure with the companionship and easy affection that you love him and he will feel secure with the companionship and easy affection that you give forth. Don't expect him to start walking as quickly as he began talking though. When he does strike forth in an upright position he will take a few steps and then make a safe-landing. Most likely he will then collapse with pleasure and joy at his own achievement squealling with delight. Sagittarius rules the upper legs and he loves to get up on them. Take care that he doesn't wander off. If he is at all curious about something he may move very quickly and be out of sight in a wink.

As a fire sign he is enthusiastic and appreciative of good things. His energy is abundant but he will burn it off rapidly as soon as he starts to toddle around the house. Maintain a nap schedule. His restlessness can cause depletion of energy of the nervous system which will eventually run the gamut in terms of spills, falls and injuries. Sagittarians are more prone to accidents than natives of any other sign except Aries and many will occur through tripping or falling (even long after he has mastered the art of standing on his own two feet). Much of them can be prevented through the maintenance of a planned diet that is geared to feed and nourish the nervous system. This tendency toward being nervous may not always be apparent. Compare his state to a thin violin string that is tautly stretched and you gain some insight into the inner forces at play. Be careful how you treat this little package. Gentleness and honesty are musts with Sagittarian children.

The most immediate problem you will have is in allowing him freedom of guided activity. He is an independent child and he could rebel against authority. It is vital that you direct his energy into the proper channels before discipline becomes a meaningless word in your vocabulary.

In the beginning the universally accepted forms of punishment are the best ways in which to show your displeasure; displaying a strong hand, withholding special treats, and so forth. As he approaches the age of reason your job will lessen considerably. Sagittarius is a thinking and talking sign. Present a logical and sensible platform and he will accede to your wishes. It may take several hours for him to complete his twenty questions—each one a "why" or "wherefore" to your every statement, so re-energize your dry cells before starting out.

A true Sagittarius child is generally a believer in the "I perceive" aspect of his personality. Larry is a real doer and a dare-devil at that. With the smallest degree of observation under his belt he immediately proceeds to try his hand (or foot, or mouth) at the new art he has mastered. He watched Dad oil a squeaky door and ran around for two days squirting everything in sight, including mother's watch, to make it less noisy. When he was finally apprehended it was "spank first and ask questions later." That was certainly a waste of strong-arm motion as Dad soon found out. Larry wanted to know why he was being punished and what he had done wrong. Once he was told calmly he understood. He stopped emulating adult activity again without asking "why" or "how".

He will have great fondness for the wide outdoors and the products of Mother Nature. Brooks, wild flowers and animal life truly fascinate him and will relax him too. Playing out of doors or taking trips into the country will have an almost therapeutic effect on the Archer. When of age he will probably win every Boy Scout badge in the books. He'll prefer a picnic or camping-out to dining in lavish restaurants or staying at a plush hotel.

His personality will attract many friends and, if you impress upon him that frankness is not always desirable in dealing with others, he will maintain these friendships. When he is enthusiastic about something he will pull out that bow and arrow and try to shoot his zealous ideas into all of his friends until his entire entourage has been intravenously fed with an arrow of thought.

Here is the ambassador of invention and the promoter of truthfulness. The Sagittarian darts that are dipped in truth can be crippling if you let them hit home and get under your skin. It is something of a struggle to teach some of these children diplomacy since they are so direct in their thinking. Find consolation in the knowledge that their frankness is not of the vicious variety. The unfortunate aspect of all this honesty is that the remarks he makes relate to faults or situations that the person he is addressing is already aware of and often does not want to face.

Larry is constantly telling friends' mothers that their houses are not as neat as his and that their children are not as well-behaved as he. "Why don't you get your dishes clean the way my mother does?" or "You always look so sloppy. How come you stay around the house in a robe all day and don't give refreshments when we play?" Naturally, the arrow never misses its target—how could it? The sad part of it all is that he is approximately 99-44/100% right. Honesty is one thing his own mother taught him but the compulsion to talk about things that hurt people should not always be followed. Logically she explained that most of the time it would make no change in the person involved.

Wise parents should impress upon this child that it is some-times better to make no comment at all and hold his tongue than run the risk of hurting someone. Early training on this subject can avert loneliness later on in life. Many enemies are incurred by the pull-no-punches Sagittarian. Few people take the time to under-stand his personality and psyche. Don't be tempted to let him have his way. At first it will be very cute for the tot to make direct comments, but many a parent has rued having let that first com-ment pass without some constructive criticism. If this tendency has not been controlled by school age he will begin to find out that other people will not tolerate his bluntness. Teach him early to hold on to that arrow once in a while instead of shooting it.

Meditation is a great Sagittarius passtime—difficult to believe with all that "honesty" spewing forth. The relatively serene con-templation will undoubtedly be accompanied by some undesirable habit such as doodling, foot tapping, nail biting or other manifesta-tions of nervousness. Remember that meditating is as difficult as studying. Both require remaining in a relatively confining state. The great thinker concentrates on a subject for at least a few minutes and then his mind runs ahead to a new dream or project.

It must be that his fiery spirit thrives on the air he so cherishes for the dreams never cease. Even when failure is a fact and no longer just a possibility he remains the eternal optimist.

You must first show him how to put away his toys. Then help him understand that he can eventually become his own enemy if he refuses to accept the responsibilities of seeing things through. Communication is your only hope. Teach him how to analyze his motivations. You will have to be the taskmaster.

Your child is gifted with imagination and this will be evident very often in his embellishment of stories. He is not a liar. He simply magnifies certain situations. A story can become much more exciting if he adds a little of his own creativity to it. This is innocently done because he likes people around him and wants to attract attention. Neatness should be stressed early in life as well because Sagittarians can become somewhat sloppy if not trained to keep things in their place.

He is bright and learning comes easily. He is one of those children who can pick things up quickly. However he doesn't want to be bothered with the routine of sitting still long enough to study or plod through a subject. Doing his homework faithfully is something that will have to be built into the Sagittarian youngster. He is apt to reneg if left to his own devices. He will start off, most likely, with quite a bit of enthusiasm but as times passes his writing will become sloppy and his interest will wane.

This child can be easily trained in any of the arts but he just won't give lessons his all unless trained to do so. If he is talented his studies come easily. A gentle nudge here and there should keep him in line if you remember to begin at an early stage. His memory will seem to fail when it comes to practicing and before you know it the week will have passed between lessons and he has accomplished little. If you are able to accomplish this successfully through his early teens the battle is won. If habits are ingrained in him in relation to an apparent talent you may have a poet or artist in your midst.

Flightiness is not an enviable trait at any age. As an adolescent being fickle is chic, period, but then the trait becomes a great handicap. He develops a reputation for being a feather-brained pigeon always flying the coop. That is not quite so chic.

Larry is a man-about-town at an early age. He is sought after by both boys and girls—especially girls. Even the young at heart feel stricken when flirted with, courted, and then dropped like a hot potato. As all women know, this usually enhances a man's appeal. With Larry it was the same story to the point that all his ex-girlfriends felt a little more insecure about romance, etc. after knowing Larry. He was a heartbreaker and cad at the age of fifteen. Larry's folks decided it was time for a man-to-man talk. He couldn't be less concerned. It was a matter of fleeting interest, he explained. After all, did they want him married off at 16? There was little for his parents to do until Miss Immovable Object would cross his path (an alias for Miss Right). Suddenly nothing could keep Larry away to make him a devoted if somewhat absent husband.

Intellectual ambition is the gift that your child has along with his intense curiosity and frankness. No emotional handicaps come packed into this bundle. He is something of an energetic daredevil a bit short of patience. While the great outdoors beckons to something deep within him, domesticity does not seem to have the same appeal. Somehow it seems that activity away from the home front is more magnetic. Here is an opportunity for the extravagance so common to Sagittarians to grab a foothold. After the first few times your youngster cannot make do on his allowance you must start imposing restrictions by letting him go without no matter how small the amount involved. Many archers have become the high-livers of our society until such time as their bank accounts run dry.

Sports will be near and dear to his heart. You, mother, must see to it that he gets adequate rest and balanced meals to provide the energy which he will burn off in his activity. The first time he misses out on rest or food you will see just how uptight and ragged his nerves can become.

Higher learning will appear to him only if you have instilled the required study habits and have exercised discipline. College under these circumstances will be great for him. Your youngster will undoubtedly have a good sense of humor and might be the class clown during his childhood. In later life this will be carried over into his career. He may be the entertaining salesman who knocks on doors or be a high-level executive salesman. Remember that he will continue to sell himself to people he likes; practically everyone.

Archers born between November 22nd and December 1st have Jupiter as their personal planet as well as their ruling planet. This child will be endowed with intelligence and a moral sense of right and wrong. His nature will be more sensitive and sympathetic than other Sagittarians, always ready to lend a helping hand or extend a warm shoulder. The double aspect of Jupiter indicates a very magnanimous and generous spirit that is full of life and fun. Keep in check any tendencies to whine or complain.

Children that arrive in the world between December 2nd and December 11th have the benefit of Mars as their personal ruler. In combination with Jupiter it spurs its subjects on to great things by injecting courage, drive and responsibility into the basic Sagittarian personality. Details and duties become a whiz to this child. He operates at the peak of efficiency more so than most of his Sagittarian brethren. Friends will be abundant and loyal to this child since he has learned to be diplomatic when he does speak.

The Sun rules the period between December 12th and 21st. It gives life and sustains energy. Here the combination of rulers lends ambition and intuition to its subjects. Experience is the only teacher for children of this period and a sense of beauty is inherent. Never a complainer, this child will share only the good and happy things with those close to him; the rest will remain buried deep down in that ever-mysterious soul. This person is anxious to please and will extend himself to the degree of self-sacrifice to do so.

THE SAGITTARIUS MOTHER AND HER CHILD

The Sagittarius Mother And The Aries Child

An Aries child can give even the most powerful personality a run for his money, and you are far from the domineering type. You'll be gratified by your child's neverending desire to be foremost in all things, but you are enough of an idealist to want your child to have more of a humanitarian basis for his plans and goals. Your child, on the other hand, will be put off by your dreams that never really seem to be put into validity in the way you have planned.

Your Aries child wants to have absolute control over his fate, and he comes amazingly close.

You two can carve out a rewarding life together as long as you both work hard to understand the likes and dislikes of the other. Your Aries child can lend some realism to your quest for self-satisfaction; and you can put a spark of enthusiasm for the newer things in the life of your child.

The Sagittarius Mother And The Taurus Child

Your relationship with a Taurus child can be a very pleasant experience as you strive to find points of common interest. One problem is that you tend to be an idealistic dreamer and your child is the epitome of the hard-nosed realist.

Your Taurus child will constantly be demanding results from all those labors of yours that may never seem to reach fruition. You'll frequently be turned off by that air of detachment with which your child seems to tackle every job. Can't that child get excited about anything?

If you two could somehow let some of your qualities rub off onto each other, then you have a very good chance of realizing a full and happy relationship, as well as becoming better people in the process.

The Sagittarius Mother And The Gemini Child

Sagittarius and Gemini can get along very well indeed since they have many common interests and goals. You as a Sagittarius have plans and dreams which give you much pleasure just going over them in your mind. Your Gemini child too has dreams and plans that are almost impossible to achieve, but mainly because he is at an age where many things are impossible.

A Gemini child can amuse himself almost completely just imagining the day when he will be able to achieve his goals. And since Gemini has a vivid imagination, he can draw others into appreciating his dreams. You and your Gemini child will have many happy hours planning your separate and joint ventures, but may run into problems when you spend so much time thinking that you may have the actual groundwork undone. Don't jeopardize the realization of your dreams by losing yourself in them.

The Sagittarius Mother And The Cancer Child

Your Cancer child will have you eating out of his hand if you are not careful to maintain authority in all affairs. Cancer has a sneaky, though utterly charming, way of bringing even the most domineering of us under his complete control. Since you, Sagittarius, are anything but the domineering type, you are more susceptible than most to the Cancer wiles.

Your Cancer child will be an unlikely participant in your various plans and schemes because, if he is anything like the majority of those born under the sign of Cancer, he will be a live-for-security type, wanting to control your much-needed freedom. He is the squirrel who wants to save for the future. You'll gain from his frugality in the long run.

The Sagittarius Mother And The Leo Child

Every Sagittarius ought to have at least one Leo child just to see many of his dreams come true in the form of this adorable and bright little child. A Leo will be the idealization of all your romantic hopes and dreams for this child will complement you in every way. You have always dreamed of having a child as gorgeous and romantic as a Clark Gable or a Raquel Welch; here is living realization of those dreams.

The one problem here is that your little charmer is so dramatic that he is almost always putting on some new act. You are going to feel left out a lot by this Leo child unless you take measures to include yourself along on these adventures.

Be sure to give your actions a bit more pizzazz when around your Leo child so that he doesn't lose patience with you and begin to treat you like a hopeless member of the older generation. Leo likes to see results, not plans; and if you care enough to have the respect of your child, you'll have to give a strict accounting of yourself.

The Sagittarius Mother And The Virgo Child

To a Sagittarius mother, a Virgo child can be both a delight and a heartache. You will love your Virgo child's highly developed moral and ethical code. but you may very likely be dismayed by your child's air of cool practicality that leaves little room for enthusiasm and wonder. Virgo could do with a shot in the arm of some kind of religious fever. You may be able to do this for your child by impacting some of your own reverence for life.

Give your child the feeling that life is more than just something to be gotten through by making him a part of all those dreams that keep your mind in high gear. If you do your job skillfully, you'll be able to see results before you know it.

Both you and your Virgo child have a well-developed sense of right and wrong and a kind of nobility that will grow stronger within each other's presence.

You will be gratified at your child's easy assumption of tasks that some mothers can get their children to do after a whole day's nagging.

The Sagittarius Mother And The Libra Child

You and your Libra child will undoubtedly have a relationship of the most rewarding nature, despite any pitfalls that may happen along the way. Neither of you is interested in rocking the boat in any way at all, and you are both likely to back down when the possibility of a confrontation presents itself.

When trouble finally does arise between you, you will both be eager to get things back to the status quo even if you both end up apologizing for the same thing. Sagittarius and Libra just don't make very good fighters, but since you both shy away from confrontation you don't have to worry about one's taking advantage of the other.

Your Libra child will be happy if his environment is free from hardship and chaos, so you will have to work a little harder to make things pleasant for this sensitive little creature. As long as things are on an even keel, you will have a wonderful life with your Libra child.

The Sagittarius Mother And The Scorpio Child

Your Scorpio child may leave you wide-eyed and open mouthed as you marvel at this dynamic little bundle who always seems to be flying off the handle at aggravations both major and minor. You will find yourself developing a crack in that usually sturdy exterior and becoming rather short-tempered with your Scorpio child if you don't schedule at least one major confrontation with him in order to lay down the law. Constant harping will do neither of you any good and make for really unpleasant relationship. Fight that domineering and formidable personality with everything you have got. Leave no stone unturned in getting your child to accept the status quo.

Eventually, he will give up trying to dominate you and will devote his energies to conquering everybody else in the world. That wouldn't be so bad because you could enjoy your child without always having to be on guard. Do try to help him make his goals more realistic, however.

The Sagittarius Mother And The Sagittarius Child

You and your Sagittarius child will have a dreamy, unexciting life together unless you both take steps to reverse that trend of spending most of your lives dreaming instead of doing. Dreams are wonderful, but they are not so great that you should sacrifice a satisfying life of action for an empty life of planning for things that you never quite have the oomph to follow through. You certainly don't want to play this role around your child, who had this tendency anyway and who will become even more entrenched in these habits by virtue of the fact that you live in a dream world and have so much influence over your little Sagittarius child.

More than likely, you and your Sagittarius child will never be far apart in distance or thought. Sagittarians have a well-developed sense and are very thoughtful about family matters and events, working hard to make these events memorable without even stopping to think about them.

The Sagittarius Mother And The Capricorn Child

Watch out that that Capricorn child of yours doesn't take over your role as parent in this relationship. You have a tendency to live a bit too much in the future, which means that you may forego a few responsibilities that lack the romanticism to which you are attracted.

Once you remind yourself that your Capricorn child has about as much love for romanticism as you do for housework, you will be in a far better position to assert your advantage as mother. Every child needs a childhood no matter how much he thinks and deceives himself that he wants all of the trappings of adulthood. It is your duty to see that he learns to enjoy his chilhood and to make it one he will always remember with affection and nostalgia. Don't back off from the responsibilities of motherhood at your Capricorn child's expense. Sharing responsibilities can be effective as long as you use careful judgment.

The Sagittarius Mother And The Aquarius Child

You and your Aquarius child are more than likely going to have a wonderful relationship, one that can maintain its strength over great distances and through long separations. You will find a great audience in your little Aquarius. There is nothing he would rather do than to listen to your marvelous plans for the future and wonderful ideas for vacations to come. Your Aquarius is a great listener.

You may wish that your Aquarius child had more drive and ambition, yet he could delight you with wild schemes and goals of his own. But this loving child is one who is content to take things as they come. Aquarius children are very soothing people to be around, and you will come to accept him the way he is just because the love between you will be so strong.

The Sagittarius Mother And The Pisces Child

Your Pisces child has delight in visions and future projections that keep you going even in the darkest moments. He is an acute dreamer whose acumen and insight help him to find an easy road to success.

You are bound to be a little chagrined at the way your little child keeps sliding through success after success while your goals are still in the planning stage. But maybe you can take a couple of hints from that little dynamo of yours and help yourself along to a more successful future.

In the process, you would be helping your little Pisces out a great deal if you would try to impart to him a little *joie de vivre* in his daily affairs. He may strike you and everyone else as far too moody and aloof. Bring his more human qualities out into the open where they belong so that he can enjoy life on all of its many rewarding levels.

STAR GUIDE
FOR
SAGITTARIUS

Symbol	●	The Archer
Ruling Planet	●	Jupiter
Element	●	Fire
Gender	●	Masculine
Key Words	●	I Perceive
Birthstones	●	Turquoise, Ruby
Favorite Flowers	●	Carnation, Poinsettia, Narcissus
Best Colors	●	Purple, Green, Ochre
Mineral	●	Tin
Favorite Music	●	Anthems
Favorite Pastime	●	Hunting
Lucky Number	●	5
Best Day	●	Thursday
Compatible Signs	●	Aries, Aquarius, Leo
Incompatible Signs	●	Virgo, Pisces

FAMOUS PEOPLE
BORN UNDER
THE SIGN OF THE ARCHER

LOUISA MAY
  ALCOTT
CHARLES A.
  BEARD
LUDWIG VAN
  BEETHOVEN
HEYWOOD
  BROUN
WILLIAM
  BUCKLEY, JR.
SAMUEL BUTLER
MARIA CALLAS
THOMAS
  CARLYLE
ANDREW
  CARNEGIE
WINSTON
  CHURCHILL
THOMAS COOK
NOEL COWARD
SAMMY
  DAVIS, JR.
CHARLES
  DE GAULLE
WALT DISNEY
BENJAMIN
  DISRAELI
JOE DIMAGGIO

KIRK DOUGLAS
DOUGLAS
  FAIRBANKS, JR.
WILLIAM LLOYD
  GARRISON
IRA GERSHWIN
CARY GRANT
WARREN
  HASTINGS
HEINRICH
  HEINE
JOSE ITURBI
BORIS KARLOFF
AGA KHAN
ALAN KING
FIORELLO
  LAGUARDIA
HENRI
  TOULOUSE-
  LAUTREC
JOHN W.
  MACKAY
MARY MARTIN
JOHN MILTON
POPE JOHN XXIII
FRANKLIN
  PIERCE
LEE REMICK

CYRIL RITCHARD
DIEGO RIVERA
ARTUR
  RUBINSTEIN
LILLIAN
  RUSSELL
GEORGE
  SANTAYANA
JEAN SIBELIUS
FRANK SINATRA
ROBERT STACK
JOSEPH STALIN
ZACHARY
  TAYLOR
FRANCES
  THOMPSON
JAMES THURBER
MARK TWAIN
MARTIN VAN
  BUREN
JOHN
  GREENLEAF
  WHITTIER
LAZARUS
  ZAMENHOF
EFREM
  ZIMBALIST

CAPRICORN·GOAT·

THE
CAPRICORN
MOTHER

December 22nd — January 19th

You are a traditional and ambitious female which will be more to your advantage as a mother than not, if you keep yourself from going to extremes. Common sense is also one of your outstanding virtues. Apply it in dribs and drabs or massive doses as needed to hopefully avert major calamities and act as a preventive medicine.

Capricorn women personify the counterpart of the strong silent type. Your persevering nature and acute intuition will carry you to the top of the mountain very methodically. It often comes as a surprise to your acquaintances when you reach your goal because your exterior easy-going maner never betrays you even when you are breathing hard from the exhausting climb.

A constant threat is posed by following the upward path. As each goal is reached your scope broadens and you become itchy to take the next step. There is your proclivity to teach, dictate, shelter and generally take charge because you possess the know-it-all. It is more than likely now and then, though, that you can be pegged a busybody or intruder. It is hardly necessary to translate the possible hazards this folly can bring you and your child. The trouble can amount to tidal waves of turbulence. You relish playing the part of Helpful Hannah with benevolence and loftiness of purpose, but with great selfishness on occasion. Be well-warned that this attitude cannot only earn you demerits with friends and relatives but will instill incredibly massive mounds of resentment in your child.

There may even be times when you may be double-tongued and prey on the frailties of those less determined in order to achieve your end. If you are already a devotee of such action, stop, look and listen immediately and do not pass go. The weakest of the weak is a child, and even with the most honorable intentions for your off-spring, you have the facility to make him a sacrificial kid. Exercise some adaptability and mold the putty to fit the situation. Mother instinct will hopefully be your salvation.

Much of the time you will be challenged to combat the Saturn influence that is instrumental in shifting your moods from one gear to another somewhat akin to a peripatetic oscillator. Convert that dynamo of determination to a symphony of symmetry. Fall back on the mother instinct if you must, but it would be far better to develop some type of instant stabilizer to help you function properly in the care and feeding of a youngster. This is a case in which your child would profit most. Resolve to combat gloom and despondency that wash over you not all too infrequently. To dispel depression should be your motto and that will not be a very attainable goal unless your little steel-trap mind decides that your child's mental health is at least as important as yours. Program yourself for a fixed course and your child will gain through osmosis.

An offshoot of your deep moods (and, in fact, also the root) is a penchant for worrying. Worry and fear are the grenades you juggle. Many positive aspects weigh heavily in your favor. It would be worthwhile for you to play accountant occasionally with your pluses and minuses instead of being a worry wart continuously. Receive compliments graciously and seriously and perhaps an increase in your self-confidence will allow you to be a bit freer in reassuring and praising your child when it is warranted. He has fears too, believe it or not. Each of you is a person of consequence with strong, salient attributes that are appreciable and appreciated. Please do not take a giant step backwards by endowing your child with fears that become insecurities and he will eventually become another worry wartlet.

Give much thought also to your own standards which are page for page reiterations of Emily Post, Hayle and Everywoman's Guide to absolute decorum. Yes, children must be disciplined from the day they first feel the presence of another human. There is, however, a compromise between military discipline and backstairs influence. Your adaptability does not always stretch far enough in this area. The practice of upholding traditions is an admirable one but devoting your life to following precedents without exception is neither admirable nor clever. Stand unrelentingly to your ideals and you may have one rebellious off-spring at an early age. Set standards and impose them, when necessary, in a framework that relates to your child and you jointly. Left to your own devices you would have a son in long pants and a tie at pre-kindergarten age or a daughter decked out in white gloves (spot-cleaned hourly) while still in a stroller. That goes against your traditional beliefs.

Your child will never be caught with sticky fingers, dirty overalls, or outside the rules of propriety, if you can help it. Through your insistence he will say "sir" and "madam", polish his apples, tame a cowlick and dutifully pay homage to his elders. By all means teach him the amenities but all in good time. Do not rob him of a playful, mischievous and normal childhood to find yourself with a six your old behaving like sixty. Some children are born wise little old men or women (you may have been one). It is cute and adorable when he is still a youngster but irritating, most unlikeable and unhealthy in an older child or adolescent. He will unquestionably be a model adult citizen for the greater portion of his years. You will see to that.

Temper your tendency to be strict and rigid. Instead, enjoy lending a hand with his trials and tribulations in the maturation process. Your time should always be obtainable and your ear available to steer him over the rough spots. As soon as you use your heart and head rather than the rulebook you can be assured of a warm and devoted two-way relationship. Forget your insecurities of what the neighbors will say and enjoy the few years of real childhood before they elude you.

It would be foolish to assume that the Good Samaritan can function properly without some cause to champion or a cub-scout group to hostess. Your forte is one of a professional social worker. Group activity is your preference. Retain some outlet for your talents in campaign or volunteer work, teaching the handicapped or whatever pleases you most. Your dreams are all realistic and you survive on the energy of sweet success. Never underestimate the value of your milk of human kindness. Just try not to overmilk the cow.

A wise Capricorn mother will keep herself in check when the

playmates your little one brings home are not socially acceptable. You can control his environment now, select his first friends and then, voila he has a mind of his own. Chances are excellent that in later years many storm clouds will gather over his friendships, attitudes and values. This is the Age of Aquarius and there is just no chance that he will see eye to eye with your straight-laced conservatism. Prepare yourself for the storms and give him freedom of latitude and independent thought. A built-in generation gap will very probably exist so it really is unnecessary to create further contributions to the chasm.

Maintaining one's composure and a dignified air at all times is not an easy task. If it is no longer a chore for you then the risk is high that your earthy nature has indeed started to cool from the outside in and a certain degree of coldness has infiltrated your character. This is not to say that you are indifferent to home and hearth, but just that the family duties are rote functions. Nothing, but nothing, is allowed to interfere with you and yours, be it out of genuine sincerity and warmth or mechanical etiquette and breeding. Perhaps a smidgeon of concentration will provide enough food for thought to melt away some of the exterior cool by starting a slow burn within. Your rational mind should easily assess the situation and apply the only proper solution to put things back in their proper perspective.

It is very possible that you may become involved and caught up with handling your child properly. Then he will probably receive little from you other than clean clothes, baths and instructions for the different types of finger-bowl service. Pour over his story-books and math problems with him and get to really know him as he is without benefit of preparation for ascension to a throne. Even learn to accept the possibility that as a child of an Earth mother he may choose to lead a more relaxed life style whether he becomes a banker or a farmer.

In cultivating his talents leave open time for some physical skills such as carpentry, plumbing, cooking or whatever, instead of just the esoteric and arty. Howard Johnson started with an unglamorous and not so chic position in life and the Jolly Green Giant does not "ho, ho, ho" consistently just because of a jovial spirit. Even if your youngster aspires to nothing greater than being a little grey midget or if he derives pleasure from a particular hobby, you must be understanding and not in the least condescending. Forget your ambition and concentrate on his, even if it changes with the wind. Work toward his advancement even if his interest is one you would not have chosen for him.

It is important to you that kudos and laurels come your way. Going unappreciated is not your style. A lack of recognition for a great personal coup has the potential of sending you into a long-lasting, murky mood. If care is given to overcome the obvious hazards you will encounter as a mother, you run an excellent chance of receiving both praise and respect on all fronts. No accolade will be as large or as loud as you would like but, nevertheless, in some instances more than what you will deserve.

Much work is required on your part, but satisfaction is guaranteed if you avoid the major pitfalls. You may even be somewhat surprised to find that you have gained more self-confidence and security from a job well done than from any overt applause.

THE CAPRICORN CHILD

"I use" are the key words for those born under the sign of Capricorn. Its symbol pictures the knees of man. The goat which is associated with this sign is in a climbing position. Like his Taurus and Virgo brethren the little kid is an Earth sign which should indicate to you that your child's basic nature is a practical one and that, unless major errors are made in his rearing, he will be able to rise up and meet the world head-on. Capricorn babies may sometimes have a rough beginning where health is concerned. They are usually born looking like old wise men or women. The typical wrinkled hospital baby is your little goat.

These children seem to give the impression that they are having a tough time getting used to being here. Sometimes you will develop formula trouble and other small difficulties when you get him home. There may be nothing really serious but he appears to be struggling and somewhat solemn about the business of getting along. Routine will not be much of a problem but there will be little annoyances connected with health.

Capricorn children are prone to hysteria, skin diseases and other ailments. Be certain that you have a competent physician whom you can consult on these occasions to find out exactly what is bothering the child. Once infancy has passed pay less heed to constant complaints of discomfort unless you care for the idea of a permanent house physician.

One thing you can do is to hold him firmly at feeding time and also when playing with him. This will give him a feeling of security. He is born sensitive to all things but particularly to food and physical contact. Once the correct recipe for feeding has been found and he feels adequately secure, he will settle down to enjoy the routine of living. Eating or sleeping problems will lessen. All his little wrinkles will seem to fade away and you will find a beautiful baby beneath it all. You'll see a quick smile now and then. However, expect your child to be serious and wide-eyed most of the time.

When he begins to set out on his two feet it will be with great caution. He is going to take good care of himself. Your encouragement will be needed here for that extra feeling of security. He is basically an active child and anxious to get going and a little prod or a big smile will do the trick. After you have finished holding his hand he will travel where he wants to go and it will be difficult for you to keep up with him. As he reaches the toddler stage he will be a busy little bee and full of curiosity. He'll be as helpful as can be and will love picking things up and putting them in their proper places or do any household errands that he can physically manage in order to please you. He's always on the look-out for that smile of approval from you. Please give it to him when he deserves it. His approach to things will be a very practical one and you will be sure that his directness is due to the amount of thought that has preceded any given action. It will be hard to deter him once he has set his mind on something he wants. A refusal will bring repercussions. Expect him to pout but not ask again until he knows that you are more receptive. He won't forget about his initial request. He'll know when to ask again without running the risk of another refusal.

Capricorn is ruled by Saturn which governs time. Let this be a guide to your little goat who can bide time like no other. You have a sixth sense about the right time to strike in most matters.

He was born cautious and you shouldn't fret about a seeming lack of warmth. What appears to be a deficiency in his emotional make-up is just conservatism and caution creeping through. This is one child that will never wear his heart on his sleeve. The inner workings of the mind will always be the master and his head supreme over the heart. Don't despair, in later life this will turn into a determination to accomplish and end up winning laurels from all.

Many times a timid streak will overshadow his innate organizational make-up. He should be gently taught to dispel qualms which ceases worrying. Very seldom does the Capricorn child let shyness triumph over his good sense. He knows wishful thinking doesn't move mountains, se he will carefully determine the best way to get what he wants in an unobtrusive manner.

His craving for security is great and will manifest itself in the form of Goody Two Shoes. Very seldom will he break any house rules or give teachers bad apples. He applies much concentration to ingratiate himself with you from his first coo on and, later, with all people. You may expire while you wait for the first sign of derring-do that requires a reprimand or some degree of discipline. To achieve security the Capricorn child uses all his might and self-restraint to be a model of perfection; never impolite, never out of line, never testing or questioning authority. He will be less mischievous and become involved in less shenanigans and scrapes than other children. Sadly too many Capricorn kidlets never have childhoods either. Even though those wrinkles at birth fade away, they are indicative of your child's advanced make-up.

He will worry continually about his homework and tests. A great deal of pride is connected with his schoolwork (as it is with all he does). The parents of this youngster have a responsibility to see to it that he learns to play more and to avoid the possibility of becoming a bookworm. All work and no play makes a Capricorn a dull child—he must learn to take time out for just plain fun. Whatever he does (even playing games) his ambition and desire for achievement make him take things too seriously. Teach him how to laugh and have a good time.

From the day Sam was old enough to recognize the difference between children and adults he seemed to be more at home with the latter. A sixth sense told him his playmates would not appreciate his conservatism and caution while these same traits would bring praise from the older folks. Not only that, but he felt that the kids were a little childish for him at times. With a little pressure and encouragement he was convinced to give organized activity with other children a fair chance and eventually mastered this problem (albeit with the attitude that he was their guide and Rock of Gibraltar).

In his own quiet way he will reach great heights although there will occasionally be an outburst of bossiness here and there with family and friends. Basically he knows he will fare better being a dark horse and end up on top through his own merits and not by pushing his weight around. His dreams will be practical ones as will most of his actions. His pastimes will not be idle or foolish games but useful and constructive projects that will delight you. Still in that same quiet manner, he will convey his upsets and displeasures. Very few tantrums will arise in infancy or in later development. Keep count of all these blessings.

Home life and domesticity are of great importance to Capricorn children. The boys are the ones that will follow Dad around with a hammer if he is doing some carpentry work. The girls will love helping mother with the cooking and cleaning. This child is very capable and organized.

Sam takes everything seriously and being a busybody is not one of the lesser problems. He loves to hear mother's friends exchanging gossipy notes and will toss in a few of his own about these same friends and his own parents.

In a sense he feels he is keeping tabs and perhaps protecting people from themselves and their own weaknesses. His mother was not pleased by what she considered to be a female trait but did nothing until the day she caught him spying on her when a distraught friend was talking of marital problems. Knowing instinctively that he would blurt out all the details at the first given opportunity she played the game of setting up "house rules" that precluded such shenanigans. Luckily he was old enough to understand and young enough to be molded. The "house rules" of course, extended to more than the physical confines of the home, else Sam would have taken her very literally.

Your youngster will also love school. Most teachers that have a few Capricorn children in their class are very pleased because they are such conscientious workers. Your goat does not learn all that easily but he works diligently at learning.

A sunny disposition is not one of his redeeming features and most probably he is solemn and unenthusiastic about everything in general. As a result the combination of repression and self-control make for a dangerous duo. While he avoids acting out for fear of incurring disfavor, he will sneakily go about his own quiet brand of mischief. Vengefulness and deceit are two major pitfalls. Neither are admirable at any age but more than slightly despicable in a child. The very first time you catch wind of such behavior it is almost too late (but not quite) to start instilling faith, hope, and charity along with a good measure of the social graces.

The model child will also run the risk of not just being a little snob but, ironically enough, a meddlesome chauvinist. It may be true that he alone holds the key to objectivity and the panacea for any problem in his back pocket, but after a while the "Answer Man" becomes a nuisance and a bore. Can you imagine the future potential in being a full-grown, fully-developed personification of Mary Worth, the Encyclopedia Brittanica, and Ann Landers in a repressed way. Since he equates your disfavor with the plague, dissolving or eradicating this tendency can be accomplished by constant application of punitive measures and "Man-to-Man" discussions. Don't for a second relegate this matter to any position other than one of top priority. Impress him too with the urgency of situations. No man (even a Capricorn) is an island and, unless curbed immediately, this proclivity could make him stand alone after alienating all friends near and far.

As far as artistic talent or developing skill are concerned he will be wonderful here, too, just as he is with school work. He will practice conscientiously without prodding. Do not expect though, that he will continue lessons in any given subject unless he feels that he can make use of it in later life. The key words of Capricorn are "I use" and there is a possibility that this interest can blossom into a career. Otherwise it will probably be discarded. What becomes a must for him at a young age is to relax and perhaps listen to music or anything that will put more fun and enjoyment into his life. Sometimes too many lessons or scheduled activities will affect him adversely. He will be unable to cope and become very nervous. Mention was made earlier of a tendency to worry about school work, tests, or report cards. This is really very amusing since he will almost unfailingly get high grades through school. He is so capable that you must wonder why he is a worry-wart. It is this very concern that makes him so capable and gets him those grades.

The Capricorn child in any family is the one who, regardless of age, will assume the responsibility for the other children at home. He will help them dress and generally keep an eye on them.

Sometimes he can become quite domineering because he is capable and knows what should be done.

The health of this progeny in later years will be good and rather rugged. His appetite will be hearty and he will not be a fussy eater; most likely he will eat everything on his plate. He responds well to the routine of scheduled meals and bedtime. Be sure to remember that time can become a hang-up with this child. If his breakfast is not ready on time he will gulp it down or even skip it for fear of being late for school. He cooperates with you, so here is an area in which you can cooperate with him and soothe his worries lest he become overly nervous.

Twitchy little Sam always had some physical ailment—real or imaginary. Once the pattern of so many illusionary ills was established mother couldn't decide whether he was just seeking more attention or was neurotic and developing psychosomatic ills. After consulting with a doctor she was aware that his high-strung but controlled nervous personality accounted for the hypochondria. It was simply a matter of constant reassurance and encouragement to placate all Sam's doubts and "worrier" tendencies. Remember he was born with a wrinkled brow. The worries can never be completely eradicated but soothed enough to eliminate some of the deeper furrows and many lesser ills in Sam's future life.

In later years the little old wise look will fade away gradually and he will age so gracefully that the glow of youth will emerge as time passes him by—very desirable for either sex but the Fountain of Youth for the females of the species.

Higher education is a definite necessity for the Capricorn child. He is proud and ambitious; pride alone would get him through college. When combined with his ambition to climb to the heights how can he lose. Start saving now for that college tuition. The choice of a profession or career is relatively wide open. He will make an excellent businessman or teacher or hold a position that requires organization. The medical field may attract him. He will start off low on the totem pole but progress quickly reaching the top remarkably fast. He will know his job inside and out and be a source of pride to higher-ups.

Consider yourself among the fortunate to have given birth

to a child of Capricorn. Little fuss or bother and virtually no instant mess come with this child. Rather much delight and pride are to be had and much comfort in your old age.

If your child's birthday falls between December 22nd and December 31st his personal and ruling planet is Saturn. Precision, endurance, and perseverance are emphasized in the personality of this child. His friends will be few but true and loyal; he is the very soul of dependability. This child can become somewhat overbearing and demand too much precision and exactitude from others. You must instill some moderation in his character to offset that ambitious streak. There will be some disappointments and he must learn to cope with them.

Babies born between January 1st and January 10th have the giver of love and beauty, Venus, as their personal planet. This child will require less prodding than most Capricorn goats to enjoy the pleasure and cheer of life. The artistic part of the nature will come to the fore as will the emotional. Family ties mean much and duties are always fulfilled. Solitude is often desired by this child. He should learn to socialize at an early age and lower his sights just a notch or two. Some things he desires are humanly impossible.

The period between January 11th and January 19th is presided over by the planet Mercury which makes your child practical and somewhat changeable. This planet controls the brain and nerves—making its subjects high-strung. He will learn quickly that happiness comes from inner contentment. Once this is realized he will be a good humor man spreading cheer wherever he goes. His life is the most well-balanced of all Capricorns. A very sympathetic nature enables him to give love and understanding readily.

THE CAPRICORN
MOTHER
AND HER CHILD

The Capricorn Mother And The Aries Child

The Aries child wants to hold the reins. His aggressive personality will prove very tiring at times. Maintain your self-confidence and remember who is in charge. Once threatened into retreat the future relationship could keep you out of the position of authority permanently.

A determined mother should treat an Aries child as just a child. Basically, he yearns to have you as master of his ship as long as you possess both the resolve and tender touch required to steer him onto the right course without fear of incident or the typical Aries rebellion.

You are the stabilizer that can change fiery flames to a safe simmer and thereby safeguard your child's future years.

The Capricorn Mother And The Taurus Child

Here is a relationship that should have more than its share of uneasy moments, with the both of you constantly trying for the upper hand and not usually by straight forward means either. Neither of you is very adept at coming right out and saying what you want. Instead you both have such faith in human nature that you assume good deeds and thoughts will bring you what you deserve. Unfortunately, life does not always work out that way, as you both will undoubtedly come to realize.

Left to your own devices, Capricorns would not be the greatest domestic wonders in the world. However, whenever anyone is entrusted to your care, you suddenly blossom forth into the very epitome of motherhood. In fact, sometimes you tend to go a little bit too far and could become overly protective if you are not careful.

This situation is not likely to develop with your Taurus child, however, since Taurus is pretty good at asserting himself when pushed too far.

The Capricorn Mother And The Gemini Child

Your natural Capricorn instincts to protect your child and dictate practically his every action will come in for some high going when you meet up with an elusive Gemini.

One of Gemini's greatest identifying features is his ability to wriggle out of just about anything. They are masters at this sort of trickery and are so skillful that they hardly realize that they are doing this. They can look you straight in the face and tell you that they will do whatever you say and then go ahead and do exactly what they want, without even batting an eyelash. Also let's not forget the Gemini's quick, mercurial mind that is constantly coming up with excuses and little white lies to enable him to escape from just about any predicament.

Once you accept this characteristic of your little Gemini's makeup, you will be much more able to deal with him. Perhaps it would be too much for you to hope to change this tendency toward irresponsibility, but you can give it the old college try.

The Capricorn Mother And The Cancer Child

Your Cancer child will soak all that special attention right up and be just what you would consider a model child. You will be so eager to please that you won't even notice when your little Cancer starts expecting this extra special treatment from you constantly—and from other people as well.

You are going to have to temper some of that indulgence for your child's own good. Give him a chance to develop some independence and resourcefulness, no matter how difficult this may be for you. Once you find a working relationship that is beneficial to both of you, you will be gratified by the results.

You and your Cancer child can have an enviable relationship marked by closeness and mutual concern for each other's welfare. Your Cancer child is extremely sensitive and will be the first to know when something is weighing or preying on your mind. You two can be a great source of comfort to each other.

The Capricorn Mother And The Leo Child

Your adventurous Leo child will fight your attempts at supervision at every turn. If you want to keep your peace of mind, you had better reconcile yourself to losing at least every other battle. Leos seem to lead charmed lives anyway, so you do not have to worry too much about their going off half-cocked and getting in serious trouble.

The luck of the Irish does not hold a candle to the luck of the Leo child. Of course, this is still pretty difficult for a Capricorn mother to follow, but you cannot be beat when it comes to threading yourself through some tight places and rough going. Eventually you will come to terms with your child's independence and admire him for not taking advantage of your complete protection. You cannot help loving Leo children anyway. Their charm and easy good looks can win almost anybody over to their point of view.

The Capricorn Mother And The Virgo Child

You and your perceptive Virgo child can have problems getting along if you are not careful. Like Leos, Virgos are completely independent types who want to take charge of their destinies at an early age. But *unlike* Leo they do not stop to bother with such compensating factors as charm and flattery. They just go ahead and do what they feel is best for them, without trying to con you into feeling better over your loss of power. It is not that they are unresponsive or insensitive to the feelings of others, but just that they do not want to sacrifice their independence for the mere purpose of assuaging your wounded pride.

If you can accept this mature child without bemoaning your almost negligible control over him, then you can be sure of a relationship that will stand the harsh test of time and give much support to both of you, especially in times of adversity and sickness.

The Capricorn Mother And The Libra Child

Your natural Capricorn instincts to mother and protect may be actually harmful to a Libra child if you do not set limits for yourself and restrain your exuberance at taking on the responsibilities of motherhood. Libra children are extremely sensitive and impressionable. They are more apt to succumb to stifling over-protection on your part than are children born under signs indicating more independence.

Libra children are very eager to please and will gladly curtail their activities with their peers if you desire more of their time. This is a wonderful tribute to a loving relationship but could have serious detrimental ramifications if your child soon begins to shun the companionship of children his own age. You will have to sacrifice some of your wants and desires for the ultimate benefit of your child.

Any sacrifices you make, however, will pay off great dividends in the future and you will never regret placing your wants behind your child's welfare.

The Capricorn Mother And The Scorpio Child

Your passionate and dynamic little Scorpio will be more than a match for you and may end up by usurping your role completely. Scorpios are persistent little creatures and will keep flailing away at your authority until you are completely worn to a frazzle. Do not feel like too much of a failure, though, because hardly anyone ever comes out a winner when matched with a Scorpio.

If you can work out a viable relationship with a Scorpio, however, you will have the relationship of a life time. You would be hard pressed to find a more stimulating and more dynamic child than this little Scorpio child who keeps you constantly on your toes.

You, Capricorn, frequently tend to be a little inhibited or shifty in your attitude toward life. Prolonged exposure to that passionate little Scorpio of yours can have beneficial effects upon this inhibition and can help you to enjoy life more fully by forcing out of your mind old misconceptions and erroneous beliefs.

The Capricorn Mother And The Sagittarius Child

Your little Sagittarius child is an adventurous and trusting creature who will give you more than your share of nervous attacks. You, Capricorn, are often worry warts with fertile imaginations conjuring up ever more horrifying predicaments for your child to fall into. Try as hard as you can, you are never going to be able to contain that boundless Sagittarius enthusiasm and energy, so you might as well learn to live with it.

Of course, this is easier said than done, and you may never be able to stop worrying to a point of nervous exhaustion. You will also worry about your little Sagittarius child's complete faith in the goodness of human nature and fear that some day your child will be sorely disillusioned and hurt. All you can do is to make sure that you will be there to offer support and consolation if that unhappy moment should ever arise. You can do a lot to minimize any crushing blow.

The Capricorn Mother And The Capricorn Child

You and your Capricorn child should in all likelihood share a relationship marked by mutual interest and concern for each other. Other mothers will envy the closeness which you and your Capricorn child share although they may not voice such admiration to you. Instead, you may hear some criticism that you and your child dote on each other too much, that you two shut others out from your lives, including close relatives.

Now a little gossip never hurt anybody, but just be sure that you *are not* shutting others out of your life, especially those who may need you just as much, if not more, than that little Capricorn who is the light of your life. It could never be your intention to do anyone any harm, especially through crippling neglect. But a Capricorn child, to your mind, is sorely tempting to devote yourself to wholly. As long as you are aware of this danger, you are responsible enough to avoid it.

The Capricorn Mother And The Aquarius Child

You, Capricorn, have ultra high hopes for your children and tend to live through them a great deal. For this reason you may be a little dissatisfied at times with this little Aquarius child of yours. Not that Aquarians do not strive for exemplary lives, but they frequently do not strive for the same things that Capricorns value so highly.

Capricorns tend to place a high value on material success and formal education. Aquarius children, on the other hand, have far less concrete goals and may seem completely aimless to you practical Capricorns. If you can bring yourself to rule out your selfish interests in your child, you will be much better able to accept him for himself alone and not take into account all of those grandiose hopes and dreams of yours that have gone unglamorously down the drain. With an Aquarius child, you will be able to bask in the glory of a mother whose child is admired by everyone for his friendliness and generosity.

The Capricorn Mother And The Pisces Child

The relationship between a Capricorn mother and Pisces child is destined to be a difficult and trying one until the child has finally discovered his niche in life. The Capricorn mother, such as yourself, tends to feel the pain her child is experiencing even more strongly than her child does, perhaps exaggerating the problem in her own mind.

You, Capricorn, are prone to take things seriously, especially things that involve your child. As soon as you learn to accept the fact that many of the things bothering your child are only the result of a passing phase, you will have a far better chance of surviving your beloved Pisces' childhood without becoming a nervous wreck or a nagging harpy. Just stay alert to the fact that Pisces children as a whole tend to have a great deal of mental distress at some time or other.

This can be attributed to Pisces' intuitive grasp of the nature of things, a quality that is bound to cause some misery sooner or later when the "nature of things" seems way off base.

STAR GUIDE
FOR
CAPRICORN

Symbol	●	The Goat
Ruling Planet	●	Saturn
Element	●	Earth
Gender	●	Feminine
Key Words	●	I Use
Birthstones	●	Garnet, Malachite
Favorite Flowers	●	Carnation, Snowdrop
Best Colors	●	Violet, Silver
Mineral	●	Lead
Favorite Music	●	Folk Songs
Favorite Pastime	●	First Editions
Lucky Number	●	7
Best Day	●	Saturday
Compatible Signs	●	Taurus, Virgo, Pisces
Incompatible Signs	●	Aries, Libra

FAMOUS PEOPLE BORN UNDER THE SIGN OF THE GOAT

ETHAN ALLEN
STEVE ALLEN
CLEMENT ATLEE
CECIL BEATON
HARRY
  BESSEMER
COUNT
  BERNADOTTE
LUDVIG VAN
  BEETHOVEN
HUMPHREY
  BOGART
RAY BOLGER
VICTOR BORGE
CARRIE
  CHAPMAN
  CATT
PABLO CASALS
NAT KING COLE
GARY COOPER
ELMER DAVIS
GEORGE DEWEY
MARLENE
  DIETRICH
PIERRE S.
  Du PONT
MILLARD
  FILLMORE

BENJAMIN
  FRANKLIN
AVA GARDNER
BARRY
  GOLDWATER
ALEXANDER
  HAMILTON
CARL SANDBURG
JOHN SINGER
  SARGENT
ALBERT
  SCHWEITZER
ROBERT STACK
ROD TAYLOR
LAWRENCE
  HARVEY
J. EDGAR
  HOOVER
JOAN OF ARC
ANDREW
  JOHNSON
DANNY KAYE
JOHANNES
  KEPLER
MARTIN LUTHER
  KING
RUDYARD
  KIPLING

ROBERT E. LEE
MAO TSE TUNG
TONY MARTIN
HENRI MATISSE
ETHEL MERMAN
MOHAMMED ALI
  JINNAH
HENRY MILLER
MOLIERE
SIR ISAAC
  NEWTON
RICHARD NIXON
LOUIS PASTEUR
ISAAC PITMAN
EDGAR ALLEN
  POE
HELENA
  RUBENSTEIN
MAURICE
  UTRILLO
HENRIK VAN
  LOOP
DANIEL
  WEBSTER
WOODROW
  WILSON
LORETTA YOUNG

THE
AQUARIUS
MOTHER
January 20th — February 19th

You are your brother's keeper and your husband's and your neighbor's, ad infinitum. To say that you are inclined to be a humanitarian or a public benefactor is not to give you full credit for your sense of obligation to the world about you. You are so people-oriented that it is doubtful you could ever be selfish or anything but giving of yourself. Altruism, determination, and intelligence are all contained within the water-bearer. You deal with life on a mental rather than emotional level.

Today you live for tomorrow and always peek around the corners of life curious to know what tomorrow will bring. It is not that you have anxieties or fears about the future. You are just terribly impatient about being kept waiting. Just as you abhor being alone and thrive on being sociable so are you restless about getting on with the natural progression of life. Charm and diplomacy enable you to make friends, keeping them with your loyalty and warm personality.

As a mother you are fundamentally as enigmatic and altruistic as you are in any other phase of your life. Your allegiance to any one thing or person is as difficult to capture as the airy atmosphere in which you drift along in pursuit of a star. Initially, you are perplexed by the prospect of being a lady-in-waiting for anyone, but fortunately you are accomodating and flexible.

Naturally, you are going to feel hampered and restricted by motherhood and robbed of your independence and freedom of movement. Your remarkable intuition will serve you well in this instance. You must realize that attention today to your child is an insurance policy for tomorrow and the rates are reasonable. Devoting your time and energy to him will hardly mean that he possesses your body or soul. Your practicality should tell you as much.

Approach motherhood with the attitude that you can best serve your fellow man (and child) with a well-rounded education and as many skills as you can possibly learn.

The role of mother will call upon you for hitherto untapped resources. Do not procrastinate but expend your efforts to fulfill your maternal obligation and they will be well repaid. All good things come to Aquarians and the stars position themselves to your advantage. Rarely will you encounter adverse situations that you cannot handle as a mother. With your child you exhibit patience, understanding and congeniality, all of which make you worthy of his confidence and trust. Surely nothing could please you more.

In the past you have been accustomed to having many irons in many fires. Now the only iron you should wield is one that brands. Provide your child with the love and attention he needs so he will know that he belongs. Impress him with your humanism and open mind. Do not put off until tomorrow . . . your sense of obligation should prevent you from becoming too lax in the care and feeding of your child's mind. You value respect for intelligence too much to allow yourself to flounder in this important function.

Amazingly enough, you will soon discover that you are not a slave to your child's demands and this should elicit a favorable reaction. Your emotional detachment must be countered with tenderness and interest. Once you become aware of the fact that you are still a free spirit you are more apt to give more affection to your child. Since you are far from the demonstrative type you must teach yourself the value of a gentle caress or spontaneous hug. Keep from being neglectful and too late in doing so. You will miss much by not allowing yourself the luxury and pleasure of expressing your feelings in this manner. You will even miss more if you ignore this function of motherhood; a deep togetherness that will make the relationship with your child a lasting one.

It is a rare Aquarius bird that lavishes too much of anything on her offspring. You will adequately attend to his needs (hopefully), care for him and hold him dear. Just don't hold him at a distance. Your innate aloofness and detachment must be curbed and offset by a demonstrative inclination which you will be forced to adopt. Softheartedness is not completely absent or void from your character—just deeply and absurdly imbedded in your subconscious—an undercover trait. Your air of detachment is only an outward manifestation of the unpredictable Uranus influence that governs your moods and manners. You are too bright to delude yourself into believing that a lack of compassion can be equated with freedom or that it can do anything but make you inaccessible and out of range to your child. Certainly, this is a far cry from serving humanity on any level.

Children see through watchful eyes that scrutinize your behavior. With all you can teach him about brotherly love you would be foolish to set an example of retirement in your private practice of love by proxy. Once you gain his love then respect and confidence follow quickly and automatically. You are clever enough not to be forced to operate under the handicap of being overly protective or compulsively propulsive. The desire for him to be a super-achiever is non-existent. You simply want him to do his best in whatever pleases him most.

It is certainly propitious to you as a mother that you have spread your interests far and wide and that you have exposed yourself to so many things in life. When your youngster begins to confide in you there are few deeds or misdemeanors that will astonish or stupefy you and none that will send you into a fit of hysteria. Your lenient and liberal nature allows you to deal with most situations with an impartial and objective point of view that will inspire further confidence from your child. This should not give you free license to let all of his actions pass without proper punishment. Respect him for being open and truthful with you. Reassure him of your understanding but use a firm hand when necessary.

You will probably be his best friend, confidante, and revered leader. His disappointments will be converted into meaningful lessons. His fears will become groundless fantasies and his funtime full of laughter and delight. You are the knowing provider and intuitive donor that fills his mind with security and his heart with joy.

Aquarian women are individuals that do not blindly accept or conform to the maxims and standards of our society. You set your own standards of acceptability that are considered bizarre or way out by most conformists. Your dilettante ways project you into a world of repeated experimentation and speculation so that your values and standards are apt to be frequently reassessed and adjusted to absorb your newly-found knowledge. Those who frown at your activities and lack of conformity are generally people who lead dull, sheltered lives and, in fact, are not living but rather walking corpses. You are unique and your friends will also be unique in their own ways, yet tuned in to your wave length. Exposure to many facets of life enables you to give to your child more fully. Just keep yourself from exposing him to people or forces that are too extreme for him to digest or too advanced for his age. The growing process is a long one and there will be ample time to teach him what you have learned over many years.

Since you are so caught up with a number of interests and activities you tend to lose sight of details and mind-cluttering minutia. This can be relatively unimportant in your own life although forgetting to pay the bills or fill the gas tank is not a matter of trivia. In your child's life, details and trivia are all-important. Unless you pay heed to little nuances, the first clues to a bad habit and the natural process of maturation (walking, talking, etc.) you will find yourself in real trouble. With a child there is no such thing as an inconsequential detail. Each move is indicative of his promise, development, and character. Many times a small detail is enough to make you exert extra effort to curtail a nasty trait. Another detail will lead you to encourage a possible talent before the opportunity has passed on. Sharpen your senses and concentrate on his activities—*not* yours.

As you are not a conformist all of the time, you may exhibit a tendency that is not socially acceptable according to the book. You establish your own values and can be quite outspoken about them with people who cannot accept criticism gracefully. When this occurs your intentions are always honorable and you mean to be helpful, but many people can feel this is but a breach of etiquette, lack of breeding, and anything but humanitarian. It will not further the cause of brotherly love. Try to reserve such comments for those you know will accept your constructive criticism for what it is, rather than what it is not. Children cannot be subjected to such blunt criticism unless it goes hand in hand with a calm, objective explanation and a kiss or two on the cheek. Then follow it up with some helpful advice on how to remedy the fault or temper the trait.

As an Aquarian female with a social conscience you express yourself through other people. As an Aquarian mother with a social conscience you express yourself through your child. His character development is structured and nurtured by you so the emerging adult can be a reflection of your capabilities. If you attend to the needs and follow the prescribed guidelines you will deliver to the world another humanitarian who fights for his brethren against social injustice. Very likely, he will find himself in public life doing what comes naturally. Without you this could not happen, and so, his bond with you will never be severed.

THE AQUARIUS CHILD

AQUARIANS have the words "I know" as their key and the mental stimulant of air as the governing element. The symbol is commonly portrayed as that of a water-bearer. It is, however, a quandary in some respects; the two wavy lines appear to represent water flowing from a jug but Aquarius is an air sign and not a water sign. These waves could well represent the wind which ripples the water's surface or currents of lightning or electricity. This sign rules the ankles and legs below the knee. The Aquarian baby born in this age of Aquarius is a delightful and perplexing little puzzle.

As an infant he will be pure pleasure and probably very comical. He will enjoy his food, your company and your attention. At the same time he can easily content himself with lying in his crib thinking great thoughts and chasing elusive rainbows. He isn't really a baby at all, but a knowing human being with eyes that study everything around him. A built-in curiosity will stay with him throughout life. You may establish your own routine for him but don't expect him to defer to your judgment or schedule. He will eat when he is hungry, sleep when he is tired, and stir when he feels like it. Try to be as persistent as he is and cultivate in him the feeling of acceptance for routine. This will be of great importance to him later in life. Complete success will not be yours, but a sense of achievement should be for whatever the degree of acceptance. His basic attitude will be negative when it comes to discipline or guidance, but he learns eventually if he is allowed to use the trial-and-error method to reach decisions.

Just when you are finally ready and secure enough to leave him with a baby-sitter for the first time you will run into trouble. He will feel the vibrations in the house and won't settle down. Uranus is his planet so expect lightning and vibrations to permeate the air and his little mind.

As an infant he will not be physically overactive, either thrashing about in his crib or in your arms. He appears to be taking his time to get his mind oriented—he dwells in a mental realm and attempts to reach out to grasp problems. Rest assured that his mind works with lightning speed even though his body may not. A strong will is his forte and most likely his first steps will come about as a result of something that has sparked his interest or curiosity—something he can see but cannot reach. Finally he will strike out and go towards it, then investigate the object of immediate interest.

As a toddler he has no sense of danger and will go where his curiosity takes him. It will be difficult to lead or direct him. He knows just where he wants to go which may be up the stairs or out the back door. You will spend much time chasing him around or retrieving him.

Any toy that challenges the mind will find a fond place in his heart. He is apt to sit enraptured and engrossed for hours with one if you happen to hit upon something that puzzles him a little. He must learn how it works and why. He will also love to be out in good weather. You may find him occupying himself by sitting on the ground watching the bustle of an ant colony or looking intently at the blossoms of a flower. His curiosity will be just as intense about machines and appliances around the house. Everything interests him.

Too often he will go further than he should in trying to get what he wants. Dogged determination steers him, but he is so lovable that you will be hard put to lower the boom and curtail some of his activities. Now hear this! Most really spoiled children are born under the sign of Aquarius. They are too cute, too cuddly and too precocious to discipline easily—all true. However, the early bird can make the worm turn and the faster you recognize the folly of not applying a firm hand the more traumas you will avert in later years.

Esther is an erratic hyperactive little Aquarian and so lovable that she was not even punished for filling the washing machine with clothes from the closet and pouring in Drano instead of a detergent. She was only trying to help and it makes such a cute story. Besides, while mother stood aghast Esther made a fast exit and was soon off shining dad's shoes with furniture polish. After that episode Esther was summarily struck with one of those shoes before she could get away. With a tender reminder of who gives the orders, the Aquarian youngster was carrying more than just a pail of water.

You could go so far as to say that Aquarians are chaotic children about anything. This chaos will extend to his toys and the odd things he may pick up that he considers as valuable as toys. You can buy him a lavish and lovely toy only to find it thrown aside in favor of an egg-beater or empty egg carton. This child can find fascination in many mundane objects. The more strange and bizarre, the more appeal an object will hold for an Aquarian youngster. You'll notice him giving constant attention to his clothing and appearance. He will be forever tucking in his shirt and setting his cap straight. The girls will constantly smooth down their skirts and comb their hair. These children do not accept routine readily. They are not overly neat but are interested in the aesthetic appeal of clothing. A hat is not just meant only to cover the head. Its appearance is of great consequence. There is no hang-up here with fashion or style, just a fetish that will be an insurmountable problem. So, devote your efforts to other areas.

Probably even before birth this airborn child had definite and deep convictions, strong positive and negative feelings. No one can ever justifiably cite this child for being wishy-washy. He would most likely sue for slander if it were to happen in his adulthood. His world consists of blacks and whites. Grays and neuters do not enter his planet and shyness is something that is also non-existent in his character. In like fashion with Sagittarius he will rarely be reluctant to speak his mind—a diplomatic career should be ruled out while you still feast your eyes on the little darling in his crib. Tact must nonetheless be introduced into his character.

The overall picture is one reminiscent of the absent-minded genius. This does not necessarily mean that he will be tops in school. His mind is amazingly brilliant and quick; he is a thinker and not a doer. Teachers easily recognize the innate intelligence of Aquarian children but become frustrated with them just as easily. While your youngster's mind can compete with a space-age computer he still has to cope with the difficulty of a structured routine. Be sure that he will always have the right answer, but insist on his arriving at that answer through his own methods. He will almost never follow the rules for finding the solution to a problem. As it is, he can calculate any problem in his mind and can never use pencil and paper. Learning to spell correctly will seem like a petty detail and of little value to him. No straight A student is here, except in the field of science. Any science teacher will appreciate this child's agile mind.

His penchant for precision makes him a master procrastinator. The concept is admirable but with an Aquarius child the details are apt to fall by the wayside and eventually this fervor leads to laxity and a leisurely neglect of duties, homework, etc., etc., etc. Kid yourself not in believing that pointing out a more direct approach will get him where you want him. He is very apt to fuss about and then deliver unto you a generous portion of the thoughts which will pour forth from his little old jug and you may find yourself all wet. Patience is not a major virtue of your cherub and that means intolerance lurks not too far away. Intolerance, unfortunately, can all too often be equated with outbursts, wrath and irascibility, more commonly referred to as violent temper tantrums. Gentle jabs will be more effective than strong whacks in such instances but the gradual and consistent use of logistics will be most effective, of course, if you don't mind cultivating another Ivan The Terrible—that is your choice!

This is another child who can be a Jack-of-all-trades. Any of the arts will make excellent use of his talents. Many Aquarians are famous musicians. They want to investigate the field to know and feel the mechanics of music and just why it is so beautiful a sound.

Aquarians rule the circulatory system and your Aquarian likes to circulate among people. He will have many friends, join groups and be a very social being. The mind of this child reaches out to grasp and solve problems at all times. Problems of humanity and the masses are his inspiration.

Many of Esther's friendships are, surprisingly, of long duration. Considering the fact that she has all the tact of a Sagittarian and is much more narrow-minded (one channel at a time, please), it's amazing that there are any longstanding relationships in Esther's circle of acquaintances. What is on her mind is on her tongue. The saving grace is that when she is a friend she is a loyal one, giving of herself, generous with all things material. The one bad feature about being a friend of Esther's is that her interests and affections are a bit migratory to say the least. Yesterday she may have confronted a teacher about an alleged injustice to Larry. Today she brushed past him in class without so much as a glance because Ronnie was off in a corner sulking. Tomorrow she may well have forgotten the two of them.

This child is endowed with more social consciousness and conscience than any other. His life revolves around society and he will likely be Tom Dooley, the Peace Corps, and Will Rogers rolled into one beautiful being. All humanity is his oyster and he a pearl, as a social whiz kid and a charming, if somewhat open, sociable adult.

He understands people, their hopes and objectives even at a tender age. He will be as interested in the driver of a garbage disposal truck as he is in the mechanics of the truck. The owner of an antique car or piece of jewelry holds as much fascination as the intricacies of the object under scrutiny. These will be his friends along with his school chums. People take to Aquarius children and are amused by their curiosity and individualistic ways. Your table should always be set for at least one guest.

Don't expect this child to be his brother's keeper; he won't serve well in the role of baby-sitter for younger members of the family. He loves you and the rest of the family but he just isn't that personally interested. He does feel that everyone should fend for himself and fight his own battles. You could try to instill a sense of responsibility in the early years. Never press too hard because he will want to escape. Freedom is all-important to these children in the Aquarius age. You must find the delicate balance for this "don't fence me in" type.

Esther's mother once tried to have her watch over baby brother. Not only should she not have been trusted to concentrate on such a job but mother certainly should not have expected it, even though it was for just ten minutes. Baby Ken got himself all tangled up in the telephone cord while Esther blithely went about her business distributing pieces of bread for the birds in the backyard. She even had a thing or two to say about her mischievous brother to boot.

Health is not usually much of a problem with this lightning rod. Believe it or not, your only potential source for physical concern lies in the realm of possible inactivity or inertia. As he grows into adolescence he will be a great thinker and reader. He will have an avid interest in mental pursuits. Unless he is actively (and subtly) encouraged to the contrary, his interest in sports will be as a spectator only. Physical exercise of some kind is vital to his body; the circulatory system needs help. These children lean toward taking the easy way out in any area that doesn't encompass the use of mental processes. Don't be too tender-hearted here.

If you can manage to prod him on for a long enough period he will make it so that it will keep him happy. A continuation of rote learning will not interest him, and will be a waste as far as he is concerned. Parents of Aquarius children would be wise to see to it that higher education is obtained. Physical labor is just not this child's cup of tea. He would be on the bread line if his income depended on the sweat of his brow.

Lady Luck usually sits in his opinionated corner sopping up some of the devotion and respect you receive from your Aquarian child with a still small voice within. He will never be derelict in his duties or obligations to mother and father alike, never remiss in dispensing warmth or gratitude.

When it gets around to selecting a career or profession, your child will shine forth as a humanitarian in any field—very likely in the world of science (his vibrations can be put to good use). Some will be teachers and will relate to and understand marvelously the children of the next generation—no gap here. Your progeny may well turn out to be the eighth wonder.

Children born between January 20th and January 31st have the double aspect of Uranus in their favor. Insurmountable mountains will be molehills to these native Aquarians. Your child will have no fears and more energy than his fellow water-bearers. Determination and pride will overcome any obstacles and he may well become a famous personality. Throughout life he will gather a host of friends that are unusual, eccentric, and diverse in their attitudes. He will be very anxious to find his place in life and set the world back on its heels with his innovations and innate wisdom.

Infants that come into this world between February 1st and February 9th have the wing-footed Mercury as their personal planet. Mercury controls the nervous system and can make its subjects somewhat excitable. These children will also be very outspoken and honest at all times. People will seek out these Aquarians for their good judgement and mental perspicacity. Your child will most likely gain great fame in the field of business or the arts. Don't despair if you find your child a flexible and fluctuating personality. He will never cease to amaze and delight you.

Venus, the planet of beauty and love, is the ruling planet for the period between February 9th and February 19th. As a result, happiness and cheer will surround this child. He will be sensitive, idealistic, and more joyous than other Aquarius children. Detail and precision will occupy his mind and filter through into his daily routine and habits as well. In infancy he should be taught to be somewhat more flexible so that he will not run the risk of becoming too demanding and exacting in later life. Mental relaxation is a must for his health just as some form of physical exercise should be.

THE AQUARIUS
MOTHER
AND HER CHILD

The Aquarius Mother And The Aries Child

To an Aquarius mother like yourself, an Aries child can be a real headache, especialy an Aries child who demonstrates all of his sign's influences to a marked degree.

You, as an Aquarius, are blessed with a philosophical attitude toward life. To you and others of your sign, success means finding inner peace and a personal sense of worth. To an Aries, on the other hand, success means nothing less than being the very best in any undertaking, no matter how difficult or competitive. You'll have a hard time understanding the depression that your child plunges into after coming away from a situation and you will try to placate your child as best you know how, perhaps with disappointing results.

One important thing is that your competitive little Aries child always have a loving home he can return to when things don't go his way. And when he does, he will do much to perk up your life, which tends to be a shade too passive.

The Aquarius Mother And The Taurus Child

You may find that your little Taurus child is quite a trooper when it comes to taking care of domestic chores that you have a tendency to let ride. Much as you loathe domestic chores, you feel extremely uncomfortable when everything piles up to the point of chaos. Aquarians do not take kindly to chaos; they prefer peace and harmony. For this reason, you will be gratified by this little Taurus dynamo who rushes to perform the necessary, but drab, chores of the household. He actually seems to take pleasure in their completion. Frequently, however, your Taurus child throws himself so wholeheartedly into the task that you become nervous just looking at him, not to mention developing a twinge or two of guilt.

Your Taurus child's devotion to work and responsibility is indeed gratifying, but, you may wish that he would develop some less materialistic goals. Aquarians tend to be humanitarians whose only desire for reward is humanitarianism itself. Perhaps you can bring your child around to an approximation of your thinking.

The Aquarius Mother And The Gemini Child

Your Gemini child and you will undoubtedly have a loving and exciting relationship that will never suffer a complete break up. Your loving nature will be able to absorb any of the possible strains that your restless Gemini child may place on the relationship. His restless and inquisitive nature will, in turn, keep your relationship fresh and stimulating.

Your child may prove disappointing to you in a few areas, but careful guidance and tutelage on your part will work wonders. Gemini children have phenomenally short attention spans and are constantly leaping from an unfinished project to a more alluring and exciting one. In so doing, they may unwittingly hurt those around them. It is your job to see that everybody is happy in the long run, even if your child requires some heavy handling.

Your Gemini child would never do any intentional harm, but sometimes he gets so caught up with things that he is just about incapable of considering the needs of others. One thing to watch out for is your Gemini child's trying to outwit you with his incomparable intelligence.

The Aquarius Mother And The Cancer Child

As an Aquarius mother, you should be forewarned about the dangers of this particular kind of relationship, mainly because Aquarius is willing to negotiate for peace at almost any cost, and Cancer is an expert at this kind of warfare. You will have to summon up every particle of your inner strength in order to keep yourself from giving in to your little Cancer's every whim just because of the threat of a tantrum.

If you can bring yourself to present a strong and unrelenting front, your child will, in time, refrain from these unbecoming tactics and become, ironically enough, a much happier and more content child in the bargain. Once you have solved this problem, you will have set the stage for a wonderful relationship with your child.

Both Aquarius and Cancer are extra loving people, so you can imagine the strength and fervor of the bonds that will bind you to your child. Do be careful, however, not to be too overly protective since Cancer children frequently need a little extra push to exercise their independence.

The Aquarius Mother And The Leo Child

There will be few mother/child relationships more rewarding than that of the Aquarius mother and the Leo child. Your Leo child will forever be the energetic type, but you can rest assured that this will never manifest itself in frustrations that could hinder a healthy relationship. The Leo child never lets frustration hold him back in any way. Leo children are so resourceful that they can maneuver their way out of any situation.

Your frequently passive Aquarius nature will benefit in many ways from close contact with your dynamic and inquisitive little Leo, and he in turn will benefit from your generous and loving nature. Leo children sometimes are so concerned with getting on with their adventures that they may overlook the feelings of others quite unintentionally. You can help them in this regard.

If both of you have the normal characteristics for your respective signs, your lives should be filled with animals; in fact, your home may quite easily become a zoo if you do not watch out. You will have enough love to go around, however.

The Aquarius Mother And The Virgo Child

You, as an Aquarius mother, will have a ridiculously easy time raising this puzzling Virgo child to maturity. In fact, you might get the impression that your Virgo child could have raised himself almost as effectively without any help from you.

Aquarius is a great admirer of independence and self-determination and will be impressed by Virgo children's display of maturity at such a young age.

What may bother you a little about this independent little creature of yours is his preoccupation with the practical and the pragmatic. It is not that your child has any grandiose ambitions at the expense of others. This singlemindedness may turn you off, perhaps to an appreciable degree. On the other hand, you could use a little bit more direction yourself. With any luck at all, you two can join forces and trade some of those qualities for the betterment of both of you. Don't regard your Virgo as a lovely child so easy to raise with a minimum of effort. Throw yourself into the relationship, nevertheless.

The Aquarius Mother And The Libra Child

Aquarius mothers will be more than capable of appreciating this delicate, sensitive, and considerate creature that is your Libra child. You may find yourself becoming a bit too over-protective of your child. You could do him much harm by attempting to shield him from unpleasantries that are, unfortunately, part of life that will always be with him, even after you are no longer there. This is not to say that you should push your child in the direction of morbidity or tragedy, but rather that you should acquaint him with the less harmonious and unpleasant aspects of life, all the while being an inspiring and supportive influence to him.

The proper course to take may seem to be a little wider than a tightrope, but you will be amazed at how easily the solution appears to be when you meet the situations head on.

Your life will always be surrounded by bleakness if your Libra child has his way. You may join in this healthy pursuit wholeheartedly, depending upon how your life is going at a particular time.

The Aquarius Mother And The Scorpio Child

Your Scorpio child will give you a run for your money, and have no doubts upon that score. This passionate, determined creature will be a complete enigma to you and leave you at the point of distraction more often than not. You will fail to see where he gets all of that driving inner force, keeping him so constantly on the go. But no matter how far and wide he searches, he still never seems to find inner peace. What you cannot understand, however, is just that a Scorpio does not really want to find out exactly what he is looking for, mainly because he is having such a grand old time searching and investigating.

You can perhaps accept this motivation of his but you will never grow to like it. Your main reason will be that you feel rejected by a child who hardly ever seems to notice you. Take comfort however, for Scorpios have a deeper capacity for love than most other children.

The Aquarius Mother And The Sagittarius Child

You and your Sagittarius child will most likely have a relationship unmarked by serious rifts or major disagreements. You, more than other mothers, are usually content with your own life and less likely to want to live through your child. For this reason, you can usually accept whatever future your child decides for himself without feeling any great disappointment if this life style runs counter to your own. And your Sagittarius child will have such great plans for himself that you would be unlikely to disapprove anyway.

Your loving and solid nature will provide just the right kind of support for this restless Sagittarius of yours. He will be constantly running off to joust with new windmills. He will appreciate the fact that you are always there waiting for him, willing to offer your strength at all times. Your Sagittarius child's goals may seem a bit too ambitious for your tastes, but you will value the stimulating relationship you two can develop over a period of time.

The Aquarius Mother And The Capricorn Child

You, as an Aquarius mother, have more than the usual share of love for your child, but you may be lacking in the area of down-to-earth duties of motherhood. You really have to watch this tendency to be a little lax, especially when you have a busy little Capricorn child. They hang around just waiting for a chance to step in and take over your duties one by one. This would be great except for one thing; once they start taking over your duties, they also start taking over a corresponding amount of authority.

If you do not put your foot down soon enough, the day might come (about 10 years early) when you find that you have no control over your child anymore. Capricorns, for some reason, have to be convinced that childhood, with its relative freedom from financial pressure and responsibility, is the best time of a person's life. We all need to learn this to some extent, but Capricorns seem to abhore dependence on others. They grow only when someone is in their care.

The Aquarius Mother And The Aquarius Child

With an Aquarius child, you can reach a plateau of understanding that will be a source of inspiration and strength to both of you. From an early age, you can detect in your child those qualities that you most admire; serenity, self-control and generosity. Your Aquarius child will be ridiculously easy to cope with as a baby, and the problems won't increase much with age.

When you meet a well-dressed, unperturbed, and casual woman with a delightfully charming and incredibly well-mannered child, you would not be going out on to much of a limb if you pegged them both as Aquarius. You, Aquarius, are fond of white and of long, flowing clothes, and Aquarius children are no exception. You will make a striking pair and will be exactly the type desired in mother/child photography. Maybe you could pick up some extra money by modelling with this (almost) spittin' image of yourself. Others will be impressed with your philosophical attitude toward life and will marvel at the little philosopher you have raised.

The Aquarius Mother And The Pisces Child

You and your Pisces child could have some rocky roads to negotiate together if you both, and you especially, don't make an extra effort to keep your relationship strong and lasting. The problem arises from the fact that you as a lover of peace and harmony would rather turn the other cheek than risk an argument. You accept a situation rather than look beneath the surface for ways in which this situation could prove unfavorable for you. To put it concisely, you would rather let people take advantage of you than think that people would be capable of such a heinous crime.

Your perceptive child, on the other hand, is always delving beneath the surface for the truth, no matter how unpleasant. Your child will lose no time in telling you point blank how much of a sucker you are being. Naturally, you are not going to appreciate this revelation, and you are going to develop some resentment toward this precocious youngster if you don't watch out. One thing will especially irritate you—your child is usually *right*.

STAR GUIDE
FOR
AQUARIUS

Symbol	●	The Water-Bearer
Ruling Planet	●	Uranus
Element	●	Air
Gender	●	Masculine
Key Words	●	I Know
Birthstones	●	Amethyst, Sapphire
Favorite Flowers	●	Lilac, Daffodil
Best Colors	●	Blue, Green, Silver
Mineral	●	Uranium
Favorite Music	●	Rhapsodies
Favorite Pastime	●	Literature
Lucky Number	●	8
Best Days	●	Monday, Thursday
Compatible Signs	●	Gemini, Libra, Sagittarius
Incompatible Signs	●	Taurus, Scorpio

FAMOUS PEOPLE BORN UNDER THE SIGN OF THE WATER-BEARER

HENRY ADAMS
MARION
  ANDERSON
FRANCIS BACON
TALLULAH
  BANKHEAD
JOHN
  BARRYMORE
JACK BENNY
OMAR BRADLEY
GEORGE BURNS
ROBERT BURNS
LORD BYRON
LEWIS CARROLL
KATHERINE
  CORNELL
CHARLES
  DARWIN
CHARLES
  DICKENS
JIMMY DURANTE
THOMAS A.
  EDISON
ZSA ZSA GABOR
CLARK GABLE
GALILEO
HORACE
  GREELEY

WILLIAM
  HARRISON
LOUIS NIZER
S. J. PERELMAN
LEONTYNE PRICE
RONALD REAGAN
JACKIE
  ROBINSON
NORMAN
  ROCKWELL
FRANKLIN D.
  ROOSEVELT
DEAN RUSK
WILLIAM
  RANDOLPH
  HEARST
VICTOR
  HERBERT
MAURICE
  HEWLETT
HENRY IRVING
JEROME KERN
EARTHA KITT
FRITZ KREISLER
JACK LEMMON
SINCLAIR LEWIS

CHARLES
  LINDBERGH
ABRAHAM
  LINCOLN
DOUGLAS
  MacARTHUR
HAROLD
  MacMILLAN
WILLIAM
  McKINLEY
EDWARD MANET
W. SOMERSET
  MAUGHAM
CLAUDE MONET
JAMES
  MICHENER
PAUL NEWMAN
FRANZ
  SCHUBERT
ABBA HILLEL
  SILVER
ADLAI
  STEVENSON
JULES VERNE
ROBERT WAGNER
WENDELL
  WILKIE

THE
PISCES
MOTHER
February 20th — March 20th

YOU are a Doris Day girl next door, a den mother and an all-round female. It is only natural then, that your maternal instinct is a strong one in the old-fashioned and traditional sense. The stereotyped Southern belle of novel fame and movie stardom must have been a Pisces. This female's strength lay in her coyness. Very seldom did she have to face the Perils of Pauline all by herself. There was usually a line of front porch Johnnies waiting to be of service even if it meant just holding her parasol.

Your symbol aptly depicts the ambiguity of your personality and the element of water only reinforces this characteristic. The fish swim through the waters in opposite directions only to be caught up by the undertow and carried off by the tides. This is somewhat indicative of a common lot for many Pisces women —many conflicts that can bring a vale of tears.

Since you are often prone to find yourself in discordant situations you have managed to develop a knack for coping with circumstances that are not always harmonious. Of course, it is impossible to maintain your composure in all adverse situations. So, you very understandably become irritable or cantankerous at times. Fortunately, you are blessed with a compassionate and supersensitive nature. It is very likely that you will restrict these tiny tantrums so that they are out of the sight and hearing of your child. You know too well what damage can be inflicted upon an infant by moods of this nature. There are possible feelings of rejection and guilt for starters.

Hopefully your fish are all together and you have learned to turn the tides in your favor so the fish slide along smoothly, now hither, now thither. You manage this with fragile fingers but a firm fist. If somewhere along the river leading to adulthood your fish were separated, then you have several problems to handle as a mother. Not certain of your own identity you constantly dive into deep waters looking for your other half, without which you are morose and forlorn. Everywhere you turn you imagine you see yourself, but it is always a mirage. Don't confuse the arrival of your child with anything more than just that. He is not a messenger or reincarnation of your missing self. Do not attempt to mold him into what you are not, with the idea that your faults are just omissions that the missing fish would possess. This is just a fantasy.

Fantasies are not restricted to the few of you with dubious identities. Each of you are deeply spiritual and aesthetically inclined. You wish to live in Paradise where all is beautiful and harmonious. Paradise is uninhabitable (if indeed it does exist) and fanciful dreams of perfection exist only in an unreal world. Infants cannot exist in an unreal world and, surprise, neither can you. Self-induced hypnosis is called for to encourage a sense of reality in you.

You have a dreadful fear of facing life head on and feel that it consists of one disaster followed by another. You have met with successes achieved through diligent effort, not the touch of Lady Luck as you prefer to believe. Examine the record and you will find that Luck has played no part in the things you have accomplished. Your mental capacity is tremendous and there is little you cannot master. Now you must learn to deal with life on terra firma for your child's sake. Adapt yourself and be philanthropic toward your favorite charity, keeping in mind that charity really begins at home.

You do not have the strength of a Scorpio, nor the determination of an Aries, but you are the most introspective and subjective of all the sun-signs. To withdraw into yourself is an escape from the world and you look within for the solution. That isn't all bad, except that the answer lies in the outside world that stretches out before you. Reaching for castles in the sky may seem easier and more inviting, but the world is where you have to be in order to provide a system and schedule to build character in your child. Try it, you'll like it.

So utterly feminine is your nature that no one can furnish such a warm, welcome sanctuary of security for your babe in arms. Once you realize just how secure is the haven, you will be bursting with pride and a glimmer of self-confidence. You should move in yourself, and henceforth castles will enter your world only in storybook fairy tales.

Your softness and tenderness provide complete serenity for your child. Never do you wish to become a domineering mother—a protective one maybe, never overbearing. Compassion is your forte and children flourish quickly in a warm environment. He will flourish further as you make him believe he can accomplish any feat, and he certainly will try, if just to please you.

When your child first tries his hand at something new you must take care to appraise him of his possibilities for success or failure. Too often you may be apt to dismiss all failures as bad luck or blame a third party. The first time you try this approach should be the last. Yes, success is not always achieved, but bad luck has nothing to do with it. Teach him that perseverance, work, and a strong will will do. Disappointments are a large part of life, and to a child they assume greater magnitude. It is necessary to explain how the world turns, that unrewarding efforts are still meritorious.

Most of the difficulties you will encounter stem from your own insecurity and lack of self-confidence. You are highly gifted artistically yet afraid to show your talents in public. Your shyness and secretiveness also relate back to the same lack. The abandonment of work or a project can occur when you reach a difficult stage. It is like the kiss of death for the work, due to the fear of failure. Seldom do you participate in group activity since you have convinced yourself that you do not possess the wherewithall to compete. The imagined pains of failure and defeat appear more acute than the embarassment of retreat.

All these things sound somewhat immature and similar to problems that your child might have to encounter. Rather, they are all yours—those of a dainty, fragile, and capricious mother of many a mood. With an understanding of the "why's for much of your instinctive behavior, you should now be able to eradicate many problems and learn to live comfortably with some of the others. Of prime importance is that they should in no way effect the development of your child's character.

Your ego needs boosting, as does his. This can best come about through the building of his character on a sure and steady footing. It is extremely difficult for you to be a disciplinarian but you must learn not to be overly permissive. Mandatory and firm guidance must replace an overabundance of understanding. To not provide these requisites for your child could constitute grounds for the SPCC to intervene for child neglect, I believe.

You will bill and coo with delight at his every movement and act. This is the time to construct those castles in the sky (as long as he is told that they are unreal). You must force yourself to become a pushy mother at this stage and coax him to stand alone. Nothing can cripple more quickly than a mother who sacrifices all so that her child may be spared the agonies and anxieties of growing up.

Your patience knows no bounds with this child and very few mothers would lend both their ears to his problems. He will cherish you as dearly as can be. Having a fantastic imagination and love for spontaniety will endear you to him even more. You understand each other well and this makes for harmony. He will never be bored and his relaxed environment should provide the perfect setting for your gentle coaxing and prodding—just a little at a time. Do not cajole or nag. He could easily bury his head and follow your example of disappearing in search of himself. If need be, allow him to soul-search at a much later age instead of going off on a wild goose chase now.

Yes, Pisces, it is better to give than to receive, but since you have such a difficult task in disciplining yourself it is advisable that you require your child to show appreciation and respect for all he receives from you. In the material sense, you give so many toys, clothes, parties, etc. that Christmas comes to your house once a week. You tend to be extravagant in your own right and pamper yourself a bit, as did that southern belle of yore. Showering your child with too many goodies will not increase his love for you. It will only bring him to expect his wish to be your command and that of others. Ultimately, this will result in a deeply-rooted selfish streak that cannot be easily wiped out.

In your own context, extravagance is a need for affection, a booster for a deflated or non-existent ego. It provides you with innumerable tangible possessions that you hope will compensate for those spiritual things you have convinced yourself you lack—not true at all. In any event, following the same spendthrift ways with your child is, in a sense, smothering him to the point that he will possibly develop insecurities or even an inferiority complex. This madness is no method for securing his independence.

You are a psychic and sensitive Pisces mother posessed of mystical and secret powers. Make your child evolve into a man without martyring yourself and you may yet move into that castle in the sky.

THE PISCES CHILD

"I believe" are the key words for this last sign of the zodiac which is governed by the element of water. The symbol of Pisces is that of two fish, one swimming upstream and the other downstream. The symbol can also represent the two feet of man which bear the weight of the human body.

Your Piscean baby will most likely be pretty, cuddly, dreamy-eyed and a sheer delight to behold. As an infant this child is the answer to every mother's prayer. He looks so adorable and delectable. This is not to say that he won't cry loudly—don't expect to bring a mute home from the hospital. He'll start with a small whimper and a bit of fussing before he lets loose with that first real cry. This child is one of the most sensitive, emotionally and physically, in the zodiac. Watch for diaper rash, a too hot bottle, and clothes that bind or are too heavy. These children are undoubtedly the first to instigate the term "tender loving care" since they demand and thrive on affection and demonstrative love. Here is another child who will be difficult to pace into a routine. He is dreamy and misty-eyed and will cry very easily at the slightest provocation, such as a harsh tone in your voice. The Piscean infant wants to eat and sleep according to his mood, so he won't take too kindly to the imposition of a schedule.

Since these children are always absorbed in their dreams and fantasies, they will be less active than the average child of the same age. There is not deep thinking like that of the Aquarian child—just pleasant reveries. You can almost see and hear the little fairies he has around him when he is in his crib cooing and jabbering away. This baby is a natural for mobiles over his crib and soft-tinkling musical toys. Your baby needs emotional love and support to feel secure in life.

As he develops he will be quite the charmer; he'll charm you and the entire family making cute sounds and faces. Keeping you so fascinated ensures having you close by most of the time. Actually, he will be almost psychic about the moods of the household. He can sense excitement, anger, anxiety, and sadness. Any mood is quickly picked up. He will always sense when something is right or wrong. This may seem like exceptional brilliance to you. In a way, it is —but he feels things like a devotee of ESP.

It will be great fun to watch when he walks for the first time. He knows exactly what to do but, nevertheless, you'll see his little feet rising way up high in the air before he steps down almost as if he is walking over invisible flowers or walking in water. You'll get the impression that he thinks he is about to float. Once he gets the knack of it he will be extremely light-footed and move around very nicely. He'll never be in too much of a hurry.

As a pre-school child he will be exceptionally easy to entertain. For this child one must have music playing most of the time. He will love all forms of music. Pretty picture books will appeal to him to no end, especially fairly tales that are illustrated. Don't be surprised if he lives every role and identifies himself with princes and princesses, fairy god-mothers and enchanted castles. Anything with an air of magic about it will entrance this child, a jack-in-the-box, or any toy that has a hidden opening. Secret hiding places for special toys will be par for the course. Lucite balls that have people, objects, or snow floating around inside will absolutely mesmerize this tot. All the dreamy, charming toys fascinate him just as he will fascinate and charm your family and friends.

Heaven on earth is the best way to describe what Hope's mother felt she had found in her crib—a fairy tale come true —and Hope was perfectly willing to go along with it all. She plays the role to the hilt and it suits her well. Disneyland might have been designed by her for her own pleasure. Pisces children are always tardy and Hope is no exception. She even delayed her entrance into the world. Reality is not within her ken but fear of the unknown is, however, and that is why Hope has some moon-child traits—

sensitivity, an excellent memory and frequent forays into magic mountains. Mother started by having labor induced, and so is not cowardly about prodding Hope into action before someone else less suitable beats her to the punch.

Nonetheless, you'll still have trouble getting your little dreamer into a routine of any kind or to take direct orders as he grows older. A word to the wise here; always suggest softly and accompany the suggestion with a love tap or a peck on the cheek. Don't be overly protective though. He must be taught practicality and to face some degree of reality before he has to face the world. Too much protection will retain those dreamy fantasies and he won't be able to cope with life on a real basis. You must differentiate for him between dreaming about something and actually doing it. Indicate that the difference is as great as that between night and day. You must also urge him to perform practical tasks around the house for you. He won't like it one bit but here is where you reason with your water-baby. Explain to him that it is your duty to teach him these things and that you would be a failure as a mother if you did not; you might just reach him. Be certain that you are loving when you try this approach. If he feels that the performance of his duties is solely to please you, he will argue that he can demonstrate his love without doing these chores.

You then must hold your ground. The responsibilities of assigned tasks disciplines each of your Pisces fishes. Isolationist tactics will only serve to send him into fantasyland again as a great martyr or his own favorite companion. Exile is one chastisement that is not going to work.

Remember the symbol of Pisces as being a sign of ambiguity or going hither then thither, and you will realize that he is flexible as well as confused at times. Playing plastic man with his pals does make him adaptable but also makes him too easily influenced by others, making him an easy prey for more wily or goulish companions. Get to know his playmates and weed out the ones that are more than just impish before junior starts to emulate them.

Hope sometimes appears to be several children rolled into one; as dreamy as a moon-child, as picayune and meticulous as a Virgo, as artistic as a Libra, etc., etc., etc. It is just this complex and flexible personality that is the troublespot. Hope would sooner fall in with someone else's scheme and a follower be (of an Aries or Leo, undoubtedly), than strike out on her own. She aims to please anyone, everyone and that only leads down the road to mischief. Every day some small prank is instigated by a ringleader that Hope obeys with few questions. Mama's little angel has all the potential for becoming a devil. Wisely, her parents learned to keep her time occupied and her chores plentiful. The problem will recur again as she cannot be tied forever to a chaperone.

As a student he may surprise you. His mind is capable of absorbing many things easily. This is not necessarily mental agility. He has the type of mind that just knows something without giving it much thought. He will learn everything presented to him and very rapidly. Expect his teacher to comment on his daydreaming in class, occurring most likely when the subject matter or teacher (possibly both) are boring him. His natural curiosity will assure that his grades will be top-notch with a creative teacher. Modern, progressive teachers and schools will make the most of your child's abilities. Here he will be able to pace himself and not waste energy trying to adapt to a rigid routine. The drudgery of basic addition and subtraction will be dull for him but he will love the intrigue related to higher matematics and problem-solving.

His mind is somewhat akin to a blotter and more likely than not he has a photographic memory. Should he, however, be one of the "have nots" rest assured that at least he still absorbs everything through osmosis. Much of the time in later years you may be annoyed by his perfect memory as he can remind you of unkept promises, contradictions, etc., but you won't squelch the expansion of his elephantomatic computer bank just because it evokes some occasional criticism of home and hearth, will you?

His health is not like that of the sturdy Taurean child. Both his psyche and his body are hyper-sensitive. He will fall victim to most of the common childhood diseases. Much good food and rest should be provided. There will be certain days when he just won't feel like going to school. He won't be able to tell you exactly why he feels miserable but he probably does. Even a bad dream is upsetting to his system. It will be as mysterious to him as it is to you. Pisces is a water sign and hence linked to emotion; not the open, heart-on-the-sleeve emotion of the moon-children, not the repressed inner seethings of the Scorpions. Do realize though that this child's waters run deep. His not feeling well enough for school is far from the typical child's excuse for a day off. He means business and is really naively honest.

Your child will undoubtedly be attracted to the arts—dance, music and poetry—he'll want to try them all. Luckily he has the ability to float through his lessons every week. He will be happy in taking these lessons and will be thrilled beyond words if he can relate this to someone he has seen in the movies or on television. He is very apt to surprise you when it comes to practicing and his performance of these lessons. Probably he will do better with his interest than he does with his school work.

Before you conclude that you were promised a sweet little blossom and have raised a rose garden in full bloom, look out for the pricklies. Tensions run high and rampant with your little fish and any new situation that removes him from his watery home causes him to flip-flop all over the place. Testing his adaptability in strange environments creates fear and tension. Testing his knowledge in school will get him up tight. Only time and tenderhearted care will temper the delirium tremors. Keep the faith. Even some of your best friends may go through life, shaking and shivering every time they have to speak before the local PTA.

Whatever you do, don't make a fuss over what you consider to be his short-comings. Underachievement is not a dirty word, and if it were, it would rarely enter your child's sphere. The only difficulty is that he seems to feel it lurking around every corner. Some children are afraid of the dark or Dracula and some fishlets dread disappointment and downfall. With his emotional make-up, melancholy and gloom move in at the most premature or imagined hint of failure. See to it that you move in as quickly with charm, charisma, and light cajolery, never patronize or condone his feelings of inadequacy or you will aid and abet the christening of a colossal complex that could eventually bring him to wrack and ruin in later life.

So sensitive and introspective is this little mite that you will actualy believe him to be possessed with ESP and psychic powers. The introspection will keep him from iterating many feelings and thoughts and as esoteric as that may be it can also mean trouble. pain, grudges and hostilities multiply faster than rabbits when confined, and are sometimes infectious. You should be thrilled when he feels free enough to throw an occasional tantrum. For him it is the equivalent of an inoculation against more serious sickness.

Hope is so super-sensitive and her mind so telepathic that she is Mother Confessor and advisor to her peers. Since she has been so precocious and proficient in helping other children (and doing it well) her parents have steered her toward working with younger children to explore this talent and to develop confidence in herself.

If his early schooling has been good and has not discouraged or repressed him this child will look forward to college and will do quite well. Many will go on to graduate school and higher degrees. He is much like that seer mentioned previously. He wants to know as much as he can about the world. He is anxious to see if some of his thoughts ring true and study is a means for finding this out. Art school or a music conservatory will be fairly probable prospects as will a general fine arts background that can be transformed into a vocation. It is also very likely that your child may rush to return to his natural habitat, seeking a career that will keep him close to the sea. Anything even remotely related to liquids and fluids is a posibility. From a fisherman to an oil tycoon, he can adapt and function superbly on any level. This is his natural realm. Don't be fooled by your little Piscean. He is no weakling, as any angler that has tangled with a sturdy fish can tell you.

Pisceans born between February 20th and February 29th have the spiritually awakening planet of Neptune as their personal ruling planet. This baby will be far more sensitive than the average Piscean (and that is going some) and his faculties for initiation and invention will be unsurpassable. There will almost seem to be a "guiding light" at times that leads him directly to his goal or objective without a wasted minute or motion. No insignificant trivia will take up space in his memory bank. Moodiness is prevalent but controllable.

Children born between March 1st and March 10th are graced with the benefits of the moon—namely the vital life sources. This child will be domestic, home-loving and especially imaginative. He will be more temperamental and fluctuating than his brethren and probably more secretive as well. Psychic powers will enable him to work marvelously in public service or in a position that requires contact with groups of people. He will find arguments and conflicts of any nature rather distasteful. Harmony in the home is of utmost importance to his emotional stability and mental health.

Birthdays of children that fall between March 11th and March 20th have Mars, the symbol of energy and war, as a personal ruling planet. Your child will be spurred on to great heights and have a personality that has more positive aspects than the ordinary Piscean child. A depth of understanding and comprehension enables this individual to achieve the goals that he feels important as mainstays in his life. Here is someone who does not dream idle thoughts; he has the facility to make all his dreams come true. Long range plans and projects take on new meanings and possibilities with this Piscean.

THE PISCES
MOTHER
AND HER CHILD

The Pisces Mother And The Aries Child

The forceful and impetuous nature of the Aries child is a difficult one for you to handle with aplomb. There will be many times when you feel completely unable to cope with his demands and tantrums. You must somehow dull your sensitivity and exercise your adaptability to conflicting situations. This relationship will have many head-on collisions.

The greatest stumbling blocks will be your compassion and passivity. An Aries child will quickly sense these weaknesses and capitalize on them with both steely determination and seemingly childish innocence. Never be reluctant to administer discipline with an iron fist—but one that is concealed under sheepskin. Pushing and pulling will only exhaust you and give vent to his energies through an intense outburst which could be verbally or physically violent.

Development of his leadership qualities and aggressiveness must be careful and concise in your approach. They should be channeled in a positive direction and balanced to prevent him from becoming the omnipotent Big Brother.

His skills are many. He will experiment and engage in a variety of activities and then lose the interest and initiative to follow through. You must sort out his most predominant talents, foster them and instill in him a constancy of purpose so that he may achieve success in later life and bring you pride.

The Pisces Mother And The Taurus Child

The Taurus child is one that requires tender and tactful handling. His basic nature is congenial and generous but he also possesses the obstinancy of his symbol the bull. Care must be taken to keep him from becoming provoked, for he is capable of seeing red when rebellious and you are the closest target within his range. In addition to agitating your psyche he is very apt to place a knapsack on his back and *not* bid you "adieu". He is, however, a listener, and if you can justify your complaint he will be quick to acquiesce to the error of his ways.

Since Taurus children are more introverted than most you should encourage him to socialize more and cultivate friendships. His need for attention makes him very responsive to love and affection. It is important to his self-confidence that it not only come from you but from his peers as well. You should see to it that his companions are extroverts and more devoted to their studies than your child. Outside stimuli are essential to bring his mental training to life and his artistic learnings to a successful performance level.

Hold his hand gently, love him dearly and Venus will almost guarantee many beautiful tomorrows filled with pleasures.

The Pisces Mother And The Gemini Child

You will spin many fairy tales and fantasies together and spend much time in never-never-land. As commander-in-chief of entertainment, you must impress your Gemini twins to distinguish, between fiction and fact so that he can find his place in reality.

This child is highly nervous and very "up-tight," so you must impress him with your tranquil and gentle personality to induce greater relaxation. His health could even be affected by his inability to unwind or rest. Undue tension will bring on fits of nervous energy and temper. You must keep him on a seesaw and alternate periods of relaxation with busy work.

You both often cloak your timidity with an outwardly bold and independent facade. So you have insight into his vulnerable areas and can recognize the first signs of trouble-a-coming.

The Gemini child has a natural proclivity for learning just so long as you provide material for study. Do not, however, leave the Brothers Grimm on his night-table too often.

Given a chance to observe your indigenous generosity and compassion, his future achievements will be many; and who said fairy tales don't come true?

The Pisces Mother And The Cancer Child

The moon-child can prove to be the easiest of the lot with whom to establish a harmonious relationship relatively friction free. You share so many common needs. Both of you are moody, supersensitive, fanciful, clingy, and have a craving for affection. There are not only all these but blessed understanding to boot. He does have a bit of an edge though on the power scale.

There will be problems, however, with such a duo. You can adequately feed the aforementioned a special diet, but be sure to add a few dashes of pepper and spice. This moon-child must learn to function on his own and is a perfect student in the school of "monkey see, monkey do". Discretion must be used to create a balanced structure that encompasses activity, stimulation, and a drive for independence. You are the teacher and all this will require a part-time change of pace and life style for you. Bolster his ego and confidence with words of love—give what you would like to receive yourself. Discipline his moods in a kindly manner and apply motivation for his lethargy in a gentle way. What you indubitably will learn from motherhood will make you eligible for *Who's Who* fame and your child will never wander too far from the celebrity he loves and admires

The Pisces Mother And The Leo Child

There will be some bumpy spots with this combination but no relationship of substance can be all smooth.

Your little Leo will rile you with his regal airs and demands but in your own mysterious and subtle way you will tactfully be able to tie him, heart and soul, around your pinky finger.

Until then, his egotism and flair for the dramatic will provide sharp contrast to your spiritual and traditional manner. These leonine traits could encourage you to start swimming upstream in search of a fuller life. He should learn to emulate your adaptability and develop compassion for the masses.

Unfortunately, Leo can be condescending far too often (as sociable as they are) and is usually charming enough to get away with it. Be your capricious self and pay no heed to the mighty roar. Chances are that he will come around purring like a kitten. Only your approval and support will keep him from slipping into despondency. Patience and prudence are in your corner. Humor the wounded lion and he will come to realize that he is not such an independent creature after all.

The admiration and respect he will come to have for you just proves that he is not a lion cub that was born free. Your newly gained self-esteem will make you seek some of the excitement and adventure you have missed for so long. Maybe it can be shared with a domesticated lion.

The Pisces Mother And The Virgo Child

A Virgo child will vex you frequently as he plods along behind you, methodically criticizing your inefficient ways. He will be slow and practical in his suggestions for your reform but his ideas will be sound and logical. So don't toss them aside too quickly.

Your acute mind will allow you to aptly impress your unemotional and straight-laced nature with some of your spiritualism and sensitivity for the beautiful things in life.

You have the advantages of wisdom and understanding that will keep you at least two lengths ahead in a mother-child situation that should be mother dominated. His stick-to-it-iveness and seriousness of purpose must be loosened up and it is your whimsical nature that can accomplish the job. Otherwise your Virgo will be an adult who at the age of five never enjoyed a childhood.

The relationship will never be the easiest for either of you but as soon as each of you realizes that it is to your mutual advantage to have your traits intertwine, the relationship will not be the hardest to live with either.

The Pisces Mother And The Libra Child

Your Libra child will probably present less problems to you than most, although he will just as probably give you a good run for your money. The harmony in the relationship will revolve around the common denominators of idealism and a love of beauty. Beyond that, be prepared.

Though the Libra child tends to be absent-minded, he is very alert. He intuitively knows how to maneuver through life wisely and well. It may take him an inordinate length of time to weigh all the odds in an issue, but invariably his decision will be the right one.

On the other hand, you tend to avoid any direct confrontation and are less than diplomatic when cornered. In traumatic or panic situations though, you are the one that can handle yourself while he will sit by meditating and proving himself to be a source of annoyance.

Once you realize that he has the strong will and the competence to achieve his goals, you will be able to respect him without fear of a coup d'etat.

The Pisces Mother And The Scorpio Child

All of your maternal instincts combined will most likely not be enough to prepare you for the uninhibited passionate thing before you masquerading as a child.

He demands much from you and more from the world. This relationship will never favor you forever but take heart in knowing that he can make the world his oyster. Once you accustom yourself to the idea that you have given birth to a human dynamo you will be better equipped to use your secret powers and inject him with subtle doses of self-control and moderation.

Do not dismiss his fierce drive and overwhelming determination as the hull of a bad seed. You could do with a little more spirit yourself. This is not to say that you should not make an attempt to curb those extreme tendencies as best you can.

The closeness in your relationship will not be based on tenderness but on the difference in your temperaments. The Scorpio child needs a solid and compassionate ally so that the two different worlds may find strength and solace in each other.

The Pisces Mother And The Sagittarius Child

This mother-child combination should be one of few emotional traumas. Each of you is blessed with congeniality and good nature. The aspects are favorable for mutual consideration and recognition of needs.

The Sagittarius archer is always aiming for a new target and should be granted a pilot's license strictly for his airborn hours. His day-dreams are continuous and lofty. You will share some time weaving wispy dreams with him but must exert some discipline to prevent him from being carried away on the tail of an arrow.

Your child is so uncomplicated and straightforward that it will not be necessary to waste any time deciphering his motivation. Since he is so transparent and open-minded, too, there will be few occasions that call for severe punishment.

Beware, for Sagittarians, young and old alike, suffer some degree of foot-in-mouth disease. To say that they lack tact and diplomacy is to say that black widow spiders are *never* dangerous.

Teach him the value of holding a tighter rein on his dreams and tongue and maybe you will be travelling companions in flight every so often.

The Pisces Mother And The Capricorn Child

Since your child possesses greater strength, the problem is akin to the Pisces symbol of the two fish swimming in opposite directions. You are the one to sink or swim, not he.

You recognize your child's maturity and competence, and therefore are very apt to subconsciously leave him on his own. He will embrace such freedom eagerly and eventually will want to asume some of your duties to demonstrate his independence. Naturally as this grows so will your dependence upon him and guess who's ruling the roost soon.

Being permissive is one thing, being lazy is another. Unless you come to terms with yourself while he is still a youngster, there will be no relationship for you to worry about because he is precocious, too.

The best way to maintain an alliance of any nature is to plan ahead and be on your best behavior. That requires attending to the duties and responsibilities of motherhood when the first storm watch appears and not when you are already in the eye of the hurricane.

The Pisces Mother And The Aquarius Child

Harmony and beauty will be the glues that bind your relationship firmly. Each of you have much to contribute to the education of the other and it is the mutual desire to do so that really counts.

You will delight in his aptitude and appeal. His manner will enable him to get away with many misdemeanors that would not be neglected with other children. He is unpredictable. Tomorrow he may change his thoughts and not be the angel and humanist he is today. So can he react to your disciplinary measures when they are exercised.

Take preventive measures to keep from shielding him against the harshness and uncertainties of the world. One indirect way is, if you are overly protective of him, to procrastinate for a lifetime and a half. Enough opportunities can pass him by during his career to make unemployment security only a memory. Prod him with a strong arm that he can lean on temporarily as a guide to proper direction.

The Pisces Mother And The Pisces Child

Birds of a feather, etc., etc., etc.—chances are definitely in favor of a satisfying and congenial bond centered around mutual desires and opinions. The life you have chosen for yourself will not be adverse for your child (unless, it's a girl Pisces—influenced by Women's Lib).

There is no doubt about the fact that there will be fewer conflicts in the rearing of this child than with any other. He will seldom question your authority or rebel against your just and fair discipline. This is not to suggest that he is selfless or wishy-washy, but rather that he is clever. He concurs with your judgment since he knows you are right. When you are not he will let you know.

Bear in mind that you must not sit back and gloat over a perfect relationship. Some see their faults in others. You may not have this capacity. Think ahead of his need to stand alone.

STAR GUIDE
FOR
PISCES

Symbol	●	The Fishes
Ruling Planet	●	Neptune
Element	●	Water
Gender	●	Feminine
Key Words	●	I Believe
Birthstones	●	Aquamarine, Pearl
Favorite Flowers	●	Lilac, Lily
Best Colors	●	Purple, Sea Green, Silver
Mineral	●	Platinum
Favorite Music	●	Lullabies
Favorite Pastime	●	Coin Collecting
Lucky Number	●	5
Best Days	●	Tuesday, Thursday
Compatible Signs	●	Aries, Taurus, Capricorn
Incompatible Signs	●	Gemini, Sagittarius

FAMOUS PEOPLE BORN UNDER THE SIGN OF THE FISH

CZAR ALEXANDER III
MARION ANDERSON
JOHANN SEBASTIAN BACH
HARRY BELAFONTE
ALEXANDER GRAHAM BELL
ELIZABETH BARRETT BROWNING
WILLIAM JENNINGS BRYANT
LUTHER BURBANK
VANNEVAR BUSH
ENRICO CARUSO
FREDERIC CHOPIN
GROVER CLEVELAND
WILLIAM F. CODY
ALBERT EINSTEIN

SAMUEL R. GARDINER
JACKIE GLEASON
KATE GREENWAY
MERLE OBERON
NICCOLO PAGANINI
POPE PIUS XII
SIDNEY POITIER
AUGUST RENOIR
RIMSKY-KORSA-KOV
JOHN RUSKIN
DAVID SARNOFF
ANDRE SEGOVIA
HANDEL
PRINCE HAROLD OF NORWAY
REX HARRISON
BEN HECHT
VICTOR HUGO
HENRIK IBSEN
ANDREW JACKSON
JENNIFER JONES
ELISHA KANE
TED KENNEDY

DAVID LIVINGSTONE
HENRY W. LONGFELLOW
GORDON MACRAE
JAMES MADISON
LAURITZ MELCHIOR
MICHELANGELO
MICHEL DE MONTAIGNE
ZERO MOSTEL
RUDOLPH NUREYEV
DINAH SHORE
JOHANN STRAUSS
JOHN STEINBECK
ELIZABETH TAYLOR
VINCENT VAN GOGH
VOLTAIRE
EARL WARREN
GEORGE WASHINGTON
GEORGE F. WATT

255

APPENDICES

MEANING
OF
PLANETS

SUN   represents life, energy, authority, health, dignity, and the ego.

MOON   represents personality, emotion, imagination, psychism, and emotion.

MERCURY   represents logic, mental activity, communication, statistical facts, and power of judgement.

VENUS   represents love, beauty, goals, fascination, society, and music.

MARS   represents dynamic energy, war, force, creativity and will.

JUPITER   represents riches, growth, justice, travel, and philosophy.

SATURN   represents contraction, business, regression, the past and guidance.

URANUS   represents inspiration, initiation, electricity, reform and the eccentric.

NEPTUNE   represents unreality, psychic capacity, nebulism, deceit, and spiritualism.

PLUTO   represents transformation, change, radical thinking, the dictatorial and the masses.

BASIC CHARACTERISTICS

The twelve basic characteristics represented by the signs of the zodiac are also symbolized by the planets, sun, and moon.

These twelve basic characteristics are separated into pairs by the positive and negative aspects of the same characteristics or the opposite phases.

ARIES
AND
SCORPIO

individualistic — initiating — aggressive.
suspicious — investigative — controlled.

CANCER
AND
LEO

introverted — timid — miserly.
extroverted — self-confident — magnanimous.

TAURUS
AND
LIBRA

subjective — sensitive — materialistic.
appreciative — indecisive — lazy.

GEMINI
AND
VIRGO

flexible — restless — communicative.
manipulative — agile — studious.

PISCES
AND
SAGITTARIUS

psychic — moody — secretive.

intuitive — philosophical — direct.

AQUARIUS
AND
CAPRICORN

progressive — innovating — clever.
conservative — ambitious — practical.

BASIC BODILY AND EMOTIONAL FUNCTIONS

	Part of Body	Type of Personality	Function	Main Goal	Encourage & Nurture
ARIES	Head	Mental	Activation	Leadership Independence	Patience Tolerance Humility
TAURUS	Neck and Throat	Vital	Perpetuation	Security Material Possessions	Judgment Imagination Flexibility
GEMINI	Arms and Lungs	Neutral	Communication	Intellect Social Accept- ability	Sensitivity Relaxation Organization
CANCER	Chest and Stomach	Mental	Cultivation	Consciousness Emotional Expression	Practicality Stability Initiative
LEO	Heart and Back	Vital	Creation	Achievement Self-Expression	Thrift Attentiveness Moderation

Sign	Body Part	Polarity			
VIRGO	Intestines	Neutral	Perception	Perfection Self-satisfaction	Liberalism Positivism Imagination
LIBRA	Kidneys	Mental	Cooperation	Balance Justice	Decisiveness, Constancy Determination
SCORPIO	Reproductive Organs	Vital	Domination	Control Courage	Sympathy, Fore-thought, Perception
SAGITTARIUS	Hips and Thighs	Neutral	Inspiration	Knowledge Exploration	Consideration Self-control Honesty
CAPICORN	Knees and Bone	Mental	Perfection	Dignity Achievement	Vibrancy Communication Sociability
AQUARIUS	Legs and Circulatory System	Vital	Coordination	Truth, Wisdom	Sensitivity Practicality Warmth
PISCES	Feet and Liver	Neutral	Consolation	Communication Understanding	Relaxation Concentration Purpose

BASIC TRAITS

Sign	Ruling Planet	Advantages	Disadvantages	Type of Sign	Sex of Sign	Positive or Negative	Season
ARIES	Mars	Consistent Winning	Physical Hurts	Cardinal	Masculine	Positive	Spring
TAURUS	Venus	Love and Loyalty	Domestic Disharmony	Fixed	Feminine	Negative	Spring
GEMINI	Mars	Magnetism Logic and Reason	Neuroses Depletion of Stamina	Mutable	Masculine	Positive	Spring
CANCER	Moon	Fluctuating Moods and Locations	Sudden Reversals	Cardinal	Feminine	Negative	Summer
LEO	Sun	Attainment of Goal	Professional and Domestic	Fixed	Masculine	Positive	Summer
VIRGO	Moon	Ascension Movement	Neuroses Depletion of Stamina	Mutable	Feminine	Negative	Summer
LIBRA	Venus	Love and Loyalty	Domestic Disharmony	Cardinal	Masculine	Positive	Fall

			Physical Hurts				
SCORPIO	Mars	Creativity and Capacity	Physical Hurts	Fixed	Feminine	Negative	Fall
SAGITTARIUS	Jupiter	Fortune and Solicitation	Dissipation, Poor Health	Mutable	Masculine	Positive	Fall
CAPRICORN	Saturn	Methodical Achievement	Procrastination, Sadness	Cardinal	Feminine	Negative	Winter
AQUARIUS	Uranus	Extraordinary Occurrences	Physical and Mental Illness	Fixed	Masculine	Positive	Winter
PISCES	Moon	Unusual Professions	Emotional Instability and Illness	Mutable	Feminine	Negative	Winter

GIRLS' NAMES AND MEANINGS

Abigail—father's joy

Adelaide—dignity

Adele—noble

Adina—gentle

Agatha—do-gooder

Agnes—chaste

Alberta—brilliant

Alexandria—keeper of men

Alice—of cheerful, noble rank

Alma—life sustaining

Amy—loved one

Anastasia—resurrection

Andrea—feminine one

Angela—messenger

Ann—grace

Anna—grace

Ardith—valuable gift

Arlene—a pledge

Astra—starry

Audrey—noble, strong

Avis—bird

Aviva—spring

Barbara—foreign, exotic

Beatrice—blessing

Belinda—beautiful

Bernadette—strength

Bertha—bright tone

Beryl—precious stone

Bess—consecrated one

Betsey—consecrated one

Beulah—married

Beverly—meadow dweller

Blanche—fair

Bonny—good and fair

Brenda—flame or sword

Bridget—strength

Britt—having strength

Camilla—noble maiden

Candida—steaming white

Carmen—song

Carol—joyous song

Caroline—greatness

Cassandra—helper of man

Catherine—the pure

Celeste—heavenly

Charlotte—greatness

Christine—anointed one

Clair—bright, illustrious

Clarinda—bright and fair

Clotilde—famous warrior

Colleen—girl

Constance—constant one

Cora—maid

Cynthia—moor goddess

Daisy—flower

Daphne—laurel

Dara—center of wisdom

Daryl—dear one

Davida—beloved

Deirdre—beautiful and unlucky maiden

Della—moor goddess

Denise—fertile

Diana—moon Goddess

Dina—one who has been judged

Dinah—vindicated

Dolores—sorrows

Dominica— belonging to Lord

Doreen—serious

Dorette—small gift

Doris—pertinent to sea

Dorothy—gift

Dulcie—sweet

Edith—valuable

Edna—delight

Edwina—good friend

Eileen—light

Elaine—light

Eleanor—light

Elizabeth—divine consecrated one

Ella—fairy

Ellen—light

Eloise—healthy

Elva—elf

Emily—industrious one

Enid—soul or spirit

Erica—kingly

Ernestine—earnest, purposeful

Estelle—star

Ester—star

Eunice—good victory

Eve—life

Faith—loyal

Faye—fairy

Felicia—happiness

Fern—feather

Florence— flowering

Frances—one who is free

Frederika— peaceful ruler

Frida—peaceful one

Gabrielle—divine strength

Gale—lively one

Georgia—farmer

Geraldine—mighty one

Gertrude—maiden with spear

Gilda—golden

Gladys—lame

Glenna—coming from glen

Glorianne—grace and glory

Greta—a pear

Gwenodlyn—of white brow

Hannah—grace

Harriet—mistress of home

Hazel—one who commands

Hedda—strife

Hedy—pleasing

Helen—light

Hilary—cheerful one

Hilda—warrior maiden

Holly—shrub of good luck

Hope—virtue

Hulda— prophetess

Inez—chaste

Irene—peace

Iris—rainbow

Isobel— consecrated one

Ivy—clinging vine

Jacqueline— supplanter

Jane—gracious divine gift

Janet—gift from
  God
Jean—gracious
  divine gift
Jessica—grace
Jill—youthful
Joan—gracious
Joy—delight
Judith—praised
Julie—youthful
Justine—just one

Karen—purity
Kate—pure
Kay—pure

Laura—laurel,
  symbol of
  triumph
Leslie—from a gray
  fort
Leta—joy
Lela—night
Linda—lovely one
Lois—famed in
  battle
Loretta—small wise
  one
Lorraine—famous
  warrior
Lynn—pretty

Mable—loveable
Madge—pearl
Marcia—
  hammerlike

Margery—pearl
Marian—bitter
Marta—lady of
  house
Mary—bitter
Maureen—dark one
Maxine—greatness
Melanie—darkness
Melissa—honey
Merle—blackbird
Mildred—gentle
  counselor
Minna—memory,
  live
Moira—the great
  one
Molly—bitter
Morna—gentle one
Muriel—bright

Nadine—hope
Nancy—graceful
Nanette—gracious
Naomi—sweetness
Natalie—birthday,
  Christmas
Nickie—victorious
Nola—noble
Nora—honorable
Norma—model

Olga—holy one

Patricia—of noble
  birth
Paula—little one

Pauline—small one
Peggy—pearl
Penelope—weaver
Phyllis—green leaf
Priscilla—the
  helper
Prudence—prudent
  one

Rachel—lamb
Reba—one who
  ensnares
Regina—queen
Rhoda—rose
Rita—peal
Roberta—shining
  fame
Rochelle—small
  rock
Rosalva—small
  rose
Rosalind—
  beautiful rose
Rosemary—plant
Ruth—a friend

Sabrina—river
Sally—princess
Salome—peace
Sandra—helper of
  mankind
Sara—princess
Selma—fair
Sherry—greatness
Shirley—from
  white lea
Sibyl—prophetess

Sonya—having wisdom

Sophie—wise one

Stella—star

Stephanie—crown

Susan—a lily

Sylvia—maid of Forest

Tamara—Palm tree

Tammy—palm

Tara—a tower

Tess—harvester

Thalia—joyous

Theodora—divine gift

Tina—a star

Trudy—maiden with spear

Ursula—she bear

Vera—true one

Veronica—true image

Victoria— triumphant one

Viola—violet

Virginia—pure or virgin

Wanda—stock, stem

Wendy—wanderer

Wilma— determined protector

Winifred—friend of peace

Yvonne—archer

BOYS' NAMES AND MEANINGS

Aaron—
enlightened one
Abraham—father of
the people
Adam—the "first"
one
Adolph—protector,
noble one
Alan—the fair one
Albert—noble and
brilliant
Aldo—rich one
Alexander—helper
of man
Alvin—a friend
Amos—the
burdened one
Andrew—manly
one
Anthony—above
praise
Archibald—
distinguished and
bold
Arnold— the
powerful one
Arthur—
courageous one

Baldwin—bold or
courageous
Barnabas—son of
Barney—
exhortation
Barry—spear
carrier
Benedict—the
blessed
Benjamin—the
fortunate one
Bernard—strong
and bearlike
Bertrand—bright
raven
Blair—from the
plain
Boris—fighter
Brandon—from the
hill
Brent—from the
high hill
Brock—the badger
Brook—stream
dweller
Bruce—the
brushwood
thicket
Bruno—brown

Bryan—the strong
one
Burl—the high hill
Byron—a cowman
Caleb—the dog
Calvin—
baldheaded one
Carl—greatness
Carter—cart driven
Carroll—the great
one
Cedric—a chief
Charles—greatness
Chester—dwelling
in a fortified town
Christopher—
bearing Christ
Clarence—clear one
Clement—merciful
one
Clayton—a mortal
man
Clifford—cliff
crossing
Clive—cliff dweller
Clyde—heard from
afar
Colin—people's
triumph

Conrad—wise counselor

Constantine— steadfast

Cornelius— horn of war

Craig—crag dweller

Curtis—well-mannered

Cyril—lord

Dale—dale dweller

Dane—from Denmark

Daniel—the Lord is my judge

Darrell—dear one

David—beloved

Dean—valley

Dennis—God of wine and fertility

Derek—gift of God

DeWitt—white and pure

Dirk—people's ruler

Donald—powerful ruler

Douglas—dweller by dark stream

Dudley—dry field

Duke—leader

Duncan—soldier

Durant—one who is enduring

Drew—trusting

Earl—noble born, leader

Edgar—happy warrior

Edmund—valuable protector

Edsel—rich one

Edward—valuable guardian

Edwin—good friend

Egbert—bright sword

Eli—height

Elias—the Lord is God

Eliot—the Lord is salvation

Emanuel—God is with us

Emery— industrious ruler

Emil—the diligent one

Enoch—teacher

Ephraim—fruitful one

Eric—kingly

Ernest—intense, vigorous

Errol—born of nobility

Ethan—strength

Eugene—well-born

Evan—grace

Everett— courageous, powerful

Ezra—help

Felix—lucky

Ferdinand— adventurer

Floyd—the gray

Francis—born free

Franklin— free-holder

Frederick— peaceful ruler

Gabriel—man of God

Gale—vivacious

Garland— triumphantly crowned

Garth—protector of garden

Gary—spear bearer

Garrett—powerful with spear

Geoffrey—divine peace

George—farmer

Gerald—mighty spearman

Gideon—great destroyer

Gifford—brave gift

Gilbert—bright hostage

Giles—shield bearer

Glen—dweller of glen

Gordon—round hill

Graham—from gray house

Grant—the great
Gregory—watchful
Guy—woody

Hans—divine gift
Harold—strong in
 battle
Harvey—bitter one
Heath—from the
 heath
Hector—holding
 fast
Henry—ruler of the
 home
Herbert—shining
 warrior
Herman—
 warrior
Hewett—cutting
Hilary—cheerful
 one
Hiram—noble
Hollis—dweller
 by holly trees
Homer—poet
Horace—keeper of
 hours
Howard—of brave
 heart
Hugh—great heart
Humbert—bright
Humphrey—
 peaceful
Huntington—a
 hunting estate
Hyman—life

Ian—gracious gift
Ira—watchful
Irving—from the
 west
Irwin—lover of the
 sea
Isaac—laughter
Ivan—gift from God

Jared—one who
 descends
Jason—one who
 heals
James—one who
 supplants
Jay—supplanter
Jeffrey—divine
 peace
Jerold—bearer of
 holy name
Jerome—sacred
 name
Job—persecuted
Joel—Jehovah is
 God
John—gift from
 God
Julian—youthful
Jonah—dove
Jonathan—gift from
 the Lords
Joseph—one who
 increases
Joshua—salvation
Justin—just

Kane—bright or
 fair

Keane—tall and
 good-looking
Kendrick—bold or
 noble ruler
Kenneth—
 handsome
Kenyon—fair-
 haired one
Kim—leader
Kirk—church
Kurt—wise
 counselor
Kyle—narrow
 channel

Lambert—bright
 land
Lamont—lover of
 law
Lance—of the land
Langley—from long
 lea
Lawrence—laurel
 symbol of
 triumph
Lee—lion
Leith—wide
Lemuel—devoted to
 good
Leonard—strong as
 a lion
Leopold—bold
Leroy—the kingly
 one
Leslie—from a gray
 fort
Lewis—famed in
 battle

Lionel—like a lion
Llewellyn—
　lionlike leader
Lloyd—gray
Louis—a loud one
Lowell—little wolf
Lucas—bringing
　light
Ludwig—warrior
Luther—famous
　warrior
Lynn—lake

Malcolm—
　disciple's servant
Marcus—divine one
Mark—hammerlike
Marshall—the
　Lord's gift
Martin—warlike
　martial
Marvin—sea friend
Matthew—divine
　gift
Maurice—the moor
Maynard—strong,
　hardy
Maximilian—
　greatest one
Michael—like a
　lord
Miles—merciful
Milton—mill town
Monroe—
　swamplike
Morgan—sea
　dweller
Morris—the moor

Morton—town on
　moor
Murdock—sea man
Murray—one from
　the sea
Myron—pleasant

Nathan—gift
Neal—a leader
Ned—happy
　protector
Nelson—son of
　leader
Newton—new town
Nicolas—people's
　triumph
Nigel—darkness
Noah—rest
Noel—born on
　Christmas
Norman—
　northman
Norton—from north
　country

Olaf—offspring
Oliver—symbol of
　peace
Omar—builder
Orson—bearlike
Oscar—leaping
　warrior
Osmund—divine
　protected one
Otto—rich
Owen—young
　warrior

Parker—park
　protector
Patrick—patrician
Paul—little
Payne—from
　country folk
Percival—valley
Perry—pear tree
Peter—a stone
Philip—horse lover
Phineas—oracle
Pierre—the rock

Quentin—the fifth

Ralph—protector
Ramon—powerful
　protector
Ramsey—wooded
　island
Randall—wolf
Raymond—wise
　protector
Reginald—sage
Reid—of red hair
　or ruddy
　complexion
Reuben—a son
Richard—mighty
　ruler
Robert—of
　illustrious fame
Robin—illustrious
　fame
Rodman—
　measurer of land
Roger—famous
　spear carrier

Roland—the country's fame
Ronald—powerful and mighty
Roscoe—swift horse
Russell—red

Samuel—name of divine
Saul—one yearned for
Scott—the scott
Seth—appointed one
Sheldon—level-top hill
Sherlock—fair-haired
Sherwood—from bright forest
Sidney—family name
Sigmund—victorious
Simon—snub-nosed
Solomon—peaceful
Spencer—keeper of provisions
Steven—crown

Stewart—keeper of an estate
Sumner—summoner
Sylvester—from woodland

Tait—happy one
Terrence—tender one
Thaddeus—praise
Theodore—gift from divine
Thomas—one of twins
Thurston—stone
Timothy—honor-bound
Tobias—the divine is good
Tod—fox
Trent—one who dwells by river

Vaughn—small
Vernon—springlike
Victor—triumphant

Vincent—conquering

Waldo—ruler
Wallace—a stranger
Walter—powerful warrior
Ward—guard
Warren—protector
Wayne—wagon maker
Wilbur—wild boar
Wilfred—peace lover
William—determined protector
Winfred—friend of of peace
Winston—friendly stone
Winthrop—coming from friendly town
Wyatt—woody

Zachariah—reknowned